MALCOLM BROWN

AUSTRALIA'S WORST DISASTERS

HACHETTE AUSTRALIA

HACHETTE AUSTRALIA

Published in Australia and New Zealand in 2008
by Hachette Australia
(an imprint of Hachette Livre Australia Pty Limited)
Level 17, 207 Kent Street, Sydney NSW 2000
Website: www.hachette.com.au

First published in 2002
by Thomas C. Lothian Pty Ltd

National Library of Australia
Cataloguing-in-Publication data:
  Australia's worst disasters.
  ISBN 978 0 7336 2278 6
  1. Disasters – Australia. I. Brown, Malcolm, 1947-.
  994.04

Cover design by Luke Causby / Blue Cork
Cover photograph courtesy of Newspix, Ash Wednesday bushfires,
South Australia, 1983
Text design by Post Pre-press Group
Typeset in 10.5/14.5 pt Sabon Roman by Post Pre-press Group, Brisbane
Printed in Australia by Griffin Press

Hachette Livre Australia's policy is to use papers that are natural, renewable
and recyclable products and made from wood grown in sustainable forests. The
logging and manufacturing processes are expected to conform to the environmental regulations of the country of origin.

Contents

Foreword

Disasters shape nations. More than any other event, tragedy changes peoples' lives and behaviours. When we look back over history, more often than not it is the disasters that we recall as the most significant events—the times when a nation stopped in horror to watch the events that unfolded. With the immediacy of the media today, those disasters are brought closer and closer to home for all of us.

In times past we may have heard distant and belated stories of events that unfolded elsewhere. We may have read about them days or weeks later in newspapers. They may have reached us as tales told by travellers. Now we see the events transpire before our eyes as they happen. No better example can be found than 11 September 2001 in New York, when the world watched as the event occurred on television sets across the globe—as the disaster that happened on the other side of the world became the disaster that occurred in our own living rooms.

Many of us spend our lives working to prevent disaster and to provide relief to those affected when the 'inevitable' occurs. Humanity will always face a superior force in Mother Nature. When Mother Nature deems a disaster to occur there is often little we can do but hold on for the ride and do what we can to minimise the impacts on life, property and the environment. Fire, flood, earthquake, eruption, inundation—these are disasters that we can only do our best to prepare for. Other disasters, though—the man-made kind—are obviously those that are among the most tragic because they are the most avoidable. It is often said that those sorts of disasters are not due to just one thing going wrong, but the confluence of many things going wrong.

From disaster also comes learning. We learn how to help deal with the circumstances that lead to tragedy in such a way as to help prevent or minimise the impact in the future. With each major event we hone our techniques, improve our equipment and enhance our readiness so that when a similar situation arises we are better prepared to meet its onslaught or to prevent it altogether. When it comes to the less preventable of disasters, we learn better how to respond in a relief capacity.

Disaster also shapes our culture and defines our character. There is little doubt that the Australian way of life has been moulded and evolved as a result of some of our greatest tragedies. The tragic cost of untamed bushfires in the late 1800s, for example, led to local residents banding together to form bushfire brigades. There are few greater examples of the Australian spirit than that which is encapsulated within a volunteer bushfire brigade—a spirit of neighbourly assistance, of camaraderie, of trust in each other in the face of incredible odds, of mateship. In many of the rural towns of Australia, volunteer fire brigades become the hub of the community. They bind people together—a bond formed through the common experience of having faced disaster and come through it by relying on each other. Disaster is a shared experience that, despite the tragedy, brings us closer together as a society. Indeed, our very sense of community is often founded on this very basis. The tribal spirit, the notion of 'safety in numbers' is built on this premise.

It is said that if we fail to learn the lessons of history, then we are doomed to repeat them. It is through examination, review, critique and hindsight that we are able to identify causes and determine the improvements necessary to mitigate repetition. Emergency services, as a matter of course, debrief after each significant event to critically review their performance, to learn from their mistakes and their successes. Coroners and governments inquire into events to review policies and practices in order to constructively improve how we operate as a society, changing laws to help change behaviours. This is how as a society we have institutionalised avoiding future disasters, but there is always more we can do and learn. Most emergency services concentrate a significant amount of their efforts on community education in an endeavour to take what we have learned back to the communities who are most directly affected. For while emergency service workers may improve their methods, it remains essential for the general public—those who are the first to be harmed by a disaster—to be as prepared and ready as possible. It is through this education that we cut the cost of disaster in terms of life and property.

Unfortunately, disasters often occur because we repeat the mistakes of the past. We often fail to learn the lessons or forget them through the passage of time. In the case of bushfires we have often found that in the period between major fires, those who lived in an area affected by fire are often no longer resident in the same area when fires return. New residents often have little appreciation of the ferocity of a bushfire or its behaviour. They have often, therefore, failed to adequately prepare or have little idea of what to do when the fire-front hits. It is this lack of continuity that demonstrates the ever-present need to remind ourselves of the dangers we face and to remain vigilant. It should also serve to remind us that we individually have a responsibility for awareness and preparation.

While few need to be experts, we must all ensure a level of personal knowledge of danger so that we can play our own role in avoiding it and helping others to do the same. This is our community responsibility. This is why we should all take the time to learn what caused tragedies of the past.

Phil Koperberg
Commissioner, NSW Rural Fire Service
April 2002

Introduction

For many people, somewhere in the past there has been a dreadful moment when their entire life has hung in the balance. They realise afterwards that they survived only because of fate. They realise that they might have been killed, but one or more of the safety mechanisms: the skill of a driver, someone's anticipation, another's alertness, back-up systems, crash barriers, rescue services or medical facilities came into operation, either averting the catastrophe or lessening its impact.

Disaster usually occurs when one or more safety mechanisms fail. Sometimes there are not many safety mechanisms. Sometimes the only safety mechanism might be a degree of caution exhibited by the people concerned, or the established policies of regulatory authorities. Two girls on a camping trip in Sydney's northern outskirts just happened to be under a tree during a thunderstorm when a branch torn from the tree crashed to the ground. The girls might have decided to abandon their camping expedition because of the storm. A young honeymooner surfing off a South Australian beach found he had chosen a patch of water occupied by a great white shark. The surfer might have taken the possibility of a shark attack into account. A girl watching the implosion of Royal Canberra Hospital was hit by a lethal projectile. The civic authorities could have refrained from declaring the demolition a public spectacle because of the outside chance of something going wrong. Obviously, in such matters, perceived probability is all important, but as this book illustrates, sometimes perceptions are flawed at the outset or become flawed over time.

Sometimes there could be no reasonable anticipation at all of danger by those who become victims. In such circumstances, however, there are still safety mechanisms involving the responsibility of other people. A woman shopping in a Parramatta department store in Sydney's west was hit by a rivet fired by a workman on the floor above who was taking poor aim at a steel beam. Obviously the workman should have ensured nobody was below him when he fired the projectile. Another safety mechanism was his skill in firing the shot. A young man lying on his bed in Queensland was hit by a bullet accidentally fired by a man playing with his rifle in the room below. The primary safety mechanism was the caution expected of the owner of the firearm—the expectation that he would ensure that the rifle was not loaded. This safety mechanism should have been reinforced by rules formulated by governments and other regulatory bodies. Unfortunately the monitoring and enforcement of such rules and regulations has often been inadequate, and the people subject to these provisions find ways of getting around them.

The *Macquarie Dictionary* defines a disaster as 'any unfortunate event, especially a sudden or great misfortune'. This definition can be extended to refer to such things as failed business enterprises, like HIH Insurance, or decisions that have serious consequences, such as the deliberate introduction of the rabbits and cane toads into Australia. It can take in catastrophes created by enemy action, such as the bombing of Darwin in 1942. For the purposes of this book we will stick to physical catastrophes that were unintended by anybody, such as collapses of bridges and buildings, collisions between vehicles, and natural disasters like fire, earthquakes and cyclones.

A large number of people killed and injured does not always define an event as a disaster, but such things are normally associated with disasters. Often whether something is a disaster or not is an individual perception. News came in late

2001 that a boat containing some 350 asylum-seekers trying to get to this country had sunk somewhere off the coast of Indonesia. The Aitape tidal wave in Papua New Guinea in 1998 killed about 3000 people. No ordinary, caring person wants such dreadful things to happen, but cataclysmic events far afield do not have the same impact as extreme misfortune close to home. Heather Finch, in Denistone in suburban Sydney, had a neighbour whose brother was killed in the Granville train disaster. 'It came home to us,' she said. 'My husband said at the time that a million people in the Third World equals a thousand people in England equals a hundred people in Australia equals one person in your street.'

This book covers events at sea, in the air, on land and underground. We have not attempted to include every disastrous event because of space limitations, but if we were to look at others we might find some of the same failings that are present in the disasters we have included. One such disaster was the wreck of the clipper Dunbar, which approached Sydney Heads in storm conditions on the night of 20 August 1857 after a voyage of 81 days. The captain and his crew decided they could cope with the conditions and enter the harbour that night instead of waiting. The ship hit a reef and there was only one survivor among the 121 people on board. The safety mechanism in this instance was the judgement and temperament of captain and crew.

Sometimes we encounter situations where, in retrospect, a disaster has just been waiting to happen. The safety mechanisms were totally inadequate, and catastrophe was averted time and again only because time and placement did not come together. In the aftermath of the event the systems of control, with all their safety mechanisms, are examined alongside other factors such as the morale, support and temperament of those in crucial positions. The conclusion is often that it was only a matter of time. This could well have been said of the Thredbo landslide disaster of 1997. When we examine other catastrophes in the nation's history, going back at least 100 years, we find that in many of these cases the conditions for disaster existed well in advance of the actual disaster— they were just waiting for a conjunction of events to trigger things.

Sometimes the dangers could have been anticipated well in advance, but reliance was placed on safety mechanisms. Then, over time, those safety mechanisms have been ignored or overridden for one reason or another: complacency, negligence, recklessness, bravado, ignorance, personality conflicts, rivalry or even simple stupidity. Some of these factors played a role in the preceding events. The explosion of the mine at Mt Kembla, near Wollongong, on 31 July 1902, which—in terms of the number killed—was Australia's worst land disaster. On other occasions there is sometimes no clear idea of what everyone else is doing, just an assumption that everyone understands what is happening or that if there is a problem, that someone, somewhere, is doing something about it. This muddle and complacency was a factor in the Sydney–Hobart yacht race of 1998.

The more complex an operation, the more likely disaster becomes. The more individuals are pushed to the limits of their ability, the greater the danger of disaster. This seems to be the case with the seemingly inexplicable phenomenon of the aircraft carrier HMAS Melbourne running down the destroyer HMAS Voyager in 1964—Australia's worst peacetime naval disaster. Similar things could be said about the Black Hawk helicopter crash in Queensland in 1996. On yet other occasions there is simply a false assumption by people involved in the supervision and operation of a project that they are up to it, when really they are going beyond their limits. This, surely was the most critical safety mechanism failure when the Royal Canberra Hospital implosion in 1987 killed a girl. Similar assumptions were made about the construction of the West Gate Bridge across the Yarra River. Again, similar assumptions, combined with a degree of negligence, cost-cutting and complacency, caused the Maccabiah Bridge collapse in Israel, which led to the death of two Australian athletes.

If a job is planned properly and previously established procedures and precautions are observed and there are competent people in vital positions—people who are capable not only of supervising but of making sensible decisions at critical moments—a project has a good chance of being completed without problems. In our research, however, we have found that such procedures and precautions have been bypassed again and again, or observed only in spirit and then at the critical moment people have done the wrong things. If only one safety mechanism remains in place, there is a chance disaster will be averted. In almost all the cases considered by this book, there was a collapse of almost all safety mechanisms. Such failures quickly combine to produce a critical situation.

The pressures that can be brought to bear do not stop with complexity and communications problems. Additional pressures can include shortage of time, shortage of manpower, scarcity of resources and political factors. The net effect of such pressures has been a tendency to push control systems beyond their capacity to cope. Things might work for a time, but sometimes the system is, figuratively speaking, hanging by a thread. When that thread snaps, there is no backup safety mechanism because the system has been strained too far.

Sometimes there is only the slightest oversight, the simplest misunderstanding. The dreadful consequences of such misunderstandings can be seen in the crash of the Air New Zealand jet into Mt Erebus, bordering Australian Antarctic territory, in 1979, which killed 257, including an Australian resident. (The *New Zealand Herald* has made a fuss about Aussies pinching New Zealand disasters, but it has been included in this book because there was an Australian killed in the disaster and it happened very close to Australian territory. The fact that Qantas was running similar flights means that the disaster has additional relevance in the Australian context.)

In the aftermath of disaster there are inevitably inquiries. Most of these come up with useful recommendations and changes are made for the better. In most inquiries, what is discovered is normally not surprising. The potential dangers have always been recognised, but people can be lulled into a sense of complacency when nothing dangerous happens.

To do something to improve safety costs money, and neither governments nor individuals particularly want to spend it. There could have been a lot more investment in maintenance of the Sydney rail network prior to the Granville collision of 1977. It was in all probability recognised for years that the way homes were built in Darwin, a cyclone would rip them apart. But because of complacency and the cost of doing anything positive about it, nothing was done to make the city more cyclone-proof. The Ash Wednesday bushfires in Victoria in 1983 were one of the loudest warnings of the potential of bushfire, but people still surrounded their homes on urban fringes with bushes and trees and built them on ridgetops. Equally, it could have been predicted at any time that if a particularly potent combination of storms hit south-eastern Queensland, Brisbane would be inundated. This lack of preparation continues. Most fierce storms that hit metropolitan areas brings down power-lines, cause blackouts, damage roofs, bring trees down across roads, cause local flooding and trap drivers in their cars. The question arises: why should the community be so vulnerable to damage from such a predictable event?

The evidence is all around us that things are learnt from disasters and there is action. I took a trip to Mt Victoria on 17 January 1997 to ride the train down on the 20th anniversary of the Granville disaster, and at most points along the lines there was work being done. The tragedy so shook the Wran Government and successive NSW state governments that maintenance on the main lines has never been in such a poor state again. When the Christmas 2001 bushfires hit New South Wales, 117 houses were lost but nobody paid with their life. There were four deaths in the previous bushfire crisis, in 1994, and at that time both the community and the emergency services were less prepared than they were in 2001. Lessons have been learned from the Thredbo landslide and it is likely anybody planning resort expansion in Alpine areas will always have them in mind.

There is always—in all industries, in all systems, everywhere—a tendency for people to be lazy, to take shortcuts, to throw up their hands when things get too difficult and assume that 'someone else will look after it'. Sometimes seemingly inexplicable accidents plague the system. The Glenbrook rail collision in 1999, when an inter-urban train smashed into the rear of the Indian–Pacific after the driver had been given approval to go through a red light, should never have happened. There was a communications 'black spot' on that section of rail. Why should that have existed at all, on the eve of the 21st century, when humanity has already managed to control robot vehicles on the surface of Mars?

We must accept that people will continue to weigh the risks against the convenience. Why else would motorised transport be tolerated after the thousands upon thousands of deaths it has chalked up in the space of 100 years? The value of having a properly trained, efficient fighting force will still force military planners to push their personnel towards their limits. The challenge of adventure will still drive people to go on round-the-world ocean races and do solitary climbs of Everest. As Hugo Van Kretschmar, the then commodore of the Cruising Yacht Club of Australia, said, if you want to ensure safety you do nothing. That is of course unrealistic. It is hoped that this book might be a modest contribution to the question of how we can do things, including things with a high degree of risk, and do them in a way that optimises our safety.

Malcolm Brown

Part One:
Ignition

Mt Kembla: Australia's Worst Land Disaster, 1902

Most Rhondda chapels were rather plain and functional from the outside, built of massive blocks of Pennant Sandstone to withstand the hazards of mine explosions, subsidence, and the window-rattling chords of the Hallelujah Chorus.

Clive Woosnam, Sydney Welsh chorister, reminiscing on his South Wales childhood

At the dawn of this century an old man stood beside the cemetery at the Soldiers and Miners' Memorial Church on Mt Kembla, a serene setting in the thickly wooded Illawarra escarpment on the south coast of New South Wales. The church overlooked Lake Illawarra to the south and the city of Wollongong to the north. Fred Kirkwood knew the area well. He had been keeping that cemetery in impeccable condition for more than 70 years. It was his way of honouring the 96 men and boys who were killed in Australia's worst land disaster, the Mt Kembla colliery explosion of 31 July 1902. It was an event not in his living memory—he was born on 25 February 1909, but he had mined at Mt Kembla his entire 46-year working life. From the age of 19 he had become involved in preserving the memory of an event, described to him from his earliest years, that had left him with what might be described as the 'death imprint'.

The Mt Kembla graves, with their faded lettering, told the story of 17 year olds David Stafford and Claude Pamay having their lives snuffed out, of Percey Hunt dying at the age of 60 along with his sons Percey, 20, and William, 18. Tom Morris had died at the age of 75, 25 days before the tragedy, but when the mine blew up his son George, 34, and grandson Frederick Smith, 14, went with it. Mary Dungey, who was to lose two sons in the Great War, went to the temporary morgue to identify the body of her Cornish-born husband, Francis. He had been decapitated and his head placed back in position. When the widow tried to hug him, the head fell away.

The entrance to the old mine was still there, but the mine had ceased operation in 1970. It was silent now, apart from the calls of birds and the rustle of wind in the rainforest. The entrance to the shaft was sealed, perhaps to block out the howl of anguish said to come from the ghost of Mickey Brennan, the one miner whose body was never recovered. There had been other tragedies since 1902. During Fred Kirkwood's working life 16 men had lost their lives in the mine. He remembered all of them. A man called Funnell had had his right arm pinned by a fall of coal in 1924. It being necessary to get him out, a workmate had chopped his arm off with a shovel, but Funnell had bled to death before he could be brought to the surface.

Mt Kembla was not the only mine in the Illawarra to experience catastrophe. In 1887 the Bulli Colliery had gone up, killing 81 men and boys, making it the biggest land disaster in Australia at that time. It was hardly an unprecedented or unusual, or for that matter unpredictable, event and it was certainly not unfamiliar to many of the miners from the United Kingdom who took up tools in the Illawarra. An explosion in South Wales' Cymmer Old Pit in July 1856 had killed 114 miners. Another at Ferndale, South Wales, in November 1867 had killed 178. A fractured pump bob at Britain's Hartley Colliery in 1862 had blocked the mine's single shaft and brought about the deaths of 204 miners from asphyxiation. Repeated explosions in the Richmond fields, Virginia, USA, killed 42 miners in 1836, 53 in 1839, 55 in 1855, 69 in 1867 and 32 in 1882. Despite these appalling cataclysmic events, sons wanted to follow fathers, and their sons after them. It was, as Kirkwood said, 'in your blood', and if you were injured or killed, it was simply a matter of your number being up.

Coal, with all its benefits, had long stamped itself on the history of Wollongong before Kirkwood came onto the scene. Explorer George Bass saw coal at Coalcliff as early as 1797. The outcrop was part of the Sydney basin, which came out at two other places: Newcastle and Lithgow. It was easily accessible at these places, though the area at the time had no natural harbour and the potential for coal mining was soon overshadowed by the developing industry in Newcastle. When the Australian Agricultural Company lost its monopoly on coal mining it also lost the right to restrict coal mining to the Newcastle fields. Coal began to be mined in the Illawarra, the first shaft going in at Mt Keira in 1849. The industry developed slowly. Mt Pleasant started in 1862 and the Bulli Coal Company started in 1863, using an ocean jetty. Four mines, employing a total of 182 men, were operating in the region by 1871.

From that point onward, there was sustained economic growth and an increasing interest in the riches of coal mining. Some of the colony's wealthiest and most influential people made speculative land purchases. In 1878 the Coalcliff Coal Company was formed. Three years later the NSW Government decided to build a railway to the Illawarra, the decision prompting a new phase of development and a rush of investment into the region. The Mt Kembla Coal and Oil Company was founded in 1878 with £100 000 in British capital. Its mine opened, with some ceremony, on 27 February 1883. The company's board was chaired by Ebenezer Vickery, an enterprising individual who was to later win a place on the NSW Legislative Council. The NSW Government legislated for a railway to be built from the mine to Port Kembla. Vickery estimated that the seam comprised 67 million tonnes of coal and could produce some 3000 tonnes weekly for a period of 30 years.

There were plenty of takers for jobs. In 1884 the Mt Kembla mine employed 198 men, including 60 who had been brought from Scotland and Yorkshire. There were huge riches to be gained. There were also risks, one of which was fluctuating coal prices, another being the questionable level of demand. The New South Wales coal mines were always plagued with the problems of overproduction. There was the question of how to transport the coal. The Illawarra lacked a natural harbour. In time at least some of these problems could be overcome. The train line from Sydney was completed in 1887 and ocean jetties were erected at Port Kembla and further north at Bellambi. Other problems were far more intractable. There was always uncertainty about the dimensions and accessibility of seams. Nobody wanted cave-ins or explosions. On the other hand, nobody wanted to be denied an income either. For many men it was a choice between accepting risks and forfeiting the chance to earn a living.

Miners were paid according to production, but by contemporary standards they were not well-off. They had to meet costs that workers a century later would expect the company to cover, such as supply of gunpowder and fuses, and timber and erected supports to prevent cave-ins. There was no money to be made out of this, so these vital safety measures tended to be put in hastily. There was neglect of important health issues. Over time, many men became victims of lung diseases related to their exposure to coal dust. Many also disguised their health problems for fear of losing their job.

There had to be an incentive for taking what on the face of it seem unbelievable hazards. Several kilometres underground, miners blasted rock or coal and were obliged to calculate whether the hole was big enough to cause a cave-in, and whether the timber struts would be capable of restraining several thousand tonnes of weight that could shift position. Add the hazards of drowning, asphyxiation, fire, explosion, being caught in machinery or blown to bits by percussion and one wonders why anyone would have bothered with it. Methane, a by-product of the formation of coal, was invisible and odourless. When present in concentrations of four to 15 percent in air it formed an explosive mixture known as 'firedamp'. Carbon monoxide, known as 'whitedamp', was also colourless and odourless, flammable, potentially explosive and highly toxic. Carbon dioxide, known as 'blackdamp', simply displaced oxygen, causing asphyxiation. Whitedamp and blackdamp mixed with air become 'afterdamp', which could catch fire and explode. Collectively, these commodities were simply referred to as 'gas'. Any gas in a mine spelt trouble.

Then there was coal dust, which normally does not present much of a hazard, but when thrown up in an explosion it would be suspended in air and surrounded by flame, making it potentially lethal. In major explosions, one lot of coal dust could explode and throw up another, creating a chain-reaction of explosions.

An obvious safety precaution, in the days before electricity was introduced, was to keep naked flame away from methane. But naked lights were taken into coal mines throughout the 19th century, beginning with candles, then replaced by tallow lamps, known as Scotch miners' lamps. This was despite of the fact that the Davy Safety Lamp had been developed in Britain in 1815, protecting the naked flame with a screen of metal. The metal cooled the flame of any ignited gas that entered the confines of the lamp, thereby preventing gas outside the lamp from igniting. An additional advantage was that if the concentration of gas was more than that of air, the flame went out. Thus, it could test for presence of gas. The disadvantage was that the metal screen so shielded the light that miners had much poorer illumination. Instead of the strong light of a naked flame they had a flickering orange glow. Miners could not see to lift the skip properly. They could have accidents and drop lumps of coal on their feet. If their lamp went out, they had to borrow a lamp and go to the surface to relight their own, which lost production time for two miners.

The problem was compounded by the system of paying by production, and by the motivation of the mine management to save money. Productivity was greater when a naked flame was used, so both management and workforce favoured it. Mine owners could have encouraged safety lamps by offering a higher hewing rate for those using them. In fact the miners said at one point if they used safety lamps, they wanted an extra 3d a ton. The owners did not want to pay it. Nor did they want the extra cost of providing safety lamps in the first place. Some mine owners made miners pay for broken safety lamp glass.

The decision to go underground in these conditions was a calculated risk. The most important calculations were made on the basis of whether a mine was 'gassy' or not. The Mt Kembla mine was not regarded as particularly gassy. For that matter, it was regarded as a 'dry' mine but not particularly dusty. What risk there was from gas could be reduced by ventilating the mine. The first ventilation technique was to have a furnace that drew air towards it, expelled it up a shaft, and maintained the direction of the air-flow via a system of doors. Later, furnaces in at least some mines were replaced by a steam-driven boiler, although at Mt Kembla the furnace was retained into the early 20th century. From the main shafts, 'headings', or tunnels going off at right-angles, were cut. The rules required that at intervals of 35 yards (31.6 metres) there had to be 'cut-through' tunnels to a parallel heading to allow for ventilation. Rules also said that any gas discovered should be reported, and that a record be kept of such reports.

The history of the early mines showed that many ventilation precautions were tokenistic. Doors meant to stop back-flow of air were put into main thoroughfares and opened frequently. The coalface was sometimes pushed beyond the limit of the established ventilation cut-throughs. Sometimes hollowed-out areas from the headings (the 'bords') were simply bricked up, a cost-saving procedure that increased the risk of gas build-up in those areas. The desire to get on with the job of making money was so great that men undercutting at the coalface often did not bother to 'spag' the coal, which involved putting in short props to prevent a premature collapse. There was even evidence of collusion between management and the men to blatantly cheat on ventilation. When government inspectors came, entire sections of the mine would be sealed off to enhance the air current at the time it was measured. There was often not much chance of a mine being caught by a surprise visit.

Some inspectors gave mine managers several days' notice that they were coming.

Another major control was organised unionism, but its history was patchy. Miners were prepared to make major concessions to preserve their employment. An Illawarra Miners Mutual Protective Association was formed, but it was not until 1879 that a Wollongong Miners' Union was formed and that collapsed in 1880. Unionism reverted to local miners' lodges. Mt Kembla miners' lodge struck on 15 August 1885 over the hewing rate of 2/9 a ton. The seam had become narrower and miners had to work harder. They wanted more money in compensation: a halfpenny per ton for every two inches that the seam fell below five feet six inches in height from the shaft floor. The men remained on strike for two months and the company made some concessions. District miners struck for six months in 1886–7, but lost. The strike was only settled by the miners agreeing to accept reduced hewing rates and to variations in the rate according to the prices that coal was getting. They had to sign rules of engagement, which some miners later claimed prevented them from reporting the presence of gas.

A fallback position was naturally to get the government interested, and to enact legislation to enforce safety measures. The New South Wales Government passed the *Registration and Inspection of Coal Mines in the Colony of New South Wales Act 1854*, which dealt with the registration and inspection of coal mines, but did not specifically address safety. In 1862 the government enacted the *Coal Mines Regulation Act 1862*, which set an age limit of 13 for males working in the mines and prohibited employment of women. All accidents were to be reported, there were to be two egresses or exits for each mine, there was to be ventilation, dangerous sections of the mine were to be blocked off and safety lamps were to be provided. In 1876 that Act was repealed and the *Coal Mines Regulation Act 1876* was substituted for it. This Act was ineffective. A Department of Mines Coalfields Inspectorate was established, but it was understaffed and among its officers were some very negligent individuals.

The government was always only lukewarm in its desire to intervene. Many of the legislators had interests in coal mines. Don Dingsdag points out in his study of the disaster, *The Bulli Mining Disaster 1887*, that 22 Legislative Councillors were directors or owners of coalmines and at least 25 of the Legislative Assembly's 124 members. The ministry of Premier Sir Henry Parkes had ten members, of whom seven were directors or proprietors of coal mines and Parkes himself owned 4000 hectares of coalmining leases at Jamberoo.

The explosion at Bulli mine on 23 March 1887 was not entirely without warning. The night before there had been a minor explosion of gas but the men involved had not reported it, possibly out of fear of losing their jobs if they did. When the disaster came, it rocked the city in more ways than one. A coroner's inquest into the explosion blamed the 81 deaths on management of the mines. It said that the deaths had been brought about by 'disregard for the *Bulli Colliery Special Rules* and *Coal Mines Regulation Act*, in allowing men to work while gas existed'. But that really would not do and the government ordered a royal commission and stacked it. There was a lot of money riding on the result. The other mine managers wanted the Bulli mine manager, Alexander Ross, exonerated because if he were to be heavily blamed it would reflect on themselves and they might be saddled with harsher government control measures.

The royal commission found that the prime cause of the explosion was careless use of explosives by the miners. Apart from some minor criticism of an overseer, it exonerated the mine management. It made recommendations regarding ventilation and amendments to the *Coal Mines Regulation Act*. It also said that only Davy lamps should be used in the coal mine and it made recommendations to improve management of the mine. The recommendations were ignored. Alexander Ross, manager of the mine before the explosion, continued to work in the mine. In 1890 Bulli mine management announced that naked flame would again be used 'until covered lights are cheaper'. The chance to thoroughly reform the system, and prevent a disaster in the future, was lost.

Unionism, which had been stronger in the northern coalfields, made progress elsewhere in the state's mining industry. In 1889 miners went on strike at Broken Hill, winning the right to have all miners join their union. One of the issues they fought over was safety. In 1890 the so-called Maritime Strike was called, a large-scale concerted action spreading across the country, dragging in the maritime, agricultural and mining workers. But the gains made by the unions met entrenched opposition from management. The colliery companies had no interest in what the men were fighting for. Through their Southern Cross Coal Owners Association, they pre-empted strike action by advertising for non-union labour. On 10 October 1890 police and soldiers escorted 75 non-unionists into the Mt Kembla mine. On hand were 160 men from the Permanent Artillery, who were equipped with carbines, bayonets, swords and machine-guns. The unionists tossed up the idea of storming the mine and carrying off the non-union labour. Ebenezer Vickery arrived from Sydney and was stoned. The mine manager John Evans threatened to sack any man who actively promoted the union, and posted a sign at the pit mouth intimating that any man who joined the union would be given notice of dismissal. The miners drew little comfort from the courts.

There were other forces at work. At the time of the Maritime Strike the industry went into recession in line with a depression in economic conditions throughout the world, and coal, which had sold at 10/- a ton in 1889, fell to 6/- a ton in 1893. Mt Kembla's owners kept the mine open while other mines closed, but the miners were at a severe disadvantage. There were fewer jobs. At Kembla Heights in 1891, census-takers found that 20 percent of the town's 220 houses were unoccupied and in one case four men were found living in one tent. Between 1892 and 1896 Mt Kembla coal production declined by an average of 0.3 percent a year and employment declined by three percent. In 1899 coal was selling at only 4/- a ton. Men needed work. The safety issue was always present, but it tended to be disregarded.

On 31 May 1892 a Mt Kembla miner, David Howie, drove his pick into the rock face and missed the seam, breaking into empty space and releasing the methane that had built up there. Howie's naked light ignited the gas and his workmate, Michael Gallagher, was burnt on the back of his hand. It was a warning, but when this was brought to management's notice, they were more concerned with the fact that Howie had breached work procedure by hewing ahead of where he should have been working. No methane was found when the area was tested, and it was assumed the mine's ventilation system was working. The fact was that the Mt Kembla coal seam was slowly releasing methane. The best safety lamps could detect methane at a concentration of one percent of the air. But Mt Kembla was releasing methane at a lower rate.

There were more sensitive hydrogen lamps available, which could detect methane in concentrations of as low as 0.25 percent, but they were expensive and dangerous if not carefully handled.

The NSW Government proposed to introduce wide-ranging legislation to bring further regulation to coal mines. One was the introduction of the eight-hour day. Another was the raising of the minimum age of employment from 12 to 14. Vickery, who had been elected to the Legislative Council in 1887, spoke against the bill. In 1893 his manager, Dr James Robertson, gave evidence before a parliamentary select committee that New South Wales mines were worked under the world's most favourable conditions. He said the coal industry was on the verge of collapse and that the proposed provisions would be 'ruinously expensive' to the miners because their fortunes were bound up with the fortunes of the mine owners. Governments throughout the colonies were sympathetic to such pleas from proprietors.

Mt Kembla's management was as hard-driven as mine managements anywhere. It took precautions but was not overzealous in such matters. As with all other operations across the nation, the cost of safety measures and amenities was measured against productivity. Mt Kembla was neither very good nor very bad in terms of safety. Between 1886 and 1889 it had had eight fatalities from various accidents. Those statistics, and those for non-fatal accidents, compared favourably with other mines. The possibility of Mt Kembla being caught by a gas explosion was dismissed as minuscule. In 1895 Dr Robertson gave evidence to a royal commission into proposed new mining legislation that the mine gave off gas 'very rarely'. Mine owners, he said, had no interest in explosions and the miners were protected from misfortune in 'a number of ways'. It was common knowledge that there was some gas in the Mt Kembla mine, but it was of low concentration, from 0.5 percent to 1.5 percent, not enough to cause an explosion. This knowledge tended to be suppressed by both miners and management because they considered that Mt Kembla would get an unjustified stigma as a 'gassy' mine and in one way or another production would be inhibited.

The *NSW Coal Mines Regulation Act* was passed in 1896, making it mandatory that the presence of gas be reported immediately, with a sanction of three months jail with hard labour for anybody found guilty of 'wilful neglect endangering life and limb'. The workman discovering the gas was to make an oral report to his supervisor. The Act said that when gas was discovered, workmen should be withdrawn from the area and only safety lamps used thereafter where a 'dangerous' level existed. Mine proprietors ignored the provisions. There was no definition of what level of gas amounted to being 'dangerous', so it became a matter for the management to make a judgement. It was ultimately up to the management of individual mines to determine for themselves whether there was 'likely to be any such quantity of inflammable gas as to render the use of naked lights dangerous'.

Inspectors were appointed who could request that things be carried out in accordance with the Act. The inspectors had the general power to request managers to remedy 'any matter, thing or practice . . . [that would] threaten or tend to bodily injury of any person'. But any inspector's decision could be appealed and the resulting proceedings, involving arbitration, could be drawn-out. In the meantime, if the inspector had found dangerous conditions, they continued to exist. There was also prejudice throughout the coalfields against anyone who brought problems to notice. In 1899 a parliamentary inquiry investigating the dismissal of a mining deputy called Bailey from Newcastle noted that he had reported firedamp three days before his dismissal. The colliery proprietors continued to push home their advantages against organised labour. The Southern Cross Coal Owners Association comprised the owners of Mt Kembla, Mt Pleasant, Mt Keira, Bellambi, South Bulli and Coalcliff mines. Vickery and Robertson urged unions to go on strike against mine owners outside this group, who were stalling on the issue of offering a lower hewing rate to the miners.

In the meantime mines continued to blow up or collapse. At Stockton Colliery in 1896 two men were killed in a fire and nine rescuers died, prompting the government to import specialist rescue equipment. An explosion at Dudley Colliery in the Hunter Valley in 1897 killed 15. In Queensland in 1897 there were a series of worrying firedamp explosions at Torbanlea, near Maryborough, and at Waterstown, near Ipswich. The statistics were positively screaming for attention. In the 20 years since 1882 there had been 546 fatalities in NSW coal mines. More than a third had come from gas explosions. Three of them accounted for 192 fatalities. Complacency seemed to be the watchword. Queensland held a royal commission into Torbanlea, which had had a second firedamp explosion in 1900, killing five miners. The royal commission into Torbanlea produced a damning indictment of Queensland coal mines generally, including the practice of taking naked lights into coal mines known to be gassy. It said, 'In the majority of cases, the persons employed to manage collieries are very much below the standards in intelligence, and knowledge of mining, than should be required.'

The chief mines inspector for New South Wales, Alfred Atkinson, who came from a mining background in Britain and from the historical record appears a cut above other mining inspectors of the period, campaigned tirelessly for stricter controls. He wrote to mine managers urging them to introduce safety lamps when even the slightest danger of gas existed. Again there was resistance from the mine owners, saying that the inspector was interfering with their operations. In 1897 Atkinson wrote, 'It would appear . . . that nothing can be done by the Inspectors except point out to the managers in those cases where they consider safety lamps might be used.' In 1901 he sent samples of New South Wales coal dust to Britain to test how readily it would ignite. The results showed that the coal dust was quite inflammable and in concentration could explode. Atkinson wrote to all mine managers urging them to water down the areas when shot-firing took place.

Innovations favouring safety represented additional costs and trouble. The Metropolitan Colliery, between Sydney and Wollongong, was exceptional in that it did introduce locked safety lamps exclusively for illumination, electric motors being regarded as an unreliable source of power for illumination. When such precautions were not taken, there were disasters. 1902 saw some spectacular coal mine disasters. One was at Fraterville, Tennesee, on 19 May, when 184 were killed. 150 men were killed at Fernie mine in British Columbia and on 10 July 112 were killed at Johnstown, Pennsylvania.

Mt Kembla placed faith in its ventilation system. It was by now accepted practice to ventilate collieries continuously, whether they were being worked on or not, in order to avoid the accumulation of flammable gases in stagnant air and the risk of sucking them through the mine at the restart of ventilation. Mt Kembla's air conditioning, which provided between 3000 and 3700 cubic metres a minute, was considered more than adequate for the 260 men and 30 horses working below. The mine was considered one of the best-equipped in the state, but Mt Kembla management did not accept the mandatory use of safety lamps. The ventilation, it was felt, would blow the dangerous stuff away. The rewards from continuing to operate the mine were apparent. At the turn of the century Mt Kembla was the second-largest producer out of 12 mines in the Illawarra district and the fifth-largest of 89 operating in New South Wales. Since it started operations, the mine had paid £100000 in dividends and shareholder return by 1901 had reached eight percent of their investment. By 1902 the mine workings covered 300 hectares, of which 100 hectares had been completely mined. Inside the mountain, the excavated areas had had their struts removed. They were known as goafs, and were left to cave in naturally.

There was a sleeper present—a hidden menace—something so quiet and unobtrusive it was overlooked in the rush to make profits. In one section a huge area, some 13.6 hectares, became a goaf. It appears that low concentrations of gas were being emitted within this goaf, and, being lighter than the air, were concentrating in the roof cavities, far from the probing of the inspectors, unseen and virtually undetectable. In early 1902 some traces of gas were found at the edge of that goaf. No written report was made on the discovery, though it was required by regulations. Rogers knew about it, as did his undermanager, William Nelson. Mine deputy John Morrison was to say later that he checked the goaf once a month. Goafs were supposed to be checked once a week for gas when people were available to do the job and when it was considered safe to do it. In his monthly inspections Morrison did the checking with a naked light, which was an unenlightened and illegal practice—had there been a concentration of gas there he would have set it off. On the grounds of safety he did not check under sections of the roof that were unsupported by props.

Leaving aside such inspections, there were other sets of eyes and ears. If there was gas in a mine, it would come to someone's attention. David Evans, the day deputy for the mining district, heard plenty of accounts from miners concerning the presence of gas. He even saw some evidence of it himself, but he regarded the quantity as too small to constitute a threat and did not report it to his superiors. Management tacitly accepted that there was gas, but they felt that with continuous ventilation, concentrations of gas would not build up to a dangerous level. Rogers was later to say, 'I knew that it was a seam that produced gas. I relied on there being no gas by reason of superior ventilation.' On 29 April 1902 inspectors did another check of the mine's ventilation system. Two days later they pronounced it to be in good order and in compliance with the regulations.

Despite all this, there was never any particular complacency about gas. As Drs Stuart Piggin and Henry Lee, authors of the most comprehensive study, *The Mt Kembla Disaster*, point out, management and workers were happy to perpetuate a public myth that there was no gas in the mine, but privately many held serious concerns. In July 1902 an arbitration hearing was in progress in Wollongong over the miners' claim for an increase in the hewing rate to compensate for the use of safety lamps.

On the morning of Thursday 31 July, the 'front' shift started operations at 7 am, intending as usual to work through to 3 pm. The 'back' shift started at 9 am and would work through to 5 pm. At 2 pm that day there were 261 men underground and 22 on the surface. At that moment, it appears from later inquiry, part of the 13.6 hectare goaf collapsed, displacing air which, with nowhere else to go, was forced along the nearest passage, the No 1 Right Road. With the air came methane gas which, encountering the naked flame of a miner's lamp, exploded. Coal dust, thrown up by the percussion, ignited as well and the succession of explosions knocked out props from the working section, causing the roof sections to fall, displacing more air, throwing up more coal dust, and spreading the explosion further.

The mine was so extensive that in other parts the explosion was not heard at all, but the rumble was heard soon enough at the surface. The ground trembled as though hit by an earthquake. It looked as though a white sheet was coming up to the surface. This was the result of water vaporising immediately before the rush of flame—one of those extraordinary tricks of nature like the lightning bolts in the plume of a volcanic burst or the wafting breezes in the eye of a cyclone that are eerily fascinating to the trapped soul who might have a second or two for contemplation. The smoke and ash roared up through the mine entrance, picking up miner John Clark, who was wheeling a skip, and hurling him and everything around him 30 metres. All buildings were wrecked and the main haulage road was blocked by thousands of tonnes of rock. Piggins and Lee relate the story of Paddy Brownlee and William Wilson who were in a weigh-cabin 25 metres from the mine entrance: 'They neither heard nor saw anything before they were suddenly thrown to their floor and their ears went numb as if something had been savagely thrust upon them. As they were scrambling to their feet a flame rushed through the window to their left, passed under the desk, burned both of them on the left of their faces, peeled the skin from their left arms, and passed out of the cabin through a window on their right.'

Dust rose high above the mine, blotting out the sun. Beneath the surface, eight men had been killed or were mortally injured and another 15 were injured less severely, as were six more who, like John Clark, had been outside the mine. But that was only the start of it. The afterdamp spread quickly, assisted by the ventilation system which, damaged but not destroyed, was inadvertently drawing poisonous gas into other sections of the mine. A number of men from the front shift who were due to stop work were walking towards the main travelling road to get out of the mine. They had not heard the explosion and walked into the afterdamp, where a number succumbed. Others crawled or dragged mates from the deadly atmosphere. Jim Powell, acting in accordance with a mistaken belief that bare feet made one more resistant to gas, got out barefoot. Other miners, feeling their legs go weak and their hearts pumping faster under the effects of carbon dioxide, fell to the ground and into even greater concentrations of carbon dioxide. Some men, so badly affected by the gas, became disorientated and behaved irrationally. James Annersley sat down to light up a pipe and died with the match still between his fingers.

Miners rushed to the scene from all over the district. In the first hours after the explosion, for every two men who were carried out of the mine alive one was carried out dead. There were so many dead that the bodies were loaded onto skips and wheeled out. Nobody had put much thought into preparation for disaster. There were only a dozen safety lamps available. Spares had to be brought from other Illawarra mines. There was no clear knowledge of the layout of the Mt Kembla mine. There were not enough stretchers. Rescuers went into the mine workings and many were affected by the afterdamp and themselves had to be rescued. Two died, one being Henry

Osborne McCabe, a former mayor of Wollongong, who had distinguished himself in rescue work after the Bulli disaster 14 years previously. Another was a night deputy of Mt Kembla mine, William McMurray. Ebenezer Vickery, having received a telegram at 2.30 pm while attending a session of the Legislative Council in Sydney, returned to Port Kembla with sinking feelings.

By 4 pm the next day all hope was lost for any more survivors. Ventilation was so poor that all further searches were suspended. The final toll, after some initial survivors succumbed to the effects of afterdamp, was 96 men and boys. Thirty-three women had been widowed and 14 children aged 14 and under were left without a father. Another 15 adults had lost lovers, partners and breadwinners.

The disaster was followed by a coroner's inquest and a royal commission. The company, following the instinct of most corporate bodies after tragedy, wanted to be exonerated. The theory most appealing to the company was that there had been a wind-blast from the collapsed goaf and no explosion. But burnt bodies and death from carbon monoxide poisoning made that theory untenable. Three royal commissioners, headed by District Court Judge Charles Murray, did not, however, find against anybody in the company—not even Morrison. Morrison's chances of finding such a low concentration of gas in the roof of the 13.6 hectare goaf, they said, were 'practically nil'. The commissioners did find that had safety lamps been used, there would have been no explosion. They said that in future even if a mere trace of gas was found, a mine should be regarded as 'gassy' and appropriate measures taken. They said that use of naked lights to test for gas should be banned, that there should be regular tests of the Mt Kembla workings with safety lamps and each three months tests should be conducted with hydrogen lamps. They ordered that a book be kept in which written records be made of every report by a miner about gas. Other recommendations concerned such things as ventilation, explosives and educational levels for the award of mine manager's certificates.

On 19 September 1902, less than two months after the disaster, 170 men presented themselves for work at the mine and on 25 September production recommenced. On 15 July 1903 Judge Charles Heydon was directed by the government to undertake an inquiry into the conduct of William Rogers, the mine manager. Heydon found that Rogers was 'unfit to discharge his duty by reason of gross negligence'. He found that Rogers had not observed Special Rule 10 for the mine, which required weekly inspections of the mine and regular checks to be carried out in 'idle places', or unworked sections of mine, for the accumulation of gas. Heydon did not find against Rogers on charges of having failed to introduce safety lamps or to recognise the dangers of the accumulation of coal dust. The penalty Rogers suffered was minor: he had his mine manager's certificate suspended for 12 months. For the next ten years almost all coal mines in the Illawarra District were worked with safety lamps, but there was intense opposition to the lamps from mine managers in Newcastle, who did not believe the problems of Mt Kembla had anything to do with them.

Other disasters were to follow. In 1912 a fire broke out in a pumping house on the 213 metre level at Mt Lyell North copper mine in Tasmania. Because there was no alternative escape route and because communications failed, 42 men lost their lives. A royal commission ruled that there should always be alternative escape routes in mines. But why was that precaution not taken beforehand? Coal mines had exploded prior to this, both in Australia and overseas. In the United Kingdom the Senghenydd mine blew up in 1913 near Rhondda in South Wales, killing 439 men and boys. One woman lost her father, her husband and brothers, her three sons and her lodger, but the miners, just as they did at Mt Kembla, went back. This writer reported on a disaster for the *Sydney Morning Herald* at the Kianga coal mine at Moura in central Queensland in September 1975, when 13 miners died and it was decided that the afterdamp problem was so serious that the bodies should be sealed in the mine. In 1979 14 men were killed in a methane gas explosion at Appin, south of Sydney. In 1986 Moura No 4 mine went up and 12 died. In 1994 Moura No 2 Mine went up, killing 11 more.

In March, 1987, a century after the Bulli disaster, a memorial service was held in Bulli's St Augustine's Church in memory of those who died. Among those present were descendants of the victims, some of them fifth-generation miners from the district. Amid such spiritual matters the conflict that could be seen in the worker–employer confrontations of a century before continued. In Melbourne a verdict was given in a key compensation battle over repetitive strain injury. In Western Australia more court battles took place over asbestos diseases. In NSW there were allegations of deaths because of poor facilities in TAFE colleges and debate over changes to workers' compensation laws. The attitudes of employers remained as ever. Cliff Reece, then NSW director of the privately-operated National Safety Council, told this writer, 'I had a project manager for a building company in here two years ago who said, "I just don't know why you are getting stuck into us. We have had only two fatalities on this project and we thought we would have had five by now." Then he realised what he had said and he added, "Oh, I did not really mean it like that." And I said, "Oh yes you did."'

Despite all the modern improvements, the most notable being the introduction of electric lighting, the kinds of accidents which had bedevilled mining the previous century have continued to occur. On 14 November 1996 four miners broke into an old mine shaft at Gretley Colliery near Newcastle, misled by an inaccurate map, and drowned in the water that gushed out. In July 2000 a huge air blast at Northparkes gold and copper mine near Parkes in central western New South Wales picked up a land cruiser containing two men and dashed it against a wall. They died, as did two others caught in the blast. The managing director of the mine's owner, North Limited, blamed 'irregular' practices. Regardless of whether such a claim was justified, the real irregularity was that mining was, as it always has been, operating at the very edges of safety. Safety is considered to be merely a single factor in a more complex equation of risk cost, profit and share price. For the industry to survive these things have to be kept in balance. The problem is, when the balance becomes distorted, managements usually only stand to lose their jobs and shareholders only stand to lose their investment. The men at the workface stand to lose much more.

2

The Implosion of Royal Canberra Hospital, 1997

Kate. In memory of a beautiful angel we never knew.

Message at the Katie Bender Memorial,
Lennox Gardens, Canberra

Implosions of buildings—watching them stagger, then collapse lopsided into a shower of dust—have caught the public imagination ever since it was realised that they are quicker and easier than using wrecking balls and bulldozers. In 1995 the United States saw a number of implosions, including the Landmark Hotel, a 31-storey needle-shaped tower in Las Vegas where Frank Sinatra had performed. At 5.40 am some 7000 people turned up to see it implode, and just before the big bang a film crew shot segments of couples running in 'terror' down the street, for a proposed movie, *Mars Attacks*. In the pre-World Trade Centre era, such events had the allure of spectacle. Australia had seen implosions, including the former Bunnerong power station near Malabar in Sydney in June 1987, and St Vincents Hospital, in Melbourne, in October, 1992.

The way the explosives were placed, the buildings collapsed in on themselves and very little debris, or 'fly', was hurled out. The fact that there might be some fly made it necessary to put up some sort of barrier, such as a 'bund wall'—a barricade, usually two or three metres high, made up of building materials. This is placed around the location of the explosives, and because the explosives are normally set at the bases of buildings, providing bund walls is usually fairly simple. It is normal as well to impose some sort of exclusion zone, which is cleared of people at the time of the blast. The bund wall is mainly seen as just a precaution. The exclusion zone around St Vincents in Melbourne had only been 50 metres, and there had been an occupied building within that zone.

Right from the earliest days of demolition there has always been a right way and a wrong way of going about things. Amateurs, or the underqualified, can be extremely dangerous in these circumstances. This applies to all kinds of demolition. This writer, reporting on a demolition at The Rocks in Sydney in 1977, heard complaints that debris was falling into the Argyle Centre, far below the site. The demolition team threatened violence for reporting the complaints in the *Sydney Morning Herald*, and the next day they vehemently denied that anything had ever fallen into the shopping centre when interviewed by a television news crew. The crew was sympathetic to them, but when interviewing people in the shopping centre they were almost wiped out by falling debris. The Royal Commission into the NSW Building Industry heard evidence in 1991 of a wall falling the wrong way and through the roof of a house during a mechanical demolition in Newington Road, Marrickville, in inner Sydney. John Sutton, Federal secretary of the then Building Workers Industrial Union, whispered, 'You can see what cowboys there are operating in this industry!' Regrettably, when it came to knocking down the Royal Canberra Hospital, located on Acton Peninsula, which overlooks the beautiful Lake Burley

Griffin, the perils of employing the underqualified were realised to the full.

By 1995 Royal Canberra was no longer wanted. Two other hospitals were fulfilling its role: Woden Valley Hospital and Calvary Hospital. The buildings on Acton Peninsula did have some significance. The peninsula had been a construction site when Canberra was being built. Medical facilities had been erected there in 1943, and they had become the Canberra Community Hospital. In 1964 a six-storey tower block had been built using thick, strong steel girders that were built for permanence. The same technique had been used to construct Sylvia Curley House, a nurses training centre erected nearby. By 1995 Canberrans had had a long association with the hospital, but things had moved on. The ACT had gained self-government in 1989 and the Alliance Government decided that it would close the hospital—a proposal initially opposed by the ALP. The closure was announced in November 1991, but rationalisation of ACT health services had fuelled bitter divisions. The buildings could be used for other things. One-time ACT Attorney-General Bernard Collaery said the premises need not have been destroyed at all. 'There was nothing wrong structurally with them,' he said. 'They lent themselves to imaginative redevelopment in the way old buildings were in Chicago and downtown New York.'

Kate Carnell, a builder's daughter and a successful pharmacist who joined the ACT Liberal Party in 1991, had been elected to the ACT Legislative Assembly in 1992. She had become party leader in 1993 and had led the party to government in 1995. Carnell's ideal was a corporatised, 'can-do' government. Personally attractive, she was publicity-minded, participating in stunts such as parachute jumps. Melbourne journalist Andrew Rule was to write, 'She had a touch of fellow Queenslander Pauline Hanson's tendency to polarise voters with her blend of populism and personal appeal, and she relied heavily on advisers and sometimes became close friends, though not always personal ones.'

In 1995 the ACT and Commonwealth governments decided on a land-swap. Acton Peninsula would go to the Commonwealth, along with lake foreshore land at Kingston for development as a housing estate. The then Prime Minister, Paul Keating, was keen on establishing a gallery of Aboriginal history on Acton Peninsula. On the weekend of 16–17 May 1995 the ACT Liberal Party met at Eaglehawk hotel complex, south of Canberra. Ideas were put forward as to future agendas. One item on the agenda was the future of Acton Peninsula, whose hospital buildings were in a state of decay. A minute record said, 'The buildings should be bombed as soon as possible and the proposed museum be allowed to get under way.' It went on to say, 'The buildings currently act as a living reminder of the closure of Royal Canberra Hospital and the sentimental baggage which that carries.' The word 'bombed' was later crossed out and replaced by a milder word.

Such ideas attracted Carnell's attention, as did such notions as a high-speed rail link to other capitals, an international airport and a venue in Canberra for Olympic soccer. In late 1996 Carnell announced that $27 million would be spent for the upgrading of Canberra's Bruce Stadium, making it suitable as an Olympic soccer venue and a contribution to the future success of Canberra's powerful Rugby and Rugby League clubs. Of the $27 million, the government would contribute $12.3 million and the private sector $14.7 million. Carnell was aware of the possibility of imploding at least the Tower Block and Sylvia Curley House. It had the attractions of savings in time and cost, though whether the prospect of a public spectacle attracted her at the time is doubtful.

The ACT's Department of Urban Services commissioned a feasibility study on demolition by Richard Glenn and Associates (RGA), a Melbourne firm. RGA, which had been project managers for the St Vincents Hospital demolition in Melbourne. They made several reports and mentioned the option of implosion. That option, RGA's engineer Ron Deeble cautioned, needed to be properly studied and if taken up would require overseas expertise. If carried out, he said, it should be at the least active time of the week when fewer people would be around.

In March 1996 the John Howard-led Coalition team won national government and Howard put forward the idea that Acton Peninsula should be the site of an Australian museum. The ACT, which administered the peninsula, was to clear it. There was continuing civil resistance, involving protesters and squatters, but the idea that there would be an implosion was then being actively put around. There were more examples of implosions overseas, including the demolition of the 10-storey Anthony Wayne Hotel in Akron, Ohio, in which shaped steel-cutting charges were used. The shaped charges were a spin-off from space technology. They had been developed to separate solid fuel boosters from space shuttles. In April the Newark Housing Authority in the United States demolished three eight-storey apartment buildings in an effort to improve public housing, bringing both cheer and sadness and a place in TV news bulletins.

On 4 August 1995 the ACT cabinet adopted implosion in principle without going into the finer details, such as the need for additional work to supplement the RGA feasibility study and the need for overseas expertise. Implosion of the main hospital buildings was estimated to cut demolition time by a month. On 11 December the Howard Government announced that the Museum of Australia would be built on the Acton Peninsula rather than its previously designated site, Yarramundi Reach. Two days later Howard announced that work on clearing the peninsula would begin immediately. The Canberra company, Project Coordination Australia Pty Ltd (PCAPL), which had long been on the scene and had assisted RGA with its studies, was engaged as the project manager. The following day PCAPL put up a fence around the site and Howard was quoted by the *Canberra Times* as saying, 'Get on with it.'

The ACT Department of Urban Services had been handling the Acton Peninsula project. On 1 January 1997 Totalcare Control Ltd (TCL), a wholly government-owned corporation, took over. Intended to streamline health administration in the ACT, it took over the functions previously exercised by the ACT Health Administration and the Department of Urban Services. It was far more autonomous in its method of operation than its predecessors, and was more inclined to work directly through the office of Ms Carnell.

The implosion idea continued to gain support. On 4 January 1997 Paul Murphy of PCAPL told the *Canberra Times* he favoured it. 'We know how it can be done,' he said. At that point PCAPL had not been appointed project manager, but its managers were confident of getting the job. *The Canberra Times* reported, 'The Tower Block on Acton Peninsula, which has sheltered the sick and witnessed thousands of births and deaths now faces its own demise, almost certainly by "implosion".' Murphy said that asbestos had to be removed before the demolition. He also said, 'Containment of debris will be an important feature, as is often the case overseas with the demolition of famous landmarks by implosion, if the use of it at Acton is made a community event and attracts a large crowd.'

On 8 January Warwick Lavers, a principal of TCL, met with Carnell's media adviser, Gary Dawson, to discuss the event. On 24 January TCL formalised the appointment of PCAPL. ACT Coroner Shane Madden said later that the selection had been a 'rubber-stamp' operation and in fact the process of making a decision had been 'a sham'. The following day PCAPL advertised for expressions of interest from prospective demolition contractors, but the advertisements did not specify implosion.

On 15 April 1997 Carnell issued a media release that there would be 'savings on Acton Peninsula'. The release contained the phrase 'celebration of change'. On 18 April Dawson, after meeting again with Lavers, decided to make the implosion a public event. At this point, as the disaster was starting its count-down, the critical responsibility for doing the job safely was being passed down the line. The ACT Government was now applying pressure, with the Chief Minister's Office leading the charge, including arrangements to pay a child-minding centre to move off the site quickly. Melbourne journalist Andrew Rule later wrote, 'Kate Carnell knew her government had problems: it represented self-government that most people did not want which had closed a hospital most people did want because it could no longer afford it. She hoped that one maverick act would kill two birds with the one stone: win her glory of getting the Kingston foreshore developed and to end the hospital controversy.'

There were a half-dozen tenderers for the demolition, one being Delta Demolitions, run by David Riddell, president of the Australian Demolition Contractors Association, who proposed using a conventional means of demolition. In his view it was feasible to strip the building, weakening the supports, then pull the building over using a bulldozer and a cable attached to the girders—an 'induced' collapse. There were many examples of this, including the ASIO building in St Kilda, Melbourne, which was demolished without trouble in 30 days using a concrete pulveriser. With one exception all firms expressing interest proposed demolition by conventional means, one even proposing to leave a single storey building around the base of the hospital to catch any debris.

The one exception was from City and Country Demolitions Pty Ltd (CCD), a company based in Newcastle, which had put in a comparatively low price and suggested an implosion. Its principal, Anthony Bruce Fenwick, had experience in demolishing, but not in implosion. Despite this he won the tender and subcontracted for the implosion to Controlled Blasting Services Pty Ltd (CBS), headed by Rodney Douglas McCracken, based in Tweed Heads. McCracken's reputation, Riddell said later, was that he was 'no mug at the game'. Early that year, McCracken had blown up the chimney of the old Nestlés chocolate factory in the Sydney suburb of Abbotsford, with spectators watching from less than 100 metres away. He had done about 200 implosions without serious complication, though at one demolition flying debris had smashed windows in a police station. Applying for the Canberra Hospital contract, McCracken did not provide much evidence of his work, certainly not in video form. Had some of it been shown it would have revealed debris thrown great distances.

McCracken got the contract, but he only had a general idea of how the buildings were constructed. No plans were shown to him. He did a visual inspection and saw concrete-clad columns, but did not realise that they were steel-reinforced and the steel was exceptionally thick. Once he found out, the presence of steel did make him think. Concrete buildings, he said, did not present much of an implosion problem. Steel did. He was to say later that when he realised steel was involved, he had withdrawn his recommendation for implosion and opted for an induced collapse. But, he said, he was ignored. Instead, he decided to take the job on and draw on his general demolition experience to make decisions along the way.

In reality, he was entering 'tiger country'—an area of hidden perils. He relied on intuition and did not take the trouble to seek advice from an engineer who had experience with implosions. He also neglected to do basic things, like having tests done to determine the properties of the steel. The fundamental point to be made about steel is that it is designed to withstand stress. This makes it resistant to destructive forces. When work began on 22 April, Fenwick did not provide a work plan as required by the project manager. This was mainly due to time constraints. The deadline had been set as 9 July, though this was later changed to 13 July. Canberra radio MIX 106.3 FM gained Gary Dawson's approval to run a competition for a person to push the plunger to set the implosion off. The Lions Club decided a good idea would be to sell bricks from the site to raise money for charity and allow Canberrans to have the chance of keeping a little piece of memorabilia.

Cameron Dwyer represented the project manager PCAPL on site. His job was to supervise contractors and sub-contractors. He was concerned about the safe viewing distance, but Fenwick and McCracken demonstrated from the outset that they were headstrong. McCracken was a forceful and confident personality. After Dwyer pressured him, Fenwick agreed to provide a statement of method, but by the time he did, on 16 May, work had been in progress for nearly a month and even then the real author of the statement was McCracken.

Fenwick engaged the services of an engineer, Adam Hugill, of Northrop Engineers Pty Ltd, to give advice on the demolition of the tower block. Hugill had no experience with explosives, but he had basic knowledge and common sense. He was aware of some of the monstrous technical difficulties, and his own limitations. He had never before advised on pre-cutting to weaken buildings. He at least checked with his own directors for approval before he proceeded to give that advice. On 22 May 1997 Hugill found that one column had been so over-cut that it placed the remaining metal at more than twice the upper level of stress, raising the danger of premature collapse. He tried to take a more prominent role, and to get his services used on a more formal basis. Instead he found that his services were terminated. Dwyer told Fenwick and McCracken that there should be no more cutting until an engineer had done an inspection. They went on cutting anyway.

McCracken was telling everyone what was to be done. Coroner Madden found that he was uncaring of supervisors and continually failed to meet deadlines or provide information. Fenwick was no more cooperative. On 29 May, Dwyer wrote to Fenwick about what he thought of using explosives. Fenwick did not reply. On 2 June Dwyer wrote to Fenwick about the question of flying debris and safe viewing distances. Fenwick made no written reply, but McCracken did contact another engineer, Gordon Ashley, from Sydney, with whom he had previously worked. Ashley made three visits to Canberra, the first on 30 May, to give advice on the stability of a weakened building, but he was not an expert in explosives. Nor did he learn of Hugill's advice. His attendance on-site hardly reflected the size and complexity of the project: four hours on-site in his first visit and brief visits on 4 July and

13 July, though he later claimed that he spent 15 hours on calculations. He was there at least long enough to recognise that Sylvia Curley House, because of the way it was constructed, was going to represent a demolition problem, but he had no contact with Fenwick.

Ashley seemed less concerned than Hugill by possible limitations of his expertise. He sent McCracken a letter saying that approximately four kilograms of explosives would be needed to strip concrete from the columns. If that had been his genuine professional belief, drawing upon his general engineering knowledge, that might have been acceptable at least as a professional opinion. But it turned out that McCracken had dictated what he was to put into the letter. Ashley said later, 'Quite frankly, I was essentially taking a transcription from Rod to put in writing so I could formally approve.' On 2 June, on the basis of that authorisation, McCracken started blasting the concrete. Ashley was not overly concerned with the bigger explosions that were to follow. He believed that the method of demolition was up to the contractor, and it was up to the project manager to ensure it was done properly.

The monitoring of the project by statutory authorities was another safety mechanism, or series of safety mechanisms, but sadly they broke down. There was some uncertainty over the status of the peninsula, now formally owned by the Commonwealth but administered by the ACT. This might have slowed the process down because of confusion regarding who had what authority. Neither the ACT Building Control nor the National Capital Authority examined the demolition proposal, and the ACT Dangerous Goods Unit (DGU) limited itself merely to issuing a permit to use explosives. McCracken showed DGU officer Tony Smith his unrestricted demolition licence issued by NSW WorkCover and powderman's licences that he held in New South Wales and Queensland. He impressed Smith with his confidence. Smith and fellow officer Bill McTernan were later to say that they had no experience with explosives. ACT Work-Cover inspectors might have provided a safeguard. But they really didn't know what they were meant to be looking for.

The real voice of concern came from the trade union movement. The Health Services Union of Australia was concerned with the safety of staff and patients in a hospice 78 metres from Sylvia Curley House. Dwyer thought the concerns reasonable and told Fenwick and McCracken that work should cease until it was decided how the hospice would be protected. A WorkCover officer, Margaret Kennedy, made inquiries and in the process found out about the broken police station window at McCracken's demolition project in Queensland. At a meeting of various parties on 2 July, McCracken said he would ensure that the hospice was especially safe. He would reconfigure the explosives in the building to ensure that no fly would go towards the hospice.

What McCracken did not address when he spoke to the meeting was the question of where fly might then go. In fact, it was more likely after the reconfiguration that fly would sail across the lake and hit some of the tens of thousands of people who would be gathered there. What McCracken did tell the meeting was that he would use 130 kilograms of explosives, including 100 kilograms of Riogel, an explosive designed for shattering rocks in quarries and not specifically designed for demolition work. Added to that would be 12 kilograms of powderfel and 18 kilograms of PE4. There was no mention of specially-shaped cutting charges. Such charges could have been obtained, but they would have had to be imported. They were more expensive, but far more powerful than the explosives used, requiring only 1.1 kilograms per steel column as opposed to up to 2.2 kilograms of conventional explosive. McCracken chose to use conventional explosives, pre-cutting the steel so that they would work the same way as the cutting charges.

McCracken did make a concession towards safety. He said he would use 50 percent more sandbags than originally intended. When questioned he admitted that there had been broken windows in his earlier Queensland job, but he claimed that that had been due to the charges being set 'too high'. Leaving aside the question of why there had been any problem at all, anyone seriously critical could have come up with a number of questions about the very diagrams McCracken presented. When the total of explosive charges that McCracken said he would lay were added, they came to some 240 kilograms.

McCracken said the maximum charge at any one point would be 2.4 kilograms. The diagrams indicated that some of the charges were greater than that amount. WorkCover, whose main representatives on-site were Margaret Kennedy and Ken Purse, could have been far more critical but as the coroner found, they simply did not appreciate the dangers. The sandbagging was inadequate. Chain mesh, which could have been wrapped around all of the columns in order to prevent pieces flying out should the metal disintegrate, was nowhere to be seen. It was later revealed that 2000 square metres of mesh would have been required. It would have cost McCracken $4000. McCracken decided that he did not need it.

On 4 July Dawson sent a series of emails to ACT public service organisations reminding them about the event. There was little doubt that the pressure was on the contractors now. In a later interview with police McCracken said that he would have been 'hauled over the coals if the implosion did not go ahead on time'. It was for that reason, he said, that he had decided to proceed without getting the shaped steel-cutting charges. There were lingering concerns in the political establishment. One was whether all the asbestos had been removed, preventing the possibility of showers of the lethal dust. An independent territory politician, Michael Moore, said that he had received unequivocal assurances from Carnell that all asbestos had been removed.

Ken Purse had continuing doubts. On 9 July he wrote to Dwyer seeking confirmation that the bund walls would be at least two or three metres high. Dwyer wrote back saying that bund walls 2.5 to three metres high would be constructed on the northern side of Sylvia Curley House, where required. Dwyer said, 'Our contractor has advised that the bund walls are not required along the full length of the building and will be formed where necessary to eliminate rock and minimise noise.' Purse could have responded by saying, 'I don't care what the contractor says. I want bund walls three metres high around the entire site or the work does not proceed!' But he did not. There was no bund wall in front of one column, C74. Another column that was later to come to notice, C30, had a bund wall that was too low to catch all potential fly material. All of the bund walls were too low and too far from the buildings to do their designated job. As the time of implosion drew closer, it would have been obvious to anyone that there was virtually no protection on the side of the buildings facing the lake. Sandbagging had been carried out around some of the columns but not all of them. There were no sandbags on the external face of C74 or C30. WorkCover inspectors could have responded to this oversight, but they did not.

On 10 July Kennedy visited the site and took photographs. The photographs, which were developed after the implosion, revealed the lack of sandbagging and wire mesh. The pictures included columns C74 and C30. Kennedy did make a note, but it was not about these critical safety matters, just that McCracken had not realised what was in the columns when he tendered and since then had been working up to 18 hours a day. In the meantime McCracken told the *Canberra Times* that the amount of explosives was now 225 kilograms, spread throughout the tower in 280 positions. The tower would be first to go, followed ten seconds later by Sylvia Curley House. According to later evidence there was even more explosive than stated—somewhere between 480 and 500 kilograms. In a relaxed mood Warwick Lavers told the media that more than 200 bottles of oxy-acetylene had been used. So much pre-cutting had been done that the entire hospital structure was measured as having sunk two millimetres and leaning two millimetres off line, but who was concerned about that, if the whole building was to go anyway? In keeping with the celebratory mood, the Lions Club said that people could take bricks from the demolished hospital in return for the donation of a gold coin.

Some people opposed the demolition to the end. Jack Kershaw, president of the community group Action for Acton, which believed that the buildings could be adapted to other uses, said the destruction of the buildings was a 'final solution'. There were nostalgic expressions from nurses who had trained and served there. Nobody was talking about whether the contractors could really be believed when they said everybody would be safe. Radio MIX 106.3 FM's competition for the right to press the plunger was won by Sue George, a Canberra mother-of-three. On 11 July Carnell suggested some good vantage points. 'The best viewing will be from the south side of Lake Burley Griffin in Lennox Gardens, the Yacht Club and round Attunga Point, or on the north side of the lake from Black Mountain to Attunga Park.' It was heralded as 'a historic event not to be missed'.

McCracken, now having been fully appraised of the publicity, embraced the idea and put fireworks into the building for effect, including drums of diesel that would spew fire from the windows. It was noted later that no permit had been issued for fireworks or any warning issued to aircraft, but such detail hardly mattered at that point. A special government-organised group, including journalist Norman Abjorensen, was invited to a vantage point close to the hospital and given ear muffs. Spectator craft went out onto the lake but the ACT Water Police said they would keep the craft at what their advice said was a safe distance. Carnell said the safe viewing distance was only 50 metres and that the government had its own people within that.

On 13 July, a fine day, with the lake surface still and mirror-like, the big event had finally arrived. Purse and Kennedy were among WorkCover inspectors who visited the site. The sandbagging was still inadequate and the wire mesh absent but they did not question it. Purse did raise the question of safety, but McCracken again reassured him, telling him at 12.30 pm that he had changed the configuration of the explosives, advice which Purse took to be further assurance that the hospice would be protected. It had not occurred to him, he said in later evidence, that the entire crowd of spectators was in danger. But even a cursory inspection of the site would have revealed the inadequacy of sandbagging and provided grounds to have stopped the implosion at that point. McCracken said that at 1.05 pm, five minutes after the scheduled time for the blast, he would be at the Canberra Yacht Club to wash the dust from his lungs with ale. At 12.30 pm, an ecumenical church service was held to farewell the building. MIX 106.3 FM put up loud-speakers for a public broadcast.

The family of Mato and Zola Bender, Croatian migrants with four children, might or might not have been among the 100 000 people, representing a third of Canberra's population, who turned up early on the Sunday afternoon. Mato was a school porter. The family comprised Mato and Zola and their children Anna, 20, Maria, 19, David, 17, and Katie, 12. They were salt-of-the-earth people, devoutly Catholic, living in Rosebery Street in the central Canberra suburb of Fisher. They had been concerned with problems in their home country, joining a rally of 40 000 people who turned up at Commonwealth Park in 1991 to protest about the Serbian invasion of Croatia. Katie, a Year Seven pupil at St Clare's College in the Canberra suburb of Manuka, was a cheerful, outgoing girl who had a keen interest in Croatian dancing. The night before the implosion she had gone dancing at the Australian Croatian Club in the suburb of O'Connor, joining the 100-strong Kardinal Alozija Stepinac group in performing traditional folk dances.

David Bender had heard the publicity about the implosion. On that Sunday morning, the family went to mass at St Patrick's Church in the suburb of Braddon and, seeing the crowd assembled, they decided they would have a look too. They took a blanket and went to the lake's edge at Lennox Gardens, some 450 metres from the hospital, which was the vantage point selected by between 30 000 and 40 000 people. The crowd was dense—people were sitting with legs dangling over the retaining wall, cameras mounted on tripods, laughing and waiting for the countdown. Abjorensen wrote later, 'When the project manager, Cameron Dwyer, was asked what would happen if it did not work, he smiled nervously and said, "We would have to go and sneak out of here very nervously."' Three small aircraft flew overhead. Warning sirens went off, by arrangement, at 45, 15 and 5 minutes before implosion. At 1.03 pm, slightly behind schedule, the countdown began. At 1.05 pm the pyrotechnics went off. Nothing else happened. It turned out that debris dislodged by the pyrotechnics had fallen and broken a cable linking the push button to the charges. The button was repaired and recounting started. The sirens sounded and Sue George pushed the button.

Abjorensen wrote, 'The building beneath us moved up and down with the shock of the blast before swaying sideways, before the old tower block crumbled.' The explosives ripped through the metal, which shattered, sending remnants into the air. Some of these remnants, after a period of perhaps five to 15 seconds, landed in the lake, making an armada of small craft look as though they were in a sea battle with shells falling into the water, sending up plumes of spray. As it turned out, these were not the first events to take place after the detonation. World War II servicemen among the crowd recognised the whine of metal flying at supersonic speed, much of it going across the heads of the crowd. 'At between 2.2 and 2.4 seconds after the implosion, you could hear the coming of the projectiles,' said Bernard Collaery.

Pieces of metal started hitting branches on the other side of the lake, hitting buildings, cars and people. One piece smashed into a car on James Flynn Drive, near Lennox Gardens, and went spinning crazily behind it. One piece smashed its way through the brick wall of a building near the hospital. A triangular-shaped piece, weighing almost a kilogram, about the size of a dinner plate, came across flying like a frisbee at an estimated speed of 150 metres per second. One spectator, Eugene Petrie, there with his family for a barbecue, saw what he thought was a brick coming through the air. 'I could see this lump flying along through the air,' he said. 'Then it dropped down, broke some branches off the trees and hit this woman. There was a lot of blood.'

The 'woman' was Katie Bender. The missile had struck the top of her head before careering into the ground, landing with a thud some six metres behind her. Mato Bender said that the family had been standing watching the explosion and Katie 'just fell down'. Katie Bender, the loveliest little girl, a smiling, bespectacled teenager, was dead before her body hit the ground. Her mother, horrified, bent down and cradled her in her arms. The crowd started screaming. Ten other people were injured. A 14-year-old boy, who was standing next to Katie, was hit in the chest and suffered broken ribs after being hit by another piece of debris.

On the lake, Jim Cunningham and Amanda Staier, and a friend from Melbourne, Joe Devlin, at least had a chance because they saw what was coming at them. Their canoe was part of a flotilla of craft 350 metres from the site. Cunningham said, 'We watched the hospital come down. That was brilliant. Then all of a sudden, it starts raining shrapnel all over the place and it's gone, we are too close. We thought of paddling out of the way backwards but before we had a chance to do that, the second blast went off that was Sylvia Curley House. We saw this thing, this material, coming straight at us. I yelled that it was going to hit us . . . we must have thought the same because, just before it hit us, we all rolled and it came down on top of the canoe, leaving a gash in it.'

At the implosion site, the people involved were not aware of the tragedy. What was obvious was that the implosion had only been partially successful. Parts of the buildings were still standing. The hospital chimney had fallen the wrong way, towards the lake instead of into the 'footprint' of the building. But news of the disaster came soon enough. Carnell, horrified, tried her best to control the situation. She said that the event had had thorough preparation, there had been 12 months of inquiries to ensure safety, and that Richard Glenn and Associates had produced studies in 1995 and 1996. But she came under immediate attack. Apart from the fact that the RGA reports had only amounted to a feasibility study, why should a demolition which carried an inherent risk, despite the best control measures, have been promoted in that way? Carnell, in a statesmanlike and compassionate spirit, visited the Bender family at their home.

When the then Opposition leader Wayne Berry started making criticisms, Carnell called on him to stop making 'political mileage' out of the tragedy, a sentiment, which to her critics fell oddly from her lips because in their view the event had been intended to gain political mileage for her. The Construction, Forestry, Mining and Energy Union accused Carnell of having exploited the event for its publicity value. The ACT branch secretary of the Health Services Union, Bert Tolley, accused Carnell of not having owned up to her government's involvement, an accusation immediately rejected by Carnell. The ACT Opposition went on the attack, saying that WorkCover had been too cowed and under-resourced to challenge the enthusiasm of government.

As the public sent bouquets of flowers to the Bender home, one delivered personally by Dr Jozo Meter, the Croatian ambassador, grim-faced engineers, police, bureaucrats and lawyers went to the wreckage of the hospital and surveyed the damage. Bernard Collaery said, 'I saw that shrapnel had stripped trees. It had cut through fencing. It had gone straight through the masonry of some buildings and out the other side. One wooden floor had been splintered. I looked at one bathroom and shrapnel had gone clean through the ceramic bowl of the toilet. At the lakeside, I could see shrapnel hits on trees at the water's edge that indicated what we call sheet flight.' Police found shrapnel 650 metres from the site. One 16-kilogram piece of metal was recovered by divers from the bottom of the lake. Stephen Thompson, from the suburb of Wanniassa, showed media a piece of metal that had penetrated the bonnet of his car, which had been parked in Flynn Drive, on the opposite side of the lake.

There were accusations of slipshod work practices. A local television station, TEN Capital TV, interviewed a man who said he had been taken off a dole queue to help lay explosives and that he had been totally unqualified. Two days after the implosion, McCracken surveyed the site in dismay. He was overheard expressing deep concern. On 18 July 17 hospice patients were moved temporarily so that a search could be conducted for unexploded charges. The next day the remaining demolition was completed. Several weeks later, Collaery met Fenwick at the site. 'Tony was the only man who forgot legal inhibitions and with great emotion said how wretched he felt, how terrible he felt,' Collaery said later. 'Those comments of his were so important to the family at the time. It was the words of a decent human being.'

A white cross was erected at the place in Lennox Gardens where Katie fell, with a simple message: 'Kate. In memory of the beautiful angel we never knew.' A memorial service at St Patrick's was packed. Katie's dancing shoes were put on exhibition at the Croatian Club. In December 1997 it was announced that a memorial garden to Katie would be built at the edge of Lake Burley Griffin.

Kate Carnell continued her own way. That month, after attending a tennis match at a winery, she suffered a car accident, which in the circumstances she could well have done without.

In the continuing inquiries into the disaster, a Queensland academic, Dr Jeffrey Gates, confirmed that the steel in the hospital was brittle and likely to shatter. It went without saying that such information should have been available at the time the ACT Government advertised for tenders.

Whatever political damage Carnell suffered, it was not reflected in the February 1998 election, when the Liberal Government won another term with an increased margin. It was noted that the report into the tragedy by coroner Madden was not to be released for another month, so none of the government's dirty linen was going to be displayed for some time. Meanwhile, there were other political storm clouds gathering for Carnell.

The inquiry soon revealed shocking inadequacies in demolition technique and in bureaucratic control. It appeared that the entire system had been depending on the final link—the man setting the explosives—to do his job properly. McCracken had not done so. He had not obtained the shaped cutting charges that would have vastly reduced the need for explosives. Mark Loizeaux, a highly-credentialed US expert, said the use of Riogel was 'not well-advised, in fact, ill-advised'. He said the shaped cutting charges had been available in the United States since the late 1960s and, had they been used, would have required less than a tenth of the explosives. 'We could have shipped it to Australia in two months or flown it over in two weeks,' he said. The shaped cutting charges could have been rushed to Australia by dedicated flight at an estimated cost of $75 000.

Coroner Madden found that the fragment that killed Katie Bender had in all probability come from column C30 or C74, columns which had had no barrier. The great miracle was that more were not killed. One expert said that the majority of projectiles had sailed just over the heads of the crowd. Madden recommended in his report on 4 November 1999 that McCracken be put on trial for manslaughter by negligence and that Fenwick be tried for being knowingly concerned in the offence of manslaughter by negligence. He was critical of WorkCover and of the engineer Stanley. He strongly criticised the Carnell Government for promoting the implosion as a public spectacle without due regard to public safety.

Release of the report was followed by a call by the then ACT Opposition Leader John Stanhope that Carnell resign as chief minister and that two other assembly members should consider resigning. Carnell continued for the time being but, at the same time she was in trouble over the Bruce Stadium development, the cost of which had blown out from $27 million to $45 million. $16 million of that had been spent without formal approval. The private sector, which was meant to have given generously, had contributed nothing. On 17 October, 2000, Carnell resigned as ACT Chief Minister, heading off a no-confidence motion that was to be moved against her, and which was to be supported by two independents on whom she had relied.

It was always going to be difficult to make criminal charges stick to the contractors. Negligence can only be established when the person should have known better. In 2000 the ACT Director of Public Prosecutions decided that the criminal charges against Fenwick and McCracken should be dropped, but it was announced that both would be summonsed for breach of the ACT *Occupational Health and Safety Act*. On 18 May 2001, McCracken pleaded guilty to a charge of failing to ensure a safe workplace. But the contractors, like anyone, anywhere, at the coalface of an operation, could only ever be expected to shoulder part of the blame. If they were to be rebuked for an inadequate performance, it should have been before the disaster, not after it, and the rebuke should have been delivered by the person or persons higher in the administrative or even legislative tree.

3

The Ash Wednesday Bushfires, 1983

Well, there's my house gone, finished.

Clifford Pannam QC, Mt Macedon resident

When the Ash Wednesday bushfires came to Victoria, salesman Kel Grigg set out to pick up the wife and daughter of a client and get them to safety. A few hundred metres down the road the three of them encountered a massive fire and because of the heat evaporating the petrol in the engine, the car stopped. The three were trapped.

'I explained to the woman that the only way we would save ourselves was by winding up all the windows of the car, lying on the floor and await the fire to burn over the top,' Grigg said later. 'We all sort of got down on the floor and sort of laid there. This worked OK until the windows started to explode. A fair amount of flames coming through the openings. The flames were licking at us. I was in the back seat and the woman was in the front driver's seat and the boy, I think, was in the front passenger seat, although I can't really remember where he was. The woman said, "I've got to get out of here." After that it was just a bit of chaos. She kept screaming out that she wanted to get out of the car. I told her she would be killed if she did. I can remember that at one stage she said, "I don't care, I can't stand it." She opened the driver's door and suddenly took off and that was the last I saw of her. The fire was pretty violent then.'

Farmer Albert Stephen Payne begged his uncle Mervyn George Thomas not to try to rescue his cattle. 'I saw him walk over to the shed when suddenly there was a violent wind change and I saw the roaring fire turn at us. It just came straight back on top of us. I could not see Mervyn and at the same time the entire area was engulfed in a mass of flames and smoke.'

Julia French rang her sister-in-law, whose house at Macedon was threatened by the inferno. 'She said nobody was coming. She said, "Nobody is going to save me. I won't leave Jack." I asked her could she go down the track. She said she couldn't go down the track as it was on fire. She then said she saw a light and someone was coming. She then hung up the phone. I rang back shortly thereafter and she answered the phone again. She said they didn't come. She said, "No one's going to come. I'll stay with Jack." She then said the front of the house was on fire. Graham [French's son-in-law] then took the phone off me and told Amy to be calm and that we were coming. She called out that the windows were exploding, and there wasn't another sound after that.'

Radio journalist Murray Nicoll broadcasted the destruction of his neighbourhood to 5DN listeners in Adelaide. 'I'm sitting in the driveway of a friend's house two doors down from my house,' he said. 'The next block to my right there's a house burning down. It's 30 feet away. It's going up in flames. There's nothing we can do. The driveway of the house I'm sitting in is so hot. I can hardly sit on it. I am so tired. I can't do anything. My neighbour Bill is shovelling dirt on a burning fence here. His house is OK. The house behind me across the road, that's gone. The one next door to it, that's gone. My house is gone. It's exploding still and I just can't bear to look at that. And the man across the road from me, he thinks his wife may be trapped in the house, and his house is burnt to the ground. He hasn't seen his wife since they left, and she didn't come out of the house at all. He ran with his son, calling for his wife, and she didn't follow him. He believes, and nobody can tell him to the contrary, that she may still be in there. Well, if she's in there she's gone.'

These are the voices of people attempting to deal with the death and destruction caused by the worst bushfires in south-eastern Australia's history. Ignited in the blistering afternoon of 16 February 1983, they directly killed 76, incinerated more than 3700 buildings and reduced more than half a million hectares of townships, forests and farmland to ashes. Some 2400 families or individuals lost their homes. More than 340 000 sheep and 18 000 cattle were lost, either burned to death or destroyed because of their appalling injuries. Figures vary, but it can be safely said that between 1100 and 2700 people were injured, many requiring hospital treatment. It has been estimated that 20 000 kilometres of fencing was lost and 1.5 million bales of hay were burnt. Insurance losses, in contemporary values, exceeded $320 million. In 2002 values, that would come to more than $1 billion.

There is no such thing as a boxing bout lasting several years, of course, but it is the closest simile we can find for the lop-sided contest between Nature and south-eastern Australia up until mid-February 1983. South-eastern Australia was on the ropes. Nature had fought it to a standstill, throwing, as the ringside commentators love to say, punches in bunches. In an appalling irony, the *Age* prepared a virtual round-by-round commentary on the contest just before the Ash Wednesday fires. Feature writers Philip McIntosh and Louise Carbines, who wrote the report, made no allusion to the disaster, even though their story appeared the morning after the devastation. They did, however, begin by saying that some might choose to call Victoria the Garden State. Nature had decided otherwise. It was now the 'drought, bushfire and dustbowl State in the tragic summer of '83'. So far this season, they innocently wrote, Victoria had experienced one of its worst droughts, some of the 'most devastating bushfires and certainly the most remarkable dust storm'.

As early as the previous August the Country Fire Authority had warned that Victoria could face one of its worst bushfire seasons. In November the CFA reiterated that not a single region of the state would be free of serious danger. Extreme fires could be expected when rainfall was more than 30 percent below average in the three months from August to October; the whole of Victoria had met that criterion, its aridity in some parts worse than at any time since records were kept.

On 24 November 1982 high temperatures were accompanied by 85 bushfires. In January 1983 two Forests Commission workers were trapped and killed by a bushfire in the Greendale area east of Melbourne. The commission said the fire, which started in the Wombat State Forest, was deliberately lit. Indeed, nature had its little human helpers, the reporters pointed out. A total of 119 bushfires said to be deliberately lit had flared across the state in the seven months prior to February. It was twice the annual average of the previous 10 years. Igniting on 31 January, a bushfire in the far east of the state had burned for two weeks, even into New South Wales, reducing 120 000 hectares of forest and grassland to ash, causing millions of dollars of damage to pine plantations and threatening the township of Mallacoota. On 1 February bushfire destroyed 18 houses on Mt Macedon without loss of life.

'But there was worse to come,' the writers guilelessly asserted. On 6 February, 98 fires were 'whipped by winds of up to 110 kmh . . .' and on 9 February, a massive dust storm swept through Victoria on a day when Melbourne's temperature reached 43.2 degrees Celsius. It cut 'power to more than 150 000 people, damaged houses, disrupted train services, ripped boats from moorings and caused Melbourne's worst air pollution in almost five years.' The cloud had a front of 500 kilometres—from Mildura in the north-west to Melbourne in the south. It measured 150 kilometres from west to east and varied between 350 and 3500 metres in altitude. On average about 95 kilograms of topsoil from far away regions of the state fell on every Melbourne suburban quarter-acre houseblock.

More than half of Victoria's 211 municipalities had been declared drought-affected areas. Many Victorian regions had lived with drought for the previous four years. Wheat farmers expected to harvest only about a tenth of the crop they had reaped in 1982. Sheep populations were well down. Casual farm work was disappearing. Service industries in the bush were dying and, by mid-February, Melbourne's eight water storages were holding less than half their normal capacity. Humidity was very low, and because of the drought, dry leaves, twigs and other vegetation that can fuel bushfires were copious. Even forest vegetation in steep gullies that were usually green and damp was also dry. Slugged and sluggish might be an appropriate description of Victoria and Victorians on the morning of 16 February. Yet another scorching day and more fires were predicted, but people looked forward to the cool change forecast for the evening. Melburnians love cool changes, but fire fighters await them in trepidation; often they just make things worse.

South-eastern Australia's high-summer runs on a classic cycle. Rotating high-pressure systems move from west to east across the continent, blowing hot air from inland Australia across the region. Temperatures increase over three or four days to the low-forties Celsius. Northerly winds can regularly blast Victoria and South Australia at up to 60 kmh. Sometimes even more fiercely. Think of a kind of planetary hair dryer; it is not beach weather. These are parching, face-reddening, skin-blistering, eye-crusting conditions. Then, as the high moves east out over the Tasman Sea, another slips in to replace it. Before that, though, the coast, including cities such as Melbourne, feels a low-pressure anti-clockwise spin off the Southern Ocean. Cool air and rainstorms sweep in from the south and south-west. When the change occurs, temperatures can drop by 25 degrees Celsius in the same number of minutes.

The first significant fire of 16 February 1983 was logged at 11.30 am at McLaren Flat, 37 kilometres south of Adelaide. It was Ash Wednesday, a chilling coincidence. South Australians had experienced an Ash Wednesday three years earlier in which bushfire destroyed 70 homes and many farmlets in the Adelaide Hills. The authorities' ears were still ringing from a long legal and administrative inquiry that followed, part of which showed that they performed poorly and were under prepared and under funded. Would Ash Wednesday 1983 be a repeat performance?

The sequence of fires continued as follows. At 11.57 am, heavy forest around the vineyards of Clare, about 130 kilometres to the north of Adelaide, was reported to be alight. Twenty-eight minutes later, vast pine forests around Mount Gambier to the far south-east on the Victorian border were reported to be in flames. In the next half-hour eight separate fires were listed in the steep and heavily-treed Adelaide Hills and Mount Lofty Ranges just north of the city. By 1 pm the Country Fire Services had declared them beyond control. In Victoria, the temperature by early afternoon had reached 40 degrees Celsius. Spotter aircraft had pinpointed dozens of fires throughout the state all morning. The CFA would attend 180 fires that day. A total of 178 would be controlled. Blasting northerly winds were driving the fires, as usual, and fire fighters, many of whom had battled for months, were professional but mechanical, doing what they could with just-adequate equipment, resources and communications. They were employees of either the CFA or the Forests Commission, which had responsibility for outbreaks in state forests. Wouldn't it be nice, many no doubt thought, if the southerlies came in with a dump of rain and quickly rebated winds.

The winds had already turned in South Australia, to come from the south in Adelaide, where they were more a nuisance than an aid, driving fire fronts up picturesque valleys towards the houses and hobby farms of South Australia's best-off families. Perhaps it was an omen. In *Who Burned Australia?* John Baxter writes that 'quick chemical bombing' from the air might have put out the most threatening Victorian fires early in their rampages. But only one specialised Hercules C130 was used that day, flying from a base in New South Wales. Four hundred fire-trucks, water tankers and bulldozers, 11 helicopters and 14 fixed-wing aircraft were eventually used to fight the fires. 'Coordination of effort, where it existed at all, was casual,' Baxter writes. On a disaster scale of one to three, the Victorian fires were for many hours declared a one, or possibly two, meaning that they were to be handled locally by the commission or the CFA.

During the afternoon the worst conflagrations were easily identified. Two fires had joined in the far west of the state between Framlingham and Warrnambool, which are 30 kilometres apart and 250 kilometres to the south-west of Melbourne. They were to burn on a 13 kilometre front through hundreds of hectares of grazing country, destroying 164 houses and claiming eight victims. Three more epic infernos were closer to Melbourne and more destructive. The first was registered at around 2 pm near the Wombat State Forest, about 70 kilometres north-west of the city centre. Fanned southward by northerlies, it could blaze for 20 kilometres or so before reaching even a hamlet. Further south it would stop, anyway, at the edge of the black scar of the Greendale fire, which had burned the month before. The second had far more catastrophic potential, starting in the heavily populated Dandenong Ranges at 3.38 pm, just 35 kilometres east of the city. More densely inhabited than the Adelaide Hills, the Dandenongs are thickly forested. A crumple of hideaway houses, steep gullies, dense bush, winding narrow roads and tracks, they are home to many permanent residents but also many wealthy Melburnians with weekend cottages. Even though the Dandenongs are seen these days as a part of Melbourne's inevitable suburban sprawl, they host giant eucalypts that are among Victoria's tallest trees. Equally, the Hills, as they are affectionately known, have a long history of devastation by bushfire. Within half-an-hour, a separate fire at Cockatoo, a village 12 kilometres further to the east, had flared. Later in the day it was to cause the greatest despair of all.

Just after 4 pm the most spectacular fire of all broke out at Deans Marsh, 115 kilometres south-west of Melbourne. A tiny timber town 20 kilometres inland from Victoria's picturesque Surf Coast, Deans Marsh is in the densely forested Otway Ranges, which roll down steeply onto the wide golden sands of famous beach resorts such as Lorne, Aireys Inlet and Fairhaven. By mid-afternoon the fires were roaring. Baxter contends that authorities were dithering. Until 7.30 pm they still regarded the fires as local problems to be dealt with by the CFA or the commission. In South Australia the situation was little better. Baxter writes that while Adelaide police were urging people to protect their homes in the northern hills, country police were keeping drivers out of the area. 'Unwitting [South Australian] radio stations broadcast advice and news bulletins which were either erroneous or out of date.'

Communications were in chaos. Adelaide police car radios were simply not up to the job. In Victoria massive use of reserves might have been tried. But each of the fire authorities thought the other had the problem under control. Neither Stan Duncan, chief fire officer of the commission, nor Ron Orchard, chief officer of the CFA, went on record to concede that the situation was out of hand. For them, the fires retained their status of one or possibly two on the state's disaster plan, not a catastrophic three. The comprehensively trained and best-equipped institution to battle the fires, the Metropolitan Fire Brigade, was called into action only when it was too late. Victoria's disaster co-ordinator, Chief Commissioner of Police S.I. Miller, was ready to ring the Federal Government at any moment for help, but, as he acknowledged on national television, he 'knew nothing about fighting fires'.

No-one asked for Miller's help, and he gave it only after the fires were beyond fighting. Nonetheless, at 7.30

pm the commission and the CFA decided that they needed more manpower. More than 16 000 fire fighters, including volunteers, had no hope of holding the line. Half an hour later Miller made his first call of the day for help from the Natural Disaster Centre in Canberra. In response to a request for troops, 350 naval ratings were made available. The Metropolitan Fire Brigade's John Perry was later caustic—10 spare vehicles and 800 off-duty firemen could have been supplied. All he needed was to make one phone call. Speaking later on behalf of his men, he said, 'They can't believe you'd call up 350 naval cadets or ratings who've had no fire training whatsoever, and they be used while we have trained fire fighters who are not required.' It was not until midnight that the ratings and seven Metropolitan tankers engaged the fires.

The cool change ripped through in the evening, reaching Melbourne at 8.40 pm. The capital's maximum wind gust blew at 102 kmh, but closer to the coastal fire it was anything up to seven to eight kmh faster. The change brought disaster, not relief. Indeed, most of the losses of life and property occurred in the 60 minutes following the wind change. Each blazing inferno did a 90 degree turn to the left and headed for the fresh fuel and targets ahead of it. For several hours the wind was even fiercer. The gales from the west and southwest also brought final recognition that a catastrophe was at hand. Frantic calls between the CFA and the commission established that the fires could no longer be considered merely local events. The CFA continued to see them as a Stage Two Disaster as did the Victoria Police. For the commission they were now worthy of Stage Three. No matter how the fires were classified, the moment to instigate any kind of palliative action was long past. It must be emphasised that only a sustained effort of manpower and equipment quite beyond anything the whole nation could have mustered would have slowed the Ash Wednesday fires after the wind change. The northerlies had caused relatively narrow infernos sometimes a score or more kilometres long. When the wind changed direction these fires became the fronts of very wide refuelled conflagrations. In the chip-dry bush of southern Australia offering up to 25 tonnes of dry vegetation each hectare, their ferocious progress was inevitable and unstoppable.

Full of eucalyptus oil, gum trees can literally explode in seconds. Oil in the trunk of a tree can vaporise if radiant heat is hot enough, the tree blasting limbs and sparks in all directions. Forests of trees can easily create a holocaust. Television footage shot from aircraft of the Otways fire showed great incendiary gouts exploding 50 metres above the forest canopy. Fire fronts can travel in winds of 100 kmh—common on Ash Wednesday—at a brisk jogging pace, consuming all in front of them. For every 10 degree uphill slope speed doubles. For every 10 degree downhill slope it slows by half. Rod Incoll of the Department of Conservation and Natural Resources told a conference in 1994 that bushfire fuel accumulates in three typical ways in eucalypt forests. First, leaves, 'branchlets' and bark build up on the forest floor. Second, bark 'flakes' form on trunks and branches and are responsible for many spot fires (fires that ignite sometimes kilometres ahead of the front). Finally, leaves and other vegetation get caught in grass and scrub. He cited data that placed Victoria with southern California and the Mediterranean coast among the world's 'leading wildfire hotspots', and summarised research that showed the impracticability of curbing a big bushfire: '[Probably] the only chance of controlling [such] a fire occurs in the first 30 minutes of its life.' The Otways fire on Ash

Wednesday, he said, progressed at 10.8 kmh. Its intensity was equivalent to placing 110000 one-kilowatt electric radiator bars on every metre of the fire's front. This amounted to a fire 30 times more fierce than was possible to control using ground tankers. Spot fires were ignited 8 to 10 kilometres ahead of the front. Other experts had remarked that flames from the windward side of a ridge were akin to a giant military flame-thrower.

For those in the paths of the fires there was nowhere to run, but there were several places to hide. In heat that fused sand to glass and melted car wheels onto the bitumen beneath them, they cowered in their houses or whatever shelter they could find. Many survived.

On the morning of 17 February, just hours after the worst of the holocaust had wreaked havoc in the Dandenongs, the first newspaper reports attempted to convey the size of the tragedy. The *Age* conservatively estimated in its opening paragraph that at least 34 people had died and about 600 homes had been destroyed. Then followed incomplete lists of numbers, names and places. A state of emergency had been declared in Victoria and South Australia, and Prime Minister Malcolm Fraser, who was in the midst of an election campaign, interrupted his schedule to fly over burnt areas. 'A panzer division going through,' he was reported as saying, 'could not have done as much damage there is nothing left.' Similar stories appeared throughout Australia's Press, the Melbourne *Sun* reporting that South Australia was 'hell on earth' as 22 people died and more than 100 houses were destroyed in the state's worst day of fire.

In the following days narratives of valour and escape dominated the media. Richard Yallop's *Age* report on the single most tragic incident, the death of 12 fire fighters by their two tankers near Cockatoo, was the most piteous. 'Their bravery had carried them into a wooded slope in defence of a house at the top of the hill. The flames leapt up the slope and enveloped the trucks. Some men died seeking shelter beneath the vehicles, some huddled against the bank of the hill In its desolation, with charred trees on every side, the site seemed a cross between a cemetery and a battlefield.'

Reporting from Adelaide for the *Age*, David Elias wrote that from the top of Mt Lofty, on which Adelaide's television towers are perched, that the ground was blackened as far as the eye could see. 'To the right, looking towards the city, the historic castle in which Kim Bonython, the Adelaide entrepreneur, lived and which houses one of Australia's best private art collections and one of the world's best jazz libraries is nothing more than a shambles. To the left the mansion owned by his businessman brother John is the same.' Greenhill, a small town that had nestled on top of a ridge about 20 kilometres east of the city, was now 'the remains of 28 fire-gutted homes, some of them empty shells, with about 15 of them nothing more than mere piles of rubble'. Irreplaceable personal papers, unpublished letters, rare photographs and books, oil paintings and 27 drawers of documents were lost from the family home of Sir Thomas Playford, who had been Premier of South Australia for an unequalled 26 years.

On the morning after the fire this writer drove through a desolate landscape, trees denuded, logs still burning, to Mt Macedon. Like dirty snow, the ash lay everywhere. There would easily have been enough of it to cross the foreheads of the world's Christians 40 days before Good Friday. Near the summit I came across Dr Clifford Pannam QC, still in the morning trousers he wore to court the day before. He leant against the boot of his chocolate-and-beige Rolls Royce.

He swept up an arm theatrically and said, 'Well, there's my house gone, finished.' Indeed it was. Huntly Burn, as it was called, bled grey smoke into the sky, a vast ruin. Nine high chimneys stood in the twisted corrugated iron and red-hot embers. Farther up the mountain another equally stately home, Cameron Lodge, was untouched. Pannam apologised for his attire, which included a red tartan lumberjacket stolen from a nearby cottage, as he fled the holocaust in a filthy singlet and riding boots over dirty feet. Advancing off the Rolls, he explained that his 30-room mansion had been a 'lovely old house built in 1874. Just a beautiful timber and lath and plaster home with 15-foot ceilings.' In there, he said, pointing to the debris of twisted iron and smouldering stumps, 'was a library the envy of every barrister of the Australian bar'. He had complete collections of many law reports, all gone. What did the loss mean to him? I asked foolishly. The response was eloquent. 'Every single personal treasure in a personal and professional life is gone.'

Within days experts opined. David Packham, who had researched bushfires for 21 years, said he 'knew this fire would happen' as he drove with a reporter through the Dandenongs. For 18 years a principal research scientist with the Commonwealth Scientific and Industrial Research Organisation, he pointed to the 'massive amounts of fuel—dead leaves, twigs and grass—that have been building up on the forest floor for so long'. Fuel was as much a factor in bushfire intensity as wind, he said. In some parts of the Hills 15 tonnes of undisturbed fuel per hectare had built up over 30 years. 'You can't do anything about the wind, but you can do a hell of a lot about the fuel,' he said. Another CSIRO bushfire researcher, Dr Caird Ramsay, said his preliminary investigation of the Surf Coast devastation showed that timber decking on a house was potentially dangerous. Fires got a foothold at the bottom corners of timber-framed windows, tiled roofs were vulnerable, hot debris easily got into guttering and eaves, and most homes did not explode in fire, as popularly believed, but were destroyed when small ignitions were not quickly extinguished. Yet another CSIRO expert, Vince Dowling, said the coast fire at its fiercest—as it passed over Aireys Inlet— would have blazed at 2000 degrees Celsius.

With *Age* colleague John Larkin this writer collected stories on the Surf Coast a week after the holocaust. Plumber Ron Diamond's was typical. He had a newly renovated home at Fairhaven, overlooking the sea. On 16 February he was watching the approaching smoke with mates. They thought the fire would burn itself out at Grassy Creek, several kilometres nearer Lorne. A police car on the highway sounded the retreat and they decided to take its advice. Ron's big Bedford truck was backed up the driveway and the men began grabbing tools—his business would not recover if he lost wrenches and $15000 worth of copper piping. In a subsequent feature article I wrote, 'Ron's windsurfer and its sail had just been thrown into the truck when an unholy noise broke out and the garage exploded, followed quickly by the house and three others nearby. Built on a concrete slab, the garage's frame was of hardwood. God knows it was a solid garage. It had been up only two months. The roof didn't peel back, the tin didn't rattle off. The garage just blew to bits. Ron and his mates found it hard to believe none of them was even scratched. In unison they dived under the Bedford and hung onto the wheels and each other.'

The truck shook in the wind, which screamed in the men's ears. There was a lull after the initial blast and they fled. Two utilities and a tip-truck hared down the hill onto the Great

Ocean Road, where they could go no further. 'The towers of flame advancing behind them were firing sporadic blazes even in the town itself. Long grass on the river flats was beginning to burn. They deserted the convoy. With the fire at their tails, they sprinted to a concrete bridge that takes the highway over a creek. Leaping into the water, they waded under the bridge, not daring to come out for four hours.'

Several Aireys Inlet residents headed for the safety of the surf. Fire fighting mates Jamie Gathercole and Charlie Carr had been resting at the fire station when chaos broke out. 'They heard an explosion and realised it must have been a house when they saw roofing iron flying through the air at the height of a four-storey building.' Outside, people were running for their cars to drive to the beach. Jamie and Charlie joined them. Charlie had driven his ute down the roughly straight track many times, but never in a pea soup fog at 50 kmh with half of Aireys Inlet bouncing around them. Headlights were nearly useless. The lights of a car behind 'shone like a cat's eyes in a wide-screen of blackness'. Above the blackness was a bright orange glow. Parking the car above the beach, they exited running, down the steep and winding path and its irregular steps of treated pine. At one point, the gale blew Charlie two metres off the track into the heath. He got up and kept running. 'They ran into the water until it came up to their necks. Inverted cataracts of flame burst out over the 20-metre cliffs above . . . The scrub around the car park and even down the track began to blaze brightly.'

Charlie saw an old woman with a bag coming down the track and waded in for her, 'his surfing shoulders thrusting back great spades of water'. He sprinted up the sand and half-carried, half-dragged the woman to safety. A solicitor and a surfboard maker joined them. 'Debris flapped above like giant predatory bats before splashing down about them. They held onto one another—five points of life committed to hellfire. They feared for their existence and yelled at each other: 'Stay together!' They were freezing, and two hours passed before they moved into shallower water and eventually onto the beach itself, where they lay on the sand exhausted.'

Coroners had the more precise and formal job of deciding causes and apportioning blame. Four inquests were held in Victoria and two in South Australia. Coroner Anthony Ellis opened the first Victorian inquest on 23 May near the Surf Coast at Geelong, Victoria's second biggest city. Witness Francis James Dowie told him that a spark from the burner at a Deans Marsh sawmill could not have caused the fire. Destroying the mill, the fire killed three people on its rampage towards the coast then along it. Dowie said the fire and the burner were at opposite ends of the mill. At 1 pm on 16 February he discovered that the burner was 'smouldering with sawdust'. He and another worker put water on the burner, which became 'totally cold'. Inside, the sawdust was 'wet, very wet'.

On the following day Ellis heard that a police motorcyclist had driven through a sheet of flame to try to lead a Telecom employee to safety. Senior Constable Steven John Williams of Colac, a major western Victorian town, was checking farmhouses on the Lorne–Deans Marsh road before meeting the fire front about 11 kilometres from Deans Marsh. He waved down a Telecom utility and told its driver, maintenance manager John Mierla, to turn around and head back to Lorne. But the fire was 'spotting' ahead of them and became a 'solid sheet across the roadway'. He had shouted to Mierla 'Come on!' before riding towards the fire at 80 kmh, changing down to third gear and laying on the tank. He 'accelerated hard', swerved around a burning tree and came out the other side perhaps 400 metres down the road. Mierla's body was found later just outside the passenger door of his vehicle.

For the CFA, Robert Johnston told the inquest that two of the victims were clearly warned more than once to evacuate their homes. Ellis returned his findings of accidental death on 27 May. He said that evidence had detailed many acts of heroism. He called Senior Constable Williams' efforts 'valiant', but he was unable to determine the cause of the fire; no evidence implicated the activities, equipment or installations at the sawmill.

Clashing overhead powerlines might have started one of the devastating Warrnambool fires, Ellis heard when he sat at the provincial city on 4 July. Three outbreaks—at Cudgee, Ballengeich and Branxholme—caused infernos that resulted in ten deaths. Assisting Ellis, Robert Webster QC told him that the 'probable cause of the fire was a clashing together of two active conductors in the last stand before (a) house.' Later, Ellis heard that six victims had died while following the recommended practice of staying in their cars with the windows wound up. Webster told him that very heavily wooded country on either side of the road might have been a relevant factor.

Twelve days into the Warrnambool inquest Detective Senior Constable Frederick Michael Hughson said in a statement that he found four bodies at around 9.15 pm on 16 February in a car burned so badly that metal from the wheels had melted into the road. The car's tyres, upholstery, dashboard and lining had been burnt away. 'There appeared to be four bodies in the car, two in the front and two in the rear. They were badly charred and unrecognisable.' Then there was Kel Grigg's story, with which this chapter opened. Petranella

Alida Anderson, 31, and her son, Gareth, 10, were the people who gave him a lift. Both died, the son in agony from burns. Anderson's charred remains were found about 52 metres from the car. Two thongs were found stuck to the bitumen 27 metres from the car. Bringing down his findings on 6 September, Ellis ruled that the State Electricity Commission was involved in two of the Warrnambool fires at Cudgee and Branxholme that killed five. The Cudgee fire started when wires on a private service line clashed. Branches of cypresses were too close to them, and Ash Wednesday's high winds had caused the clashing. It had happened before. While the property's owner Raymond Anderton had a duty to ensure that a dangerous situation did not exist, the SEC had been told five years before of the hazard and had done nothing about it, said Ellis.' I am of the opinion that some form of follow-up procedure was an obvious and necessary adjunct,' he continued.

The Branxholme fire, he continued, started when an SEC pole carrying live wires was blown down. The pole had been rotten at its base and had had a noticeable lean. Moreover, local residents had been worried about the condition of SEC poles before the fire. The causes of the two fires revealed 'a degree of negligence which falls short of criminal negligence'. As to the cause of the Branxholme fire, Ellis returned an open finding, saying that neither a road-roller seen near the fire's seat nor a nearby electric fence could be ruled out. He recorded findings of accidental death, death by burns accidentally received and an open finding on a man who might have contracted legionnaire's disease while fighting the fires. Some 160 writs were lodged immediately in the Warrnambool Supreme Court.

Seven people had died at Mt Macedon because fire fighters had not warned them of the approaching bushfire, Ellis decided on 29 September. There was no 'logical reason or excuse' for the lack of warning. Sitting in the inland town of Kyneton, Ellis said that six of the victims were found in or near their homes and the seventh had been trapped in his car near his home. They were either ignorant of the danger or transport to evacuate them was unavailable. Ellis said the fire had been caused by the clashing of SEC wires near East Trentham. The same stretch of line had ignited a fire the year before, and several SEC employees had failed to notice that it was too close to a tree. The fire entered the Wombat State Forest and turned left with the wind change to burn towards Macedon. The deaths occurred about eight hours after it had started. The Forests Commission and the CFA could have warned Macedon residents from the time they knew of the evening wind change. Experienced foresters thought the fire would die down and fail to cross the four-lane Calder Highway. But it was a difficult view to accept, he said. 'It was known to be a crown fire travelling at great speed, devouring treetops, and it must have been known by these officers that previous experience with those fires had shown that fires are capable of traversing wide highways. Yet persons possessing this expertise saw the unexpected happen yet again.'

Ellis said that it was difficult to understand that the deaths occurred because of insufficient warning in 'this age of advanced technology'. People outside the Macedon area were having 'horrific conversations' with 'persons who were about to be consumed by fire'. It was understandable that the commission and the CFA had separate powers. But it did appear 'patently obvious that this independence should cease in emergency situations.' Following the Macedon findings, Victoria's Energy Minister David White said the SEC needed to intensify its fire-prevention activities. The line that caused the fire had been inspected, but the degree of the hazard had not been properly gauged. White added that the SEC was reviewing training so that its officers were 'fully equipped to identify such hazards'. It was also reassessing reporting procedures.

At the fourth and final inquest in November, held in the lower Hills town of Pakenham, on Melbourne's south-eastern outskirts, Ellis heard from a police officer that he found the bodies of a man and a woman who died apparently embracing one another during the Cockatoo bushfire. The following day the officer found another body in the remains of a car, the man's wristwatch stopped at 9.07 pm. On 8 February 1984 Ellis brought down an open finding on the deaths of 27 people in the Ash Wednesday fires at Belgrave, Upper Beaconsfield and Cockatoo. In particular, he decided that the two tankers of the 12 CFA fire fighters who died near Cockatoo had been in good mechanical condition. The fire fighters were probably trying to help people escape when they themselves were trapped. He decided that he could not determine the cause of the fires. There was probably some human involvement in the Cockatoo fire, but implicating evidence fell far short of any acceptable standard of proof. He was aware that criminal charges had been laid against a person about two smaller fires in the Hills on Ash Wednesday that had been quickly extinguished.

Ellis said many lessons had been learned from Ash Wednesday. Amendments had already been made to legislation and a media campaign to increase public awareness had been launched. He recommended that likely wind changes on fire-ban days be 'made public in the same way as total fire ban days', that municipalities develop disaster plans and that municipal property officers be granted the power to order the clearance of fire hazards.

In South Australia, State Coroner Kevin Ahern's findings were similar. He decided on 14 December in Mt Gambier that at least four of the south-eastern bushfires, which had claimed 14 lives, were ignited by State Electricity Trust power lines. He recommended the removal of rows of trees from around power lines in the radiata pine forests that covered much of south-eastern South Australia. Furthermore, police had been placed in 'great personal danger' during the fires because of a breakdown in radio communications, which had not been fully effective at any stage. Radio equipment used in the south-east was between nine and 15 years old. One of the largest south-eastern fires, he found, had been started by molten metal after conductors in power lines had touched and arced. The distance between the conductors was less than that recommended by the Standards Association of Australia. In other fires, tree or branches had fallen on power lines and ignited undergrowth. Thirteen of the 14 victims had died of burns, the effects of smoke or oxygen deprivation, while the fourteenth had died of a heart attack induced by the events of 16 February. In Adelaide, Ahern's findings of 20 July 1984 were similar; power lines were implicated in all five of the Adelaide Hills bushfires that killed 14. He recommended that the trust increase tree-lopping and considered using spreaders to keep lines apart. He criticised the Country Fire Service for information breakdowns, adding that headquarters had too little say in the sometimes substandard equipment country units bought.

Long-term and short-term human error in response to natural threat was present all around. Electricity authorities in both States paid out millions of dollars in claims in the years following Ash Wednesday. By March 1984, the SEC had settled 959 claims amounting to $45 million, a further $5 million having been offered to settle 168 outstanding complaints. The SEC, which has since been broken up and privatised, adopted stricter controls on vegetation near powerlines, checked its poles more closely and scattered the state with spreaders. Very soon after Ash Wednesday the CFA had new trucks and tankers with protective heat shields along their sides where previously there had been only handrails. In South Australia the State Electricity Trust improved its surveillance and standards.

Late in 1983 the *Homeowner's Bushfire Survival Manual* was published by the Victorian State Government in conjunction with the newspaper publisher Herald and Weekly Times. For $2.95 you got 52 colour pages of practical, detailed advice on designing and maintaining houses and gardens that were of least risk in bushfires. It was important.

Of 32 Victorian civilian deaths on Ash Wednesday, 22 were aged 50 or more. All five Mt Macedon victims who lost their lives in houses were over 55. Only seven of all Victoria's Ash Wednesday deaths occurred in houses. Eighty-two percent of occupied houses at Mt Macedon survived the fire but only 44 percent of unoccupied houses were unscathed. Even in severely burnt areas up to 40 percent of houses survived. If ground cover was cleared near houses and occupants were able-bodied, houses made good shelters. Staying inside a well-prepared house was much safer than last-minute evacuation, experts stressed. Moreover, people who returned to their homes after the fire front had passed were able to improve the chances of their houses' survival or at least reducing damage.

In April 1984 the Bushfires Review Committee, chaired by Chief Commissioner Miller, made 21 recommendations, none of which referred directly to the SEC. Essentially administrative, they shook up official responses to bushfires, recommending, for instance, several 'motherhood' notions such as that 'effective utilisation and management of resources be regarded as a major objective' in future. The three-stage Displan categories were replaced by 'Alert', 'Standby' and 'Action', and a Bureau of Meteorology officer would be stationed with the Country Fire Authority on total-fire-ban days. In time, all the recommendations were implemented, as, of course, they should have been.

In his 1995 review of government reports on bushfires written for the Australian Fire Authorities Council, Stephen Petris pointed out that, in Victoria, '85 percent of the total losses caused by bushfire are the result of just 0.1 percent of all reported fires over one hectare'. Bushfires capable of holocaust were unpredictable and capricious, he seemed to be saying, and in the case of Ash Wednesday even major firebreaks such as four-lane highways 'had no impact on the run of the fire'. Being prepared was the key. As the Victorian Government's Department of Natural Resources and Environment points out on its website, bushfires 'as severe as the Ash Wednesday fires appear to occur six to ten times a century'. If that is true, then south-eastern Australia is long overdue for another inferno.

Part Two:
Collision

4

The Sinking of the HMAS Voyager, 1964

*Voyager came on headlong, like a steel javelin of 3500 tons . . .
her red port light like a mocking danger signal.*

Tom Frame, Where Fate Calls

Maritime disasters have always been part of Australia's history. They were inevitable during the time of sea transport, which was wholly dependent on wind. Wind could keep ships embayed for days or weeks, could shred sails and could drive the vessels relentlessly to their doom. Steam and diesel power gave control and reduced losses. They also created the opportunity to build much bigger ships, which increased efficiency of transport but which also created the potential for huge individual losses when things went wrong. As with any type of vessel, there was always the human element—mistakes and miscalculations in an intrinsically unforgiving environment.

War brings with it the intention, at least on the part of one party, to create disaster, but seamen and sailors have also managed to create disasters for themselves. The first naval casualty suffered in World War II occurred when His Majesty's submarine *Triton*, at sea off the Norwegian coast on 10 September 1939, managed to torpedo and sink His Majesty's submarine *Oxley*. In his autobiography, *We*

Seemed to Get There!, veteran merchant seaman Captain Herbert Bolles recounts some of the accidents that occurred during the war, including a collision on 20 December 1940, when the Melbourne Steamship Co passenger ship *Duntroon*, moving to sea through Port Phillip Heads in gale conditions, cut a 223-tonne minesweeping trawler in half, killing five officers and 19 ratings.

The Royal Australian Navy (RAN), established in 1911, has built a formidable record of success, but the war cost the RAN three cruisers, including HMAS *Sydney* and its entire crew of 645, who were lost in 1941 when they engaged a German raider, *Kormoran*. Other naval losses included three destroyers. The RAN went on to serve in the Korean campaign and in the Malayan Emergency. Following a relative lull, when its numbers dropped from a wartime peak of 337 ships and 40 000 personnel to 40 ships and 10 000 personnel in the late 1950s, the RAN became more relevant to the national defence debate in the mid-1960s. The 'downward thrust of Communism', as the government of Sir Robert Menzies called it, was very real in the minds of many Australians. There had been some question about government defence priorities. 'Forward defence' was the accepted wisdom, expressed in the saying, 'It's better to fight them up there than wait for them to come down here.' From 1959 navy personnel numbers increased to 12 800 and its retention rate vastly improved.

The RAN's aircraft carrier, the 19 930 tonne former British light fleet carrier HMAS *Melbourne,* commissioned in 1955 as a flagship, was an enduring symbol of national naval might. In its role as leader of Australia's maritime defence, Melbourne set out from Sydney on 5 February 1964 with the 3550-tonne Daring class destroyer HMAS *Voyager* to practice manoeuvres off Jervis Bay on the south coast of New South

Wales. It was to be a 40-day 'working-up' program intended to get officers and crew—many of whom were serving in their positions or on an aircraft carrier for the first time, or who were working together for the first time—to mould themselves into operational units. The ships were to exercise with Gannet anti-submarine aircraft and Venom aircraft from HMAS *Albatross,* the naval air base at Nowra, which would do 'touch-go' landings on the carrier: approaching the deck, touching with their wheels and taking off again.

Exercises were expensive. Steaming time had to be budgeted for. The armed services needed to get maximum value from them. To do this, it had to replicate operational conditions as far as possible, which included flying operations at night and in varying weather conditions. It is incumbent on commanders, then as at all other times, to do these things as safely as possible.

On 10 February the ships were operating efficiently. The commander of the *Melbourne,* Captain Ronald John Robertson, 47, had been in the Navy since 1930 and had distinguished himself in World War II. At the time of his promotion in 1956 he became one of the RAN's youngest ever captains. Robertson did have one career blemish, from the time when he was commander officer of the destroyer HMAS *Vendetta.* In 1958 an order he gave while the *Vendetta* was alongside a wharf at Williamstown in Victoria was wrongly interpreted and the ship nearly crashed through a dock wall. For that, Robertson 'earned the displeasure' of the Naval Board. In 1960 and 1961 Robertson served as Director of Plans in the Navy Office. On his appointment as commanding officer of the *Melbourne* on 6 January 1964 he was going to sea for the first time in three years. It was also his first time in command of an aircraft carrier. In the armed services, with their constant turnover of staff through retirements, resignations and transfers, many things are being done for the first time, so in itself that was nothing remarkable.

On the *Voyager*, a ship commissioned in 1957, was Captain Duncan Herbert Stevens, 42, a World War II and Korean War veteran. Stevens, in the Navy since 1935, and recently serving with the Royal Navy, had glowing reports. An ebullient, outgoing man, son of a senior army officer, he was looking forward to the night-flying exercises. According to procedures of the day, when in manoeuvres a destroyer escorting the carrier was subject to the carrier's direction. In normal deployment, it was in a position ahead of the aircraft carrier either on the port or starboard side, protecting the carrier. There might have been several destroyers forming a screen, so not all destroyers needed to be ahead. If the carrier intended to change direction it would signal the destroyer or destroyers, which would turn accordingly. This was known as a 'turning signal'. The destroyer or destroyers would adopt a range and direction that kept them in the same position relative to the carrier. Once the carrier decided to operate aircraft and a destroyer was nominated to take 'plane guard position', that destroyer had to move to the rear of the carrier on its port side, at a distance of 1000 to 1500 metres, where it could see any mishap involving aircraft and steam quickly to the assistance of the air crew. Plane guard position was always to the port side because the carrier's launching was angled from the starboard quarter to the port bow. The direction and speed the destroyer was to adopt in the plane guard position was signalled from the carrier before it shifted.

What the carrier sent was the 'flying signal'. How the destroyer executed it was normally a matter for the destroyer's captain. He could turn away from the carrier and do a 360 degree turn, giving the carrier time to pass before slipping into the plane guard station. Or he could turn away from the carrier and continue in a straight line at right angles to the direction of the carrier, giving the carrier time to pass, then turn 180 degrees and come back so as to reach the plane guard station. This manoeuvre was known as 'fishtailing'. A destroyer on the forward starboard position had another option, which was simply to turn towards the direction of the carrier and go across its bows, wait for the carrier to pass, then slip into plane guard position. It was not a favoured option because crossing the bows of a carrier, especially at night, involved obvious hazards.

When large ships travelling at close to top speed are working closely together, there is always a relatively small margin for error. If one ship miscalculated, the time available for remedial action was usually limited. Additionally, taking into account night-time visibility, weather conditions, battle, communication breakdowns and the human elements of lapse of concentration or misjudgements, there is always potential for disaster. In his book, *Where Fate Calls,* naval historian Dr Tom Frame recounts that in 1952 the destroyer USS *Hobson* was doing a night-flying exercise with the carrier USS *Wasp* when it turned the wrong way, going to port instead of to starboard, taking it under the *Wasp's* bows. The *Wasp* hit the *Hobson,* which sank in four minutes, killing 176. A subsequent inquiry found that the captain, Lieutenant Commander W.J. Tierney, had 'lost the tactical picture'.

On the *Voyager,* at 7.20 pm or 7.25 pm on the night of 10 February 1964 Captain Stevens ordered a steward, Barry John Hyland, to bring him a double brandy. This seemingly inconsequential event came to assume enormous significance later, even though there was no evidence that Stevens drank any more than that, or that alcohol was a factor in what was to transpire. As later evidence revealed, he did have a duodenal ulcer that may have been troubling him, and he might have taken brandy to relieve the discomfort.

What was of concern to Robertson that night was that the conditions were not greatly suited to flying. The wind was light, and the lighter it was the more difficult aircraft found it to take off into it. At 8.30 pm the *Melbourne* was on a course of 190 degrees, travelling at 21.5 or 22 knots—close to top speed. Robertson ordered the *Melbourne* and *Voyager* to turn to 020 degrees. Then he ordered another turn to 060 degrees. At this point the *Voyager*, being smaller and requiring less room to make its turns, was not in station in relation to the *Melbourne*, but quickly corrected this.

Stevens was on the bridge of the *Voyager* along with a team of officers, lookouts and communications officers—at least nine people. He had taken command in January 1962 for a tour of the Far East. He had served 18 months as executive officer on the Melbourne, so both ships were familiar to him. His team all had good references, though in some cases there were gaps in their experience. His First Lieutenant, Lieutenant Commander Ian McGregor, was described as an officer of exceptional ability. His navigation officer, Lieutenant H.D. Cook, was 'competent and experienced'.

The Officer on the watch, Lieutenant D.H.M. Price, to whom the entire ship was entrusted if the captain or executive officer were not there to countermand him, had not been watch keeper on a ship as big and as fast as a destroyer before. Nor had this seconded Royal Navy officer ever done manoeuvres like this at night. There were other weaknesses in the arrangement of personnel. Stevens only had previous experience working with only one person on the bridge: the signaller, Tactical Officer Gary William Evans. Such factors, including the youthfulness and inexperience of people in key positions, needed to be fully appreciated by the captains.

There was no moon on the night of 10 February, but the sea was calm and visibility extended up to 30 kilometres. Ships at night are not easy to assess in terms of direction and speed, especially when lights are kept at a minimum. This is especially so for an aircraft carrier, because of its size and irregular shape. On this occasion the ships had only been together for four days during the working-up period. The manoeuvre they were about to attempt could have been left for a later stage in the exercise, when the crews were more familiar with each other.

Many of the *Voyager's* 320 crew were off-duty. It is normal for sailors to work shifts of four hours on, four hours off. Many had gravitated to the cafeteria area and were playing tombola, a form of housie. *Voyager* was having difficulty with its radar. Leading Seaman Michael James Patterson said later there had been a 'blind spot', which he had noticed when he came on duty at 8 pm and which had got worse as the evening progressed. He had been unable to pick up the *Melbourne's* position, but it was not a serious enough failure to call off the exercise.

At 8.39 pm a signals operator on the *Melbourne*, Leading Tactical Operator Robert Trevor Everett, inquired by radio telephone about *Voyager's* speed. The answer he got was '21 knots', which matched the speed of the *Melbourne*. At 8.40 pm Robertson signalled to the *Voyager* that the flying operation, a phase in which the *Voyager* would be required to deploy to the plane guard position, would be delayed by five to ten minutes. When the flying signal was given, *Voyager*, because it was on the starboard side, would have to move to the carrier's port side.

At 8.45 pm *Melbourne's* meteorological officer, Lieutenant Commander Cedric Wallace Johnston, then measuring wind speed, saw that the *Voyager* was 1000 metres ahead of the *Melbourne* to starboard, where he expected it to be. Five minutes later Lieutenant Commander Gordon McPhee, in command of flying operations, assessed that the *Voyager* was 1500 metres away. He went to *Melbourne's* port side to prepare for flying operations.

Wind conditions were still not satisfactory. Robertson decided to continue with the flying operation and to revert to the bearing of 020. There was some discrepancy in later evidence as to what happened then. The turning order was given. The ship's log said it was given at 8.52 pm, but the communications officer's log said 8.53 pm. Very soon after ordering the turn, Robertson decided that the 020 gave the best wind and ordered it to be designated as the 'flying course'—the speed and direction the destroyer would adopt once it had moved into the plane guard position. The evidence is that this was also communicated to the *Voyager*.

Precisely what happened on the *Voyager's* bridge in response to these signals will never be known. It is possible the *Voyager's* communications officer took the turning signal down wrongly, as 200, or 220. It is possible that the *Voyager* took the 020 correctly but decided it was the flying signal rather than the turning signal. There was no checking mechanism whereby an order was repeated to the person who had sent it to ensure it was correctly understood, though such a mechanism did operate in a ship's internal communications, as in the case of an order from the helmsman to the engine room.

What did happen is that the *Voyager* starting turning to its starboard, contrary to what would be expected if it had received an order to turn from 060 to 020 degrees. The turn mystified the bridge of the *Melbourne*. Robertson said to his navigation officer, Acting Commander James Maxwell Kelly, 'What is the *Voyager* doing?' Kelly said, 'She is possibly taking up a plane guard position.' The turn to starboard turn did not last long and *Voyager* started turning to the port. It remains a mystery as to why it changed direction. A possible explanation is that one officer countermanded another.

Had the *Voyager* settled on 020 it would have been consistent with the turning signal from the *Melbourne*, but the *Voyager* kept turning towards the west, sending it on a heading which would take it across the path of the *Melbourne*. The question remains as to whether it settled on that course or was turning further, but it became increasingly obvious that unless it made a radical change, it was in danger of collision.

There were perhaps two minutes, possibly as little as 90 seconds, in which remedial action could be taken. The *Melbourne* could have sounded a series of five warning blasts, the recognised signal that the *Voyager* was heading into danger. They didn't. The *Voyager* could have seen the *Melbourne* looming ahead to its port and changed direction, preferably by turning to starboard, away from the carrier's path. They didn't. Because of the size and speed of the ships, if no action was taken immediately, they would be at the 'point of no return'.

The *Voyager* seemed oblivious to what was happening. Stevens stepped from the bridge and referred to something on the chart table. There was a watch, but nobody seemed to know where the *Melbourne* was. *Voyager's* signaller, Tactical

Operator Robert John Burdett, had been signalling to the *Melbourne* by lamp about the need for replenishments. The *Melbourne* had been to the port side and to the rear of the *Voyager*. At 8.53, as the *Voyager* made its starboard turn, Burdett said that the *Melbourne* had 'disappeared behind us', and he had decided to wait until he got a clear view of it before he resumed signalling. He walked up to the bridge and saw the *Melbourne* again to the port side, some 500 or 600 metres away.

Lieutenant Price saw the *Melbourne* but because of his inexperience he might not have appreciated the fact that the gap between the two ships was closing. Patterson said in later evidence that at 8.54 or 8.55, Lieutenant Commander McGregor had called from the bridge, asking whether he could see *Melbourne* or the submarine HMAS *Tabard* on the radar. He told McGregor that he could see neither, and he thought that McGregor had sounded 'concerned'. On the *Voyager's* portside lookout, Ordinary Seaman Brian William Sumper saw the *Melbourne* to the port but could not estimate how far away it was. Stevens was at the chart table. It is possible that the officers had the mistaken idea that both ships were turning together.

On the *Melbourne*, officers on the bridge, including Robertson, who was on the starboard wing of the bridge, could see *Voyager* coming across ahead and did not know what it was doing. After the *Voyager's* turn to 270, there was no immediate alarm. Kelly looked up from his wind gauge and estimated that the *Voyager* must have been 600 or 700 metres away. Then, according to his later evidence, he heard that the flying course was 020 and had not looked up again, expecting that the *Voyager* would then deploy to the plane guard position. Lieutenant Commander Johnston, seeing the

Voyager's port lights some 300 to 400 metres away, realised that if the *Voyager* did not speed up, it would collide with the *Melbourne*. He thought the *Voyager* was doing an extraordinary thing, crossing the bows of a carrier at night.

Kelly looked up again and saw the *Voyager* continuing on its course, which seemed to be more and more perilous. He said, 'Christ, what's the *Voyager* doing?' Chief Yeoman Robert William Barker, who had been compiling a flying course, said that when he first saw the *Voyager*, it was 200 to 300 metres away and he thought it was cutting it 'a little fine'. The First Officer of the watch, Sub-Lieutenant Alex Bate, had responsibility for the ship. But until Kelly called out, he had been looking at the port side, the opposite direction to where *Voyager* was coming from. He later said that he was looking for merchant ships that might have been in the area. The Second Officer of the watch, Sub-Lieutenant F.M. Jeffries, was attending to other duties.

Robertson had been expecting the *Voyager* to make a turn, either to its starboard, away from the course of the *Melbourne*, or to the port, which—provided the turn was made early enough—would have taken it down the *Melbourne's* side. Kelly felt 'exasperation', as he later put it, and went to check the *Voyager's* bearings. Robertson remained 'rooted to the spot', taking perhaps longer than he should have to realise that the 'incomprehensible' was going to happen. Lieutenant Peter Robert Bowler turned to Sub-Lieutenant Hudson and said, 'By golly, she is cutting it fine!'

Seconds later, Kelly shouted, 'Stop both engines! Half-engines astern!' Robertson, rushing in, countermanded with the order with, 'Full astern both engines!' At that point, with a collision imminent, he was concerned only with evasive action. He was later criticised for not signalling that he was going astern (three short blasts), but by then signalling was well down on his list of priorities.

On the *Voyager* Stevens, looking up and seeing the *Melbourne*, rapped out a command. 'Order the ship full ahead, both engines and wheel hard to starboard.' He followed with, 'Wheelhouse, this is an emergency!' Barker said later, 'I realised she was going to collide with us. She was possibly 80 yards away. She was almost on us, and I told the yeoman, 'We're going to hit her!' Burdett said later he felt that *Voyager* did start making the turn to starboard, but there was no time. The *Melbourne* might have reduced its speed by a single knot and the *Voyager* might have altered its bearing from 270 to 290 degrees. Burdett, seeing the *Melbourne* towering above, grabbed hold of something. Officers on the *Melbourne's* bridge could see their counterparts on the *Voyager's* bridge.

At 8.56 pm *Melbourne* hit *Voyager* amidships, at an angle of between 90 and 100 degrees, causing the *Voyager* to lurch sideways before breaking. The mast came down and the funnel collapsed. In later evidence Lieutenant Commander Johnston said, 'There was a wall of steam and smoke, she rose in a solid wall up to 100 feet ahead of us in which there was a bright flame which glowed for a while and at the same time there was the sound of a coined explosion.' On the *Voyager's* bridge, Stevens fell and was crushed. From the air, Lieutenant Commander Thomas Dadswell, pilot of a Gannet aircraft, saw a flash of orange shooting up into the darkness. In the engine room, Lieutenant Engineer John Kendall Perrett saw 'the intense glow of molten metal and sparks and heard a dull crunching sound'. Water poured into the engine room.

In a moment, the *Melbourne* had gone right through the *Voyager*, the *Voyager's* forward and stern sections floating down each side of the carrier. The *Melbourne* travelled another boat length before stopping. Dadswell said to his observer, '*Melbourne's* collected the *Voyager*!' He radioed Nowra, and in the confusion a wrong direction was given: '292 Point Perpendicular 20 miles', a position that might have come from the *Melbourne* and in fact would have sent rescuers inland, but it was remedied.

Inside the *Voyager's* forward section, which had gone over to the starboard and was not righting itself, men tried desperately to get out. 'The A boiler room and engine room were flooded, there were chaps trying to get out everywhere,' said Chief Naval Shipwright Melvin George Maine. It was then apparent that some things had been neglected. Some hatches had no spanners with which to open them. Mop handles and marlinspikes had to be used. There were lifeboats, but in some cases no knives to cut them loose. All the lifejackets were in a central location and men were risking, and probably losing, their lives to get to that area.

There were examples of selflessness and courage. Lieutenant Engineer Perrett and an artificer used a crowbar to free two men trapped by a fallen catwalk. The canteen area had taken a direct hit and when one hatch was finally opened, the 64 men who had been inside lined up in disciplined fashion to take their turns getting out. One crewmember, William Thomas Grundy, got through a hatch and was washed back in again. A locker fell on him and he had to be freed by shipmates. The forward section, weighed down by its gun turret, remained afloat for 15 minutes. When it finally succumbed to the embrace of the ocean, there were still men inside, including 30 in the cafeteria section. Able Seaman Keith John Hamilton, who got out through an escape hatch after opening it with a marlinspike, was in the water when he heard men inside the hull banging the sides and screaming as the section went under.

Out in the ocean, men had got life rafts out, but they had no idea how to operate them. One officer had to read instructions from a pamphlet while treading water. Men were swimming in oil. Petty Officer Geoffrey Percival Worth heard men calling for help. Some were injured and some simply could not swim. It later transpired that only two men had successfully completed the 'deep water' swimming test, which tested ability to stay afloat in rough conditions. Three or four men who got off the ship drowned. One of them was midshipman, Kerry Marien, who reached one lifeboat, then finding everyone safe on board, swam off to find someone else. Patterson, who was in the water, was later to say that heard a man he could not positively identify calling out again and again, '*Melbourne* ordered us to turn to 270 but did not turn herself.' Could that have been the *Voyager's* signaller, Gary Evans? The question was never to be answered.

The *Melbourne* had drifted 1000 metres and then started drifting back, forcing Robertson to use *Melbourne's* engines to avoid a collision. The emergency boats were brought out, but again there were examples of negligence. The carrier had one whaler instead of two, and the one whaler put over the side sank, either because it had been damaged in the collision or because someone had forgotten to put in the bung. The rescue crew had to scramble out and get into one of the *Voyager's* inflatable life rafts. Two of the *Melbourne's* three power cutters were inoperable, one because it had been damaged in Sydney, the second because its motor would not work. The third had been holed in the collision but was serviceable.

There could have been more efficient systems on shore. At HMAS *Creswell*, the Royal Australian Naval College at Jervis Bay, Commander Ian Herbert Richards, executive officer at the base, received a message about the collision at

9 pm but had no direct means of communicating with three minesweepers in the bay. He signalled with his car lights and dispatched a boat. On his estimation, the minesweepers did not get the message until 9.50 pm. At sea, the frigate HMAS *Stuart* did not get the information until an hour and 19 minutes after the collision, and then made an error in calculating the position. After a 20-minute delay in bringing the *Tabard*, which it was exercising with, to the surface, the *Stuart* arrived at the disaster area at 11.45 pm. Despite all that, 12 rescue vessels and 18 aircraft did arrive and men were plucked out of the sea. The stern section sank at 12.17 am the next morning. Only three bodies were recovered, including that of Stevens, and the *Melbourne*, with 158 of the *Voyager's* 239 survivors on board—and a hole six by 18 metres in its bow—returned to Sydney. The men lost comprised 81 naval personnel and one dockyard employee.

The disaster caused uproar and the Menzies Government lost no time in calling a royal commission. Headed by the Chief Judge of the Commonwealth Industrial Court, Sir John Spicer, it began proceedings on 25 February, 1964.

During the hearing it was forcibly put to Spicer by Laurence Street QC, appearing for the family of Duncan Stevens, that there was a mix-up in the signalling, that the turning order of 020 had been misinterpreted on the *Voyager* as an order to go to 270.

Evans, the *Voyager's* signaller, had sustained a fractured skull and ribs, lacerations and bruising and had been in so much pain following his rescue that he had to be given morphine. He told the royal commission he had received the signals correctly, the 020 turning signal and 020 flying signal, with a prescribed speed of 22 knots. He could not be precise as to when he received the flying signal, because the records had gone down with *Voyager*. He thought it might have been 8.52 pm, but if the *Melbourne's* log said it was 8.54 pm, that would be 'probably right'. The extent of Evans' injuries did cast doubt on the reliability of his evidence. There was speculation that the man Patterson said he heard calling out in the water that the *Melbourne* had ordered the *Voyager* to turn to 270 degrees had been Evans. But the person who might have said those words was never identified and Patterson's evidence, ultimately, could have no weight attached to it.

Spicer's report on 26 August 1964 found that the personnel on the *Voyager's* bridge had not maintained an adequate watch. He also found that those on the *Melbourne's* bridge could have kept a better lookout. Bate should have seen *Voyager* at a much earlier stage after it changed course. Kelly should have paid more regard to the *Voyager's* movements. Spicer could not dismiss the idea that there should have been a simple warning. During the hearing of final submissions, he said, 'I cannot get out of my mind the sort of feeling that you reach where there is half a chance of avoiding a collision and that you can take evasive action yourself to warn the other fellow.' Why could Robertson not have picked up the radio telephone and asked Stevens what he was doing? He said, 'The incredible need not have happened if 45 seconds before the collision, they had given five blasts on the siren.'

In the end, Spicer was only mildly critical of Robertson, saying that when he could see there was going to be a collision, he should have sounded a warning signal, even if in the last seconds that would have constituted three short blasts to indicate he was going into reverse. Spicer remained firm that some sort of warning should have been given. The fact that it had not 'may be that his inexperience, coupled with his knowledge of the capacity of Captain Stevens, led to some hesitation himself on this particular occasion.' He commented that Robertson had done the right thing in reversing engines, and said that if there had in fact been a mistake in communications leading to the turn to 270 degrees, it had been made on the *Voyager*. It was not possible to say definitively why it had turned in that direction, but he was inclined to the view that it was a mistake, at some point, in transmission of the signal.

In the aftermath a decision was made that those criticised could not be tried by court-martial, but any criticism of Robertson was devastating to him professionally. He was transferred to a shore posting, as commander of an anti-submarine training school in Sydney, HMAS *Watson*. Considering it a demotion and considering himself a scapegoat, he resigned, and in doing so attracted a legion of supporters, and the special interest of a retired Royal Navy vice-admiral, Harold Hickling.

Hickling, having himself been in Robertson's position during World War II when in command of an aircraft carrier that sliced a destroyer in two. He took up Robertson's case in a book, *One Minute of Time*. The book incorporated evidence from a former officer, Peter Cabban, who had read that Stevens had had brandy earlier on the night of the collision and believed it was his duty to bring forward what he believed to be evidence that Stevens had a significant alcohol problem. Hickling made a very pertinent point, that Robertson could have done many things to warn the *Voyager* had he had any time. Once the point had passed where a warning would have helped, Robertson had to adopt other measures. 'Had he fired a broadside at the destroyer, it would not have made the slightest difference when she had passed the point of no return, when she was committed to her act of self-destruction,' he said.

The case was taken up by a number of Federal Liberal backbenchers, including Victorian John Jess and Harry Turner and Edward St John of New South Wales. St John suggested in parliament that the truth of the disaster was that it had really been a case of drink-driving on Stevens' part. The pressure finally persuaded the Federal Government to order a second royal commission, which began on 18 May 1967, with three commissioners, headed by the Chief Justice of Tasmania, Sir Stanley Burbury. Some of the evidence made headlines, in particular an account of a birthday party that had been given in Stevens' honour in harbour on 23 March 1963, during the tour of the Far East. Cabban said that Stevens had been so affected by alcohol that he had crawled across the floor. Evidence was given that Stevens had been confined to his bed for periods, and that Stevens had been aggressive in preventing any word of his illness getting out. This included a statement that Stevens would 'completely fix' the civilian career of a medical officer, Michael Clifford Tiller, if that officer made a sick report on him. On 3 August 1967, a former naval doctor, John Roger McNeill, said that Stevens had duodenal ulcer symptoms in 1959. He said he should have reported those symptoms but had not, and he could not explain why he had not.

On 28 July 1967 Robertson told the commission that if Cabban's evidence was to be accepted, then the Spicer Report would have to be rewritten, as the condition of Stevens, and his drinking, would have provided a 'different thrust' to the view that could have been taken of the evidence. On 8 August 1967 Surgeon Rear Admiral Robert Caplan said that if Cabban's evidence was correct, Stevens had suffered from a chronic ulcer and was 'making a fight of it', but in fact was unfit to command; he should have been posted ashore

immediately. Stevens' condition had not come to the attention of the higher command. On 10 October 1967 the then
Chief of the Naval Staff, Vice-Admiral Sir Alan McNicoll,
said nothing had come to his attention during the trip to the
Far East to suggest that Stevens lacked the qualities required
of a destroyer captain.

Burbury and fellow commissioner Justice Kenneth Asprey
(the third commissioner having by then become ill), hearing
the final submissions, were not inclined to accept that alcohol-
ism was a factor. That, said Burbury, was more a question of
behaviour, which was not the business of a royal commission.
Asprey said that the days upon which the alleged drinking
incidents took place only amounted to a minute proportion
of the time of the cruise. There was no evidence that Stevens
drank significantly at sea. The commissioners did, however,
place a lot more weight on Stevens' physical condition.
Burbury accepted that had the information on the duodenal
ulcer emerged, Stevens would have been downgraded in his
classification. Gordon Samuels QC, representing Robertson,
submitted that this could be linked to the *Voyager* disaster.
He submitted that Spicer's assessment of the evidence had
been 'vitiated by the erroneous assumption of fact regarding Captain Duncan Stevens' complete competency, alertness
and concentration'. He went on to say that Stevens had been
under a misapprehension of his position in relation to the
Melbourne, and had apparently thought *Voyager* was on the
port side rather than the starboard side of the *Melbourne*.

In their report on 26 February 1968, Burbury and Asprey
did not go so far as to say Stevens' condition had caused the
collision, but they did say that the position of commanding a destroyer in these circumstances should not have been
occupied by an officer who was less than fit. They did turn

the focus onto Stevens, and exonerated Robertson, along with Bate and Kelly. Burbury and Asprey said that the turn by *Voyager* was in response to the 020 flying signal, not the 020 turning signal. They found that the turn to 270 degrees was not in response to a misinterpreted turning signal but in response to a flying signal. In their reconstruction Stevens had been making a deliberate deployment in order to get into the plane guard position. The commissioners accepted Samuels' submission. They said that the reason *Voyager* had turned in front of the *Melbourne* was that, like the US commander Tierney in the 1952 collision, he had 'lost the tactical picture' and had not known where the *Melbourne* was. They agreed with Samuels that Spicer's premise was that no officer of Stevens' experience, which included his competence and fitness, could have made the error suggested. They agreed that Stevens had turned in the wrong direction under a misapprehension of where the other ship was.

The commissioners were careful to qualify what they said. They wished to make it 'abundantly clear' that they could not determine the 'true cause' of the collision. 'Whether it was made because of some error of judgement or visual observation so confidently made that the taking of a bearing was superfluous, cannot now be definitely determined,' they said. 'We are unable to identify with complete confidence by whom the error was made, although we think it probably was made by Stevens.'

It is always of course convenient to blame a dead man, but Robertson, who had taken a rewarding civilian job, felt vindicated. There remained, however, the question of what he might have done in the 90 seconds or so when his actions could have made a difference. Sir Alan McNicoll, writing in the *Sydney Morning Herald* years later, said that the then

Chief of the Naval Staff, Sir Hastings Harrington, had declined to reappoint Captain Robertson to the *Melbourne* after the conclusion of the first royal commission. One reason was the disruptiveness of changing command, since the ship had been commanded in the interim by Captain P.H. Stevenson. But there was another reason, McNicoll said. 'Admiral Harrington was afraid that Robertson was accident-prone, by reason of over-confidence and slow reaction. He thought that both qualities were in evidence with Robertson standing on the wing of the bridge, 'puzzled but not anxious', watching the *Voyager* steaming towards him on a collision course.' McNicoll claimed that Harrington had felt that those same failings might have been evident when the *Vendetta* hit the Williamstown dock gates.

Tom Frame, having had access to confidential signals records, was later to write that *Melbourne* had sent the critical signal, which had resulted in *Voyager* making its fatal turn to 270 degrees, at 8.54 pm, and that the signal had been misinterpreted. According to Frame, *Melbourne* had sent the signal, 'Foxtrot corpen 020 Tack 22', which was information that a flying course would be set on 020 degrees and that the speed would be 22 knots. An executive order that the destroyer was to deploy to adopt a plane guard position at that bearing and speed, would have been 'Corpen foxtrot 020 Tack 22'. Frame's belief was that the two words, 'Foxtrot corpen', were transposed, and that Stevens had thought the *Melbourne* was ordering *Voyager* to take up plane guard position immediately.

Frame's interpretation might at least make the *Voyager's* actions explicable in terms of Kelly's comment to Robertson, that the *Voyager* appeared to be taking up a plane guard position. If Frame is right, then Stevens' actions are consistent with the findings of the second royal commission, that he did not know where he was in relation to the *Melbourne*, and that in steaming off to the port, he thought he was sailing away from the *Melbourne* instead of towards it. In doing so, he had indeed lost the picture, but the picture would soon be lost once again.

The *Melbourne*, with its bow repaired, put to sea again, with Captain Stevenson in command, and in 1969, with the Vietnam War now raging and Australia's role among the South East Asia Treaty Organisation countries very important, took part in a joint exercise in South East Asia. The exercise, Sea Spirit, involved 40 ships from six countries. The *Voyager* disaster hung like a spectre above the Australians. Stevenson hosted a gathering of captains at Subic Bay before the exercises and warned them of the dangers. The then Flag Officer commanding the Australian Fleet, Rear Admiral Gordon 'Buster' Crabb, insisted that destroyers in the screen ahead of the carrier should turn away from the direction of the carrier when required to take up plane guard. He said he would sack any Australian destroyer captain who turned towards the carrier on the spot.

On the face of it, nobody could have done more than those Australian officers to avert a repetition of history, but it was as though fate was playing a taunting game. On 1 June 1969 a US destroyer, USS *Everett F. Larson* turned towards the *Melbourne* and, warned by Stevenson, was missed by a whisker. Crabb ordered the destroyers to be further from the *Melbourne* during the screening, moving them from 2000 to 3000 metres. In the early hours of 3 June the US destroyer *Frank E. Evans* was ordered to take plane guard and an almost unbelievable chain of events started. The captain, Albert McLemore, was asleep and two very junior officers,

Lieutenants Ronald Ramsey and James Hopson, decided to execute the manoeuvre themselves.

The *Evans*, under the control of a totally inexperienced and unqualified Hopson, turned to starboard towards the *Melbourne*, instead of to port. Stevenson sent a signal that it was on a collision course but the *Evans* kept coming, going just in front of the bows. Ramsey, intervening, ordered the *Evans* to turn and inadvertently brought the destroyer back under the *Melbourne's* bows. Stevenson ordered the ship's wheel to hard left and sounded a warning siren. On the *Melbourne's* flight deck, Flight Deck Chief Stan Heares, in the same spot he had been when Melbourne hit the *Voyager*, saw it happen again. The *Evans*, cut in two, sank with 74 dead. Stevenson, despite all his pleas, his alertness and his warning signal, was court-martialled on a charge of having failed to put his engines into reverse and failing to give the *Evans* a clear direction when he saw it was on a collision course. It was an action seen by some to have been a sop to the Americans. Evidence showed that it would have taken six minutes for both engines, put astern, to have had an impact on the speed and as with the Robertson's failure to sound *Melbourne's* siren in 1964, it was regarded as irrelevant.

Stevenson was honourably acquitted, but his career, like Robertson's, had ended. He was given a shore posting, which, like Robertson, he saw as a demotion. He requested permission to retire, which would have assured him his pension. The then Minister for the Navy, Jim Killen, told him that the government would refuse, but the then Prime Minister, John Gorton, approached by John Jess, intervened in favour of Stevenson. Journalist Ben Hills, writing in the *Sydney Morning Herald* in 1999, said Stevenson had been scapegoated, because of the need Australia felt at the time to preserve a 'special relationship' with the United States, though it is arguable. Tom Frame flatly rejects this contention, stating that he never found any evidence that Stevenson had been scapegoated.

The *Melbourne*, completed her service and was decommissioned in 1985. Compensation battles for survivors were fought and, over the years, resolved. On 30 January 2002 Malcolm McKenzie, who was 19 when he stood on the flag deck of the *Melbourne* on the fateful night in 1964, was awarded \$450000 compensation for post-traumatic stress. Bitterness was felt after both collisions, when on each occasion the government and naval establishments felt compelled to point the finger. The reasoning seemed to be that some individual, or individuals, had to be found at fault, otherwise 'the system' was at fault, which carried implications that nobody in the service wanted to know about. Perhaps the ultimate blame lay with something more than individuals, more than conjunctions of circumstances. Perhaps, as the *Evans* disaster appears to have demonstrated, fate had simply decreed that these accidents would happen.

5

Erebus: The Air New Zealand Crash, 1979

The weather conditions had a high potential for a 'whiteout'.

Aircraft Accident Report 79-139, *New Zealand Transport Accident Investigation Commission*

On a Tuesday on an early summer evening in 1979, Jim Collins sat at the dining table in his Auckland home, surrounded by charts, a copy of *The New Zealand Atlas* and his two teenage daughters, Kathryn and Elizabeth. The girls could sense their father's excitement as he explained to them the 8000 kilometre flight he would make the next day as the captain of a 250-tonne Air New Zealand DC-10 jet that would carry 257 sightseers and crew to perhaps the loneliest place on the planet and back home in time for dinner. He was about to fly to the great frozen wasteland of Antarctica at the bottom of the world, more than 3200 kilometres south of New Zealand's southern tip, a beautiful, brutal, mysterious place of vast ice deserts and soaring white blue mountains. It was to have been the last Air New Zealand flight to Antarctica for the year.

That night, Air New Zealand was also completing its planning. Eight kilometres away from Collins' home, in Air New Zealand's Navigation Section, last-minute adjustments were being made. The airline had begun flying to the Antarctic two years before, with passengers paying several hundred dollars for the experience, and they had proved popular. In Australia, Qantas had also started flights to Antarctica at about the same time. It was a rather brilliant marketing idea. In the era of big jets, with their increased passenger capacity and fuel capacity, the countries close to the Antarctic had little trouble getting people there so that they could drink in the spectacle. There was obviously none of the danger, none of the privations of the Antarctic pioneers, no problems with dog sleds, crevasses or frostbite.

In a warm cabin with a glass of champagne in hand, a lightly-clad passenger could gaze down upon a world where life survived at the margins. It was possible to embark upon this adventure with a laid-back attitude, but it was essential that the technology required to perform this feat was in the best possible working condition. There was always the thought at the back of everyone's mind that things would go wrong. Those thoughts were no more significant than the subconscious misgivings of anybody who steps aboard an aeroplane but Antarctica, with its environmental extremes and remoteness, made such misgivings a little more pertinent. Peter Spooner, a prominent Sydney journalist who boarded the first Qantas flight to the Antarctic, knew he was very ill, and in fact he had less than three years to live. His words before he left were that if he didn't come back, it really did not matter.

For the Air New Zealand flight scheduled for 28 November 1979, Air New Zealand's planners decided on a small change to the computerised flight path. Instead of going over the 60 kilometre-wide McMurdo Sound, it would now go directly over Antarctica's tallest peak, 3780 metre Mt Erebus, an impressive, active volcano on Ross Island, whose name in Greek meant 'Hell'. The new route would take the plane more than 41 kilometres east of the usual flight path, but, weather permitting, it would allow passengers to see this most extraordinary study in extremes: a volcano in the middle of the ice, a smouldering crater where the lava deep below contrasted dramatically with the environment it might have erupted into.

Collins, at 45 years of age, was one of the airline's most experienced and respected captains. He had had 24 years of flying experience, beginning with service in the Royal New Zealand Air Force. Just under 183 centimetres tall, dark-haired and handsome with shining blue eyes, he was fit and confident. His instructions to fly the plane to the Antarctic had come two weeks before, and not having done the trip before, he had been delighted.

The big, sleek, wide-bodied McDonnell Douglas DC-10, powered by three mighty General Electric jet engines, would not land on the ice continent. There was an ice runway, but that was used only by ski-equipped Hercules and Starlifter transport aircraft of the United States military that flew summer resupply flights to the American scientific base at McMurdo Sound, the gateway to Antarctica. The Air New Zealand flight would, weather conditions permitting, descend from its cruising altitude of 35 000 feet (imperial units are universally used in aviation) and make several low passes over the ice to allow the passengers a chance to see sights such as Mt Erebus and Mt Terror. They might also have been able to see the huts of the early Antarctic explorers, Robert Falcon Scott and Ernest Shackleton. With the onset of summer bringing both the American and New Zealand scientific bases on Antarctica to life, perhaps they might even sight a dog sled or two.

Air New Zealand's DC-10s were near-new aircraft with advanced airframes and navigational systems. Powerful, responsive and long-legged, they were ideal for Air New Zealand which flew some of the longest oceanic routes in the world. They were accepted as good aircraft though queries had been raised about their history which had become rather chequered. Made by McDonnell-Douglas, the DC-10 had entered service in 1971 but had soon seen disaster. In 1974 a Turkish Airlines DC-10 had crashed shortly after takeoff near Paris, killing 364. In May 1979 a DC-10 had crashed on takeoff at Chicago's O'Hare Airport, killing 273. If passengers were still ready to board them, the joke went around that people on board them 'don't talk' in case the sound of their voice caused them to crash.

Collins, who had been flying DC-10s for five years, shared the confidence of other pilots in their capabilities. His faith had been bolstered by an incident two years before, when a bolt of lightning had struck the DC-10 he was commanding out of Los Angeles. The bolt hit the aircraft with an enormous crack and blew off two of the heavy cargo bay doors, causing the aircraft to buffet violently. Collins calmed the passengers over the PA system, explaining what had happened and that he would dump fuel over the sea before returning to Los Angeles. There was no panic and the passengers did not realise how dangerous their situation was until they read about it in the *Los Angeles Times*. To those who knew him, the unflappable manner in which he coped with the situation was vintage Jim Collins.

Collins and one of his two co-pilots, the tall, laconic Greg Cassin, 37, had done the appropriate research for the flight. Nineteen days before takeoff, they had attended a day-long briefing at Air New Zealand's Route Clearance Unit. They had also done flight simulator training. When the flights to Antarctica had begun, Air New Zealand had followed military practice and required all flights to be commanded by a pilot who had previously flown to Antarctica. Because of the realism that could be created in the flight simulator and the accurate navigation system, it had dropped the requirement. Collins had taken his black-bound atlas with him to the briefing. An audio-visual presentation showed that they would make landfall at Cape Hallet, outside McMurdo Sound. From there, they would fly almost directly south up the smooth, flat sound where they could safely descend to view the ice. The briefing included a display of a series of slides, showing the route over the McMurdo Sound sea ice. The high ground of Ross Island would be to the east. The pilots were never told that their route would take them over Mt Erebus.

Air New Zealand never took any of its expeditions lightly, least of all those to the Antarctic. Normally Air New Zealand's DC-10s were crewed by a captain, a co-pilot and an engineer. An extra co-pilot and engineer were required on Antarctic flights, making a total of five in the flight crew. The purpose was twofold. The aircraft was flying at low level into unfamiliar and potentially dangerous territory. Because big jets burn increased fuel at low altitudes, fuel management would be critical to allow a safe return, and the more 'heads' involved in managing things, the better. It also gave the opportunity for crew to be relieved during the 10-hour journey.

The morning of the flight dawned fine and calm. Captain Collins' DC-10—registration ZKNZP—was parked at the airport's Gate 2. At Air New Zealand's flight despatch office, the flight crew were going over their preparations, paying special attention to factors of weather and fuel. The 237 passengers were filtering up to the check-in counter for Flight TE-901 to Antarctica. Their excitement bubbled over. Some were obviously prosperous, like the party of 24 Japanese which included two doctors, two optometrists, a dentist, a retired university professor and two honeymooning couples. Others, like New Zealand policeman Trevor Maskelyne, had won the trip in a raffle. Others still had received their ticket as a gift. Seven tickets for the flight had been bought in Australia, 24 in Japan, one in Canada and two in London. There was only one Australian resident on the flight: June Davies, 42, wife of Captain R.M. Davies, warden of the Burnie Marine Board in Tasmania. The passengers were dressed mostly in light casual clothes and had only carry-on luggage, but just about everybody had a camera slung over their shoulder and plenty of film.

The flight down the length of New Zealand's two mountainous islands had its own excitement to offer. Passengers, catered for by the 15 cabin crew, would be served a champagne breakfast that included 'Peach Erebus'. They would be shown a documentary film, *The Big Ice*. The jet, weighed down with 109 tonnes of fuel—enough for 11 hours flying, would slowly swing around to a southerly route. If the weather was clear the passengers would be primed for the ice by overflying the Southern Alps, the great chain of high mountains that form the spine of New Zealand's south island. Once clear of the South Island the jet, by now at its cruising height of 35 000 feet, would overfly the rugged and desolate islands south of New Zealand and adjust its track to head almost directly south over the wild Southern Ocean. It was understood by passengers and crew that they would reach McMurdo Sound in four hours. Once there, the DC-10 would take advantage of the great, flat expanse of sea ice and drop down, initially to 16000 feet, then as low as 1500 feet, swooping up the sound for hopefully dramatic views. Safe navigation would be assisted by the American air traffic controllers on the ice runway, who operated a radar capable of picking up aircraft in the McMurdo Sound area that were flying at an altitude of less than 6000 feet. They were used to seeing Air New Zealand sightseeing flights pass low up the sound.

As the five crew took their places in the cockpit, it would already have been decided that Cassin would be Collins' co-pilot for the flight south and over the ice. Cassin was senior to the second co-pilot, Brick Lucas. While Collins busied himself with reported weather conditions for the ascent over New Zealand, the two co-pilots moved through the pre-flight technical checks of the aircraft. This included loading Air New Zealand's computer-generated flight plan into the DC-10's navigation system. The flight plan consisted of evenly-spaced waypoints—geographic positions which the aircraft's navigational computers read and hold to all the way to Antarctica. When the plane's automatic pilot system was switched on it drew on the waypoints to guide the aircraft exactly along the chosen route. The first waypoint was the spot where the aircraft was parked in Auckland.

As the jet rose from the Auckland runway, Collins turned her toward the south and, after her speed and altitude had built up, flicked a cockpit switch to engage the automatic pilot. The system was one of the marvels of modern big jets. Its centrepiece was the inertial platform, a gyroscopically stabilised platform that had small sensors fitted. All of the aircraft's movements in all directions were monitored and measured by sensors that then sent signals to the automatic pilot system. The automatic pilot would make corrections and keep the jet locked onto the route the pilots entered into the computer. If, as was common practice, the pilots turned off the automatic pilot so as to deviate from the pre-set route, the system registered those deviations and when the deviation was finished it simply guided the aircraft back to the route.

Collins had also taken on board somebody who, possibly better than any other New Zealander, knew the geography of the Antarctic. An Antarctic explorer and mountaineer, Peter Mulgrew had been contracted by the Air New Zealand to add spice to the sightseeing flights by giving passengers a running commentary from the flight deck as the aircraft flew over the ice. A reserved but restless man, he had lost his legs and fingers while climbing in the Himalayas in 1960 with Sir Edmund Hillary. His injuries had not dampened his passion for sailing large ocean racers, nor his fascination with Antarctica.

Less than two hours after takeoff, when the DC-10 had left New Zealand's southern tip behind, the passengers did not have much to see from their cruising altitude. In telling what happened next, we have to rely to an extent on reconstruction, because nobody is alive to give an account. Based on this reconstruction, Mulgrew addressed the passengers, telling them to keep an eye out for the desolate Auckland Islands some 600 kilometres south of New Zealand. These were uninhabited and were often blasted by shrieking southerlies from Antarctica. This is the beginning of the bottom of the world. The DC-10 was now very much alone. Soon after passing the Auckland Islands, the cabin crew drew the window visors to darken the cabin and showed the Antarctica documentary. Some passengers, jolted by their early morning start in Auckland, snatched some sleep. Two hours further on—about four hours since take-off—the cabin was roused. The cabin crew lifted up the window visors so that the passengers could get their first glimpses of the Antarctic's advance outpost. Below would be the Balleny Islands, on the ice continent's rim. They might get their first sight of drifting pack ice, and perhaps an iceberg. What the passengers did notice was the colour of the upper atmosphere, which had changed to the milky white of the far south.

At this point the DC-10's crew made radio contact with Americans on the ground at McMurdo Sound. The Americans informed the crew that they would be entering less than ideal weather. The cloud was down to 3000 feet, but visibility of up to 64 kilometres was more than adequate for sightseeing. There was a ripple of caution among the crew, although no cause for alarm. Air traffic controllers at McMurdo Sound had assisted other Air New Zealand flights to go below such cloud.

On a clear day the peaks of Mts Erebus and Terror would have been coming into view over the horizon from the left, but the cloud extended to a height of some 15 000 feet, and nothing was visible from 35 000 feet. Collins decided to begin the first phase of the DC-10's descent. Throttling back, he angled the nose by a few degrees and allowed the airliner to begin a gentle glide towards a cruising altitude of 16 000 feet, which was higher than any peaks in the area. He allowed the autopilot to hold the aircraft on what he thought was its pre-set route toward McMurdo Sound, west of Mt Erebus. Cassin was having trouble raising the McMurdo air traffic controllers (their base being referred to as Mac Centre) on the normally used Very High Frequency (VHF) radio band. He managed to make contact on the High Frequency (HF) band. The Mac Centre weather forecaster come told him the weather had deteriorated. Cloud was now down to 2000 feet at McMurdo Sound and light snow was falling, although visibility was still good up to 64 kilometres. The controllers gave permission to come lower. Mac Centre offered the services of their approach radar once the aircraft dropped below 6000 feet.

With the cloud so low, Collins knew there would be little to see until the aircraft had reached a low altitude. His passengers deserved to get their money's worth. He decided to begin his descent well outside the Sound, over the flat ice of the Ross Sea. Once they were below the cloud, they would be in a better position to assess conditions for the planned low level fight up the sound, with the assistance of Mac Centre controllers and their radar. The cockpit voice recorder taped the deliberations of the crew. One engineer said, 'A low overcast over McMurdo.' Collins expressed mild reservation. 'Doesn't look very promising, does it?' Then the radio crackled to life. Mac Centre sent a message that it could use its radar to get the DC-10 to well below the cloud, down to an altitude of 1500 feet, once it was within 64 kilometres of the McMurdo Sound Tower. Collins' response was, 'That's what we want to hear.'

By now Collins had cut back the speed of the DC-10 to 260 knots (a knot is one nautical mile, or 1.85 kilometres, per hour) from its 500 knot cruise speed. Low-altitude flying in the Antarctic called for special skills. The big wing flaps of passenger jets are usually extended at low speed to increase lift and permit slower flying, but they could not be used in Antarctic conditions because of the danger that their mechanisms might freeze, jamming the flaps in the extended position. If that happened, the drag on the aircraft would increase enormously, forcing a huge increase in fuel consumption. Cassin, meanwhile, was still having difficulties getting VHF contact with Mac Centre. VHF transmissions, relying on line-of-sight radio waves, were commonly used, but the system was known to have difficulties. In this case it seemed to the crew that either Mac Centre's transmitter was low in power or the atmospheric conditions were interfering with communications.

In fact the difficulties in communication were far more ominous. They had their origins the night before in Auckland, when Air New Zealand's Navigation Section had adjusted the aircraft's final waypoint, now keyed into the DC-10's navigation computer. The change had been from longitude 164 degrees 48 minutes east, to 166 degrees 48 minutes east. This had the effect of moving the DC-10's final destination waypoint 43.2 kilometres to the east. Instead of the programmed flight path taking the low-flying aircraft on a course directly to Ross Island and up the flat expanse of McMurdo Sound, it placed the jet on a potential collision course with Mt Erebus. The DC-10 was now at about 18 000 feet, but nobody among the crew was aware that it was on the changed flight path. They had not been told. Nor did they realise that the VHF signal was being blocked by Mt Erebus itself.

From his seat on the left had side of the cockpit, Captain Collins could see the cloud front drawing closer and knew that he would need to descend further so as to fly visually to McMurdo Sound and over the ice runway. He tried again to raise Mac Centre on the VHF, but could not get through. At 30 minutes after noon, local time, he told his crew, 'I'll have to do an orbit here, I think.' The manoeuvre was designed to allow the jet to descend further over what Collins and his crew were certain was the Ross Sea, at the entrance of McMurdo Sound. In fact they were 43.2 kilometres to the east, over the approach to Lewis Bay. Mts Erebus and Terror, obscured, were almost directly in front of them.

By now Peter Mulgrew was in the jump seat at the rear of the cockpit, scanning the breaks in the cloud so that he could work out where they were and give his best commentary to passengers. The jet's right wing dipped as Collins began the first turn of his orbit. The captain's reassuring voice broke the excited hubbub of the passenger cabin. 'Captain, again, ladies and gentlemen. We're carrying out an orbit and circling our present position and will be descending to an altitude below cloud so that we can proceed to McMurdo Sound.' Cassin, using the HF radio, called up the ice runway controllers at Mac Centre. He told them he could not raise them on either of the two VHF channels, and that they were about 69 kilometres to the north of the control tower and descending through cloud. The controller at Mac Centre was unconcerned about the difficulties with the VHF radio. He reassured the crew there were no problems with the descent. Clearly the American air traffic controllers also believed the aircraft was on the normal Air New Zealand flight path approach to McMurdo Sound. The controller said, 'Roger Kiwi New Zealand nine zero one. VMC [visual meteorological conditions, or flying visually] descent is approved and keep Mac Centre advised of your altitude.'

By now, everybody in the cockpit, including Mulgrew, were intent on picking up geographic markers from the ice that would confirm their position. In another terrible twist of fate, the crew was fooled. A veteran Air New Zealand Captain, Gordon Vette, was later to provide an explanation of what happened. Working with experts in weather and in Antarctic terrain, and the transcript of the plane's cockpit voice recorder, he later demonstrated conclusively that Mulgrew and the crew were duped by the terrain they saw into believing they were exactly on track. There were cruel, uncanny similarities between the terrain at the entrances to McMurdo Sound and Lewis Bay.

There was yet another false reassurance. The DC-10's cockpit radar transponder suddenly lit up, indicating that the McMurdo Sound's approach radar had locked onto the jet, which indicated to the crew that the McMurdo Sound controllers had their aircraft on their screens. If there was a problem with their position, then the DC-10 crew could expected to be alerted. The crew did not know that their appearance on the McMurdo Sound radar screens had been so brief that the controllers were later to claim they did not see it. The aircraft had been captured on the radar only momentarily, as it completed the first turn of its orbit. Their last chance to be saved by those on the ground had just evaporated. Now they were totally subject to the tricks of geography and weather.

By now the DC-10 was descending through 10 000 feet. They were still in cloud. They would have to go lower to establish visual flying conditions. Collins turned the DC-10 left so that it was backtracking and heading north, away from Antarctica, in another orbit to lose altitude. A few minutes later, at 43 minutes past noon, he began turning the DC-10 left again to bring it back on course for its swoop southwards. The crew expected this to take them across the flat safety of the Ross Sea and McMurdo Sound. As he completed this last turn, the cloud began to break up and the crew could see the Antarctic coast line ahead. Peter Mulgrew who was sitting behind the crew in the cockpit said, 'There you go! There's some land up ahead!'

The aircraft's flight data and cockpit voice recorder indicate that Mulgrew then thought he had sighted Cape Bernacchi, on the western side of McMurdo Sound. It was certainly what the crew were expecting to see, based on their pre-flight briefing. Mulgrew did not realise he was looking at Cape Bird, on the edge of Lewis Bay. Had he done so, he would have realised that disaster was minutes away. In the meantime Cassin told the controllers over the HF radio that the DC-10 was descending through 6000 feet to an altitude of 2000 feet. He said the crew were now on VMC, that they had found a gap in the clouds and that the crew could see their way ahead to the rapidly rising Antarctic coast. What they could not see was Mt Erebus, 56 kilometres in front of them.

What the crew and the passengers did see was comforting enough. The terrain through the cloud breaks was flat and clear. It was what they were expecting the white, watery expanse of McMurdo Sound to look like. Mulgrew believed he was looking at Taylor Valley, on the western side of the entrance to McMurdo—again, what the crew expected to see. He was in fact looking at the cliffs of Cape Tennyson, on the western side of Lewis Bay. These mistaken geographical identifications were reinforcing the apparent signals from the navigation system that the jet was on the right track. Mulgrew took up the cockpit PA microphone and, with the aircraft still descending through the broken cloud, said, 'This is Peter Mulgrew speaking again folks. I still can't see very much at the moment. Keep you informed soon as I see something that gives me a clue as to where we are. We're going down in altitude now and it won't be long before we get quite a good view.'

While Mulgrew's choice of phrase might seem to suggest he had no idea where the DC-10 was, it seems that he was certain of its general position but could not yet see specific items of interest to the passengers. In the cockpit, flight engineer Gordon Brooks asked Mulgrew, 'Where's Erebus in relation to us at the moment?' Mulgrew, calculating Mt Erebus' position from where he assumed the plane was, replied, 'Left, about 20 to 25 miles.' Brooks said, 'Yep, yep. I am just thinking about any high ground in the area at the moment.' There was no mountain in view, just a vast, flat expanse of white. The DC-10 was now flying not far above 2000 feet. It had entered the folds of Lewis Bay, which resembled the enveloping coast line of McMurdo Sound, 44.8 kilometres to the west. Mount Erebus was just 24 kilometres ahead, three minutes and 15 seconds of flying time away. Mulgrew was still certain of their general position. It still fit with the crew's reading of their navigation instruments. Mulgrew saw what he thought was Ross Island to the east, but it was Cape Tennyson. He was about to mention that he had seen Ross Island when Collins injected, 'Actually, these conditions don't look very good at all, do they?' Brooks agreed, 'I don't like this.'

The crew had begun to encounter an Antarctic weather phenomenon that none of them had ever encountered before. It is called whiteout. The view ahead looked white and flat and there appeared to be high cloud cover, but the light was unusual, eerie, sapping the usual texture and surfaces of the terrain ahead, making it look like sea ice. This polar phenomenon occurs in overcast conditions when cloud layers diffuse the direct rays of the sun, causing shadows on snow and the horizon to disappear. When this happens pilots lose their mental ability to define the surface and measure distances, even though they may be in clear air.

Collins was puzzled, even concerned, that the DC-10 had not been able to raise the McMurdo air traffic controllers on the VHF radios and that contact with McMurdo's approach radar had been lost. Something was not right. He decided to turn away from his run up what he still thought was McMurdo

Sound, telling his crew, 'We'll have to climb out of this.' Cassin, peering out of the window to his right, said, 'You're clear to turn right. There's no high ground if you do a one-eighty.' Collins replied, 'No, negative.' He seemed to be weighing up the situation. He knew that, according to the flight plan, the clear sea of McMurdo Sound was below him. Suddenly the shrill alarm of the ground proximity warning system (GPWS) in the cockpit sounded and an electronic voice coupled to the warning said, 'Pull up, pull up!' Collins lunged for the DC-10's power levers. The three engines increased their power and the DC-10's nose began to lift. Gordon Brooks, monitoring the panel of instruments and dials on the cockpit's side, calmly but briskly called the aircraft's altitude. 'Five hundred feet,' he said. They were 500 feet above ground. The GPWS continues to sound its alert. Brook said, 'Four hundred feet.' The GPWS continued. Collins called out, 'Go around power, please!' The GPWS abruptly stopped.

Mercifully, the shock wave from the impact with Mt Erebus, 760 metres from its base, killed everyone in the space of less than a second. It is possible to believe the passengers, at least, died enjoying themselves. The last instruction from Collins for 'go around power' indicates something of the atmosphere in the cockpit at the moment of impact. The instruction was for Brooks to set the engine maximum power settings at a point below which the engines would be exposed to damage by over-boosting. It was a calm, deliberate instruction, delivered in an unworried tone by a captain who obviously saw no mountain and who believed the white expanse he could see in front of him was the 30 kilometres of sea ice that lay between him and the US base. What he was seeing was whiteout, the last player in what appeared to be a deadly conspiracy that would seal the fate of 257 people.

In Wellington, some 8000 kilometres north, Air New Zealand's popular, feisty chief executive, Morrie Davis, was hosting the country's premier golf tournament, which was sponsored by his airline. Shortly after 2 pm, a grim-faced staff member took him aside. The Americans at McMurdo Sound had just radioed. The DC-10 had been meant to report in every 30 minutes but the controllers had not heard from it for more than an hour. Davis quietly left the tournament and flew 600 kilometres north to his Auckland office. Air New Zealand's concerns mounted. There was some hope the aircraft was merely experiencing radio communication difficulties, but by 6 pm, the airline's management and executive pilots were dreading the worst: Flight 901 was due to land in New Zealand in about an hour but nothing had been heard from it since shortly before 1 pm.

By 8 pm the first news flashes about the missing DC-10 went out on radio and newspapers rapidly called in staff to remake their front pages. Air New Zealand's executives knew that by 10 pm the DC-10's fuel reserves would have been exhausted, but Air New Zealand held off making any announcement conceding that the plane had been lost. Just before 11 pm, a ham radio operator in Wellington, who had equipment powerful enough to monitor the transmissions of US military helicopters in Antarctica, heard the news first. An American pilot was calling Mac Centre. He said, 'We have found the DC-10. It is on the back side of Erebus. There appear to be no survivors.'

The news did not take long to reach Morrie Davis, who slumped at his desk, his head buried in his hands. At his Wellington home that night, New Zealand's chief inspector of air accidents, Ron Chippindale, a tall, sharp-featured man with a moustache and ramrod-straight back that betrayed his military background, packed his outdoor gear for what he was certain would be a journey to Antarctica. The next morning, along with 35 others including New Zealand police rescue teams, mountaineers and a TV crew, he boarded a New Zealand Air Force Hercules transport for a flight to McMurdo Sound. Ferried to the crash site by US helicopters, he was staggered by what he saw.

The DC-10 had disintegrated to such an extent it was little more than a black scar running over 600 metres up the lower slopes of Mount Erebus. It had been the path of a cascading fireball. A deep imprint of the aircraft's underbelly, wings and engines had been left in the snow where the scar began. The aircraft itself had shredded, scattering metal far up the slope. The rear engine, attached to the tail, had flown on after impact and the tail remained intact far up the slope, bearing the proud insignia of Air New Zealand, the Maori Koru motif. Representatives of the California-based McDonnell Douglas and General Electric were quickly on the scene. McDonnell Douglas was already reeling from the DC-10 crashes in France and America.

The Air New Zealand DC-10's flight data recorder—the black box—and its cockpit voice recorder were quickly recovered and analysed. They showed conclusively that the DC-10 was functioning perfectly when it flew into Mount Erebus.

Flying colleagues in Air New Zealand were dumbfounded. They could not believe that the meticulous and cautious Jim Collins could have flown into a mountain. They refused to believe that he could have been at fault. Theories abounded as to the cause: swirling, destructive winds near Mount Erebus, an inexplicable decision by Collins to descend through dense cloud, illness affecting the flight crew. All would have to await the results of Chippindale's investigation, and for

Chippindale, required to begin his inquiries in a bleak, uninhabited environment with no survivors, it was a daunting task.

Unknown to Chippindale, a quiet panic overtook Air New Zealand's management, because they were getting the true picture. Within two days of the crash they discovered that their own flight navigation section had made a terrible mistake, changing the final waypoint of Flight 901's route on the eve of the flight so that the last part of the flight plan took the plane directly over Mt Erebus. The section had been acting on flawed information from their superiors and had attempted to correct what they thought was a minor mistake on the last portion of the flight path. The section had inadvertently downloaded an old Antarctic flight plan that took aircraft over Mt Erebus, from their computer. That flight plan, disused since late 1977, had been restored, but nobody had bothered to tell Collins.

It was claimed later that the airline began to shred documents and that the executives directed that no word of this discovery be made public. There was no doubt that the executives could see a public relations disaster for the company, but claims that they were involved in a conspiracy to cover up the facts were examined later and ultimately rejected. Chippindale did discover the computer error, but he was inclined to accept that the primary cause of the crash had been Collins' decision to descend through cloud when he was unsure of his position. He did have other evidence to consider. Flight 901 may have been the most isolated big jet disaster ever, but it was also among the best documented. Investigators recovered rolls of film from the crash site and were able to develop some 900 photographs, a unique record of the progress of the flight, documented to the moment of impact. A passenger had actually photographed the impact, the picture showing the body of the DC-10 intact but fuel from the rupturing tanks spurting onto the windows. What the photographs also showed was that the aircraft was flying in clear air before it hit Mount Erebus.

A coroner's inquest was conducted in Auckland in January 1980. Auckland Coroner Allan Copeland found that the passengers and crew of Flight 901 had died of multiple injuries when the plane struck Mt Erebus. 'I find that the force of the crash was such that nobody could have survived and that nobody died of exposure or burns,' he said. The court made formal findings on 14 people who had not been identified or whose bodies were lost on the mountain.

Chippindale made his report public in March 1980, finding grave fault on the part of Air New Zealand, not only in its last-minute change of route but in its briefings to pilots going on Antarctic flights. But he found that the primary cause of the crash had been Collins' decision to continue the flight at low level toward an area of poor surface and horizon definition when the crew was not certain of their position. In other words, the primary cause was pilot error. Confronted with the photographic evidence, he could not say Collins had been flying in cloud, but his finding nevertheless strongly stated Collins was still at fault, an accusation that was devastating to the families of the dead crew, who were joined by many of the airline's senior pilots in their feelings of outrage. The New Zealand Government decided to have the accident investigated by a royal commission. The royal commission would be chaired by a quietly spoken but—as would later be revealed—tenacious judge, Peter Mahon, who when appointed royal commissioner privately surmised that he was expected to uphold Chippindale's findings.

What followed was vastly different. Gordon Vette, who had flown DC-10s and had been one of Collins' closest friends at Air New Zealand, decided to dedicate himself to proving Chippindale wrong in his criticism of Collins. His argument was three-pronged. He claimed that because of the computer error, the crew had been misled about the route they were expected to follow. Working with the passengers' photographs and the cockpit voice recorder, he was able to demonstrate that the DC-10 crew had been misled by the geographical features into thinking they were on the right path. He argued that far from being uncertain of their position, Collins and his crew had at all times been very certain of their position because they were relying on their pre-planned route briefing, the aircraft's navigation system and what they could see of the terrain.

The problem was how to explain an aircraft hitting a mountain whilst flying in clear air. Vette made a detailed study of visual perceptions in the Antarctic. Aided by weather experts, Antarctic pilots and psychologists, he came to the conclusion that the crew had experienced whiteout. In his book, *Impact Erebus,* Vette was to say that in their final moments the crew of Flight 901 were looking out on a scene which had every appearance of being a vast, snow-covered clear expanse of flat sea ice stretching 40 to 60 miles ahead, under a cloud ceiling of 2000 to 3000 feet. The terrain in front of them was uniformly white, except for two or three strips of black rock on the snowy ice floor, which were indistinguishable from sea water or which may have been concealed by drifting ice fog. The reality was that the crew had been looking at a coastline which did not exist.

Mahon flew to Antarctica in November, 1980, exactly a year after the crash. A United States helicopter took him to the crash site. What followed amazed him. While flying toward the mountain, on the same route as the DC-10, a high cloud cover rapidly moved in. The cloud began to cover the top of Mt Erebus' peak and then concealed the distinctive ice cliffs at the base. The shadows disappeared. The helicopter crew, who were below the cloud and flying in clear air, could not define the surface ahead. The mountain became invisible and the diffused light created a false horizon. It looked as though they were flying across flat, snow-covered ground. It was a whiteout. Mahon believed he had encountered, quite by chance, the conditions Collins and his crew had encountered. Inevitably that impression would receive full exposure in his report.

In mid-1981 the then New Zealand Prime Minister, Sir Robert Muldoon, who was also chief shareholder on behalf of the government in Air New Zealand, was orientated towards damage control. He publicly warned New Zealanders that they should prepare to stand by their national airline. He knew Mahon's report, which would be released next day, would be scathing about the airline and would not support what the airline had claimed, that the crash was due to pilot error. Indeed, that was how the report turned out. Mahon completely exonerated Collins and his crew from blame. He found they had been victims of Air New Zealand's navigational blunders, that they had been fooled by the Antarctic's geography and had fallen victim to whiteout. He saved his strongest words for Air New Zealand. The airline, the Royal Commissioner's Report said, had embarked upon a pre-determined plan of deception at his inquiry in an effort to shift blame to the aircrew. He said, 'I am forced reluctantly to say that I had to listen to an orchestrated litany of lies.'

The criticism rocked the airline. On 4 May 1981, in the wake of the report Davis announced his retirement, but Air New Zealand was not prepared to accept the judgement. On 22 December that year five judges in the New Zealand Court of Appeal took the side of the airline and unanimously quashed the finding that there had been a 'premeditated plan of deception'. The court found that Mahon had exceeded his jurisdiction, and that there was no wholesale conspiracy to commit perjury. In the wake of the finding Mahon offered his resignation and on 27 January 1982 Muldoon announced that the government had accepted it.

Air New Zealand, which had removed all billboard posters advertising the trip soon after the tragedy, never sent a flight to Antarctica again. Qantas cancelled its own Antarctic flights and would not to resume them for 15 years. Mahon retired and wrote a most eloquent book, *Verdict on Erebus*, published in 1983, bringing scornful comments from Muldoon that his literary ability was better than his ability as a royal commissioner. Gordon Vette's book was published the following year. On 8 July 1988, a US District Court judge, Harold Greene, dismissed claims totalling $A40.17 million against the US Government by relatives of 16 of the 20 crew members, who had claimed that the radar operators at McMurdo Base should have warned Collins that he was off course. Greene blamed the airline for changing the original flight plan without briefing the crew. He also blamed the crew's failure to use its internal navigation device and weather radar system.

On a mid-August afternoon in 1999, three women, all widows, gathered in the public gallery of the New Zealand Parliament: Maria Collins, Anne Cassin and Margarita Mahon, the first two the wives of the pilots, the latter the widow of Mahon. They were there to witness New Zealand Parliament's formal acceptance of Mahon's report. They heard New Zealand's Minister for Transport, Maurice Williamson, tell Parliament that the report should have been tabled years earlier. Williamson said, 'Some people say why bother after all this time? I have no better explanation than this: those who cannot remember the past are condemned to repeat it.'

6

The Queensland Black Hawk
Collision, 1996

*The noise of a helicopter dying is, it's very hard to describe it,
almost sounds like a dying animal.*

Corporal Gary Proctor, SAS

The problem of getting troops to the required location without
them being shot at, shelled, bombed, speared or stoned along
the way, or without confronting a fully-alerted adversary on
arrival, has taxed military brains from the dawn of military
science. Arriving unexpectedly against an unprepared enemy
has normally given an advantage, often a decisive one. The
Greeks achieved it with deception at Troy. Kayaking commandoes achieved it with stealth in World War II. The
Japanese tried it with mini-subs in Sydney Harbour in 1942.
The Allied forces used gliders in Operation Market Garden
in 1944, attempting to capture a string of bridges and thereby
facilitate the invasion of Europe.

Helicopters, which became available after World War
II, appeared to be the answer to a vast number of military
problems. They were noisy and visible, but they were fast and
they could hover. They needed no landing strips or favourable wind directions, they could hug the terrain and they
had carrying capacity, firepower and precision. Had they

been developed some years earlier, they would have undoubtedly changed the course of the World War II. By the time the Korean War erupted helicopters had become indispensable. No weapon better symbolised the exhausting struggle in South Vietnam between 1965 and 1975 than the Iroquois helicopter with its M-16 door guns. In June 1970 helicopters took Israeli commandoes deep into Egypt to attack the military base at Bir Araida in the Gulf of Suez; in February 1973 helicopters sent a task force into Egypt to capture officers for interrogation, flying so tightly in formation that the Egyptian radar did not recognise the force for the size it was.

Helicopters do have their drawbacks. They are not streamlined like planes, and as objects they do not particularly want to fly, tending to drop if they lose power. They require enormous power because they often hover over treetops or buildings and are as subject as any aircraft to the vagaries of wind-shift, allowing them relatively small margins for error. Add to that the complexity of mission and the heightened anxiety of battle or counter-terrorist operations, it can be appreciated that they are vulnerable to accident. In 1980, after the Iranians stormed the US Embassy in Tehran, the US forces sent eight Sea Stallion helicopters from the carrier USS *Nimitz* to rescue 53 hostages. Following the withdrawal of three helicopters, two of which had developed mechanical problems, the mission was aborted while the assault force was still at a remote airstrip south of Tehran. In the night-time withdrawal, a Sea Stallion and a Hercules crashed, bursting into flames, with the loss of eight lives.

The Sikorsky UH-60 Black Hawk helicopter, developed in response to specifications laid down in 1972 by the US Army, became the new generation of helicopter for battlefield operations, replacing the durable Iroquois and Chinooks of the Vietnam era. Developed at a time after the first moon landing, it represented the high hopes of brilliant new technology. 'Ballistics tolerant', it could sustain an amount of enemy fire and remain operational. Powered by twin General Electric T700-GE-701C turbo-shaft engines, it had infra-red countermeasures, radar detectors, an exhaust system that dissipated heat, duplicate sets of electrical and hydraulic systems, and a main transmission that could run at full operation for 30 minutes with no oil. It could crash-land on its wheels and it had built-in buffers to limit the effect of the impact on those on board.

The Black Hawk could be equipped with a 7.62 mm Gatling Gun, 30 mm cannon, Hellfire missiles and a .50 calibre machine-gun. Able to carry up to 11 000 kilograms gross weight and 4500 kilograms in external loads, it could also sling-load light vehicles and equipment, convey the wounded and perform a variety of other tasks. Its most important function was troop transport. It could seat up to 15 fully-equipped troops for fast-rope insertion or high or low parachuting. Demonstrating their potential for the first time in October 1974, the Black Hawks quickly won accolades. The Connecticut manufacturer, Sikorsky, made its first delivery to the US Army in 1978 and the 2000th in October 1994. The Black Hawk had a baptism of fire in during US invasion of Grenada in 1983, and from there went on to serve with distinction in US military operations in Panama, Somalia, South-West Africa, Haiti and Bosnia.

The Australian Army had long married commando-type activities to helicopters. The Special Air Service Regiment (SASR or SAS), based in Perth and modelled on its British counterpart, had been formed in 1957 to build on the skills developed by Australia's irregular forces in World War II and had first seen action during the Malaysian confrontation in 1965. That deployment, which saw the SAS based in North Borneo, gave the SAS a chance to develop the rappelling skills that were to become standard practice. The SAS distinguished itself in Vietnam and was later to be represented in Somalia, Rwanda and Cambodia. The demands on men were high. It was hard to get into the SAS. Training had to be as realistic as possible, which meant it could be dangerous. If the SAS lost few men in combat, it lost more of them in training accidents. In 1978, when the Hilton Hotel bomb killed three men, the Australian Government resolved to form its own counter-terrorist (CT) capacity. The job fell to the SAS. They were required to train for efficient operations in all manner of environments: in the air, underwater, in streets, tall buildings, on oil platforms, deserts, jungles, storm canals and ships at sea. In most operations, the Black Hawk was an indispensable tool.

Black Hawks were sold to countries friendly to the United States. Australia bought 39 Sikorsky 5-70/A 9 Black Hawk helicopters for $500 million. The first was delivered in February, 1988, the last in January, 1991. This writer went on one, during war correspondent training in North Queensland in 1991. The speed—some 250 kmh at a height of 20 metres above treetop level—was exhilarating if a little unnerving. We did a rapid ascent at 30 metres per second to avoid a simulated rocket attack. 'Suppose the pilot miscalculates, at this speed and so near the ground,' I asked the major sitting next to me. 'Don't worry,' he replied. 'You won't feel a thing.' Prior to 1989, the Royal Australian Navy (RAN) had provided helicopters for offshore operations while the Royal Australian Air Force (RAAF) provided helicopters above the size of reconnaissance helicopters for land operations. In 1989 the army assumed responsibility for Black Hawks, acquiring transporting techniques and procedures from the RAAF, though the RAAF still had a role in maintenance. Because the SAS and the Black Hawk were so interlinked, it seemed only natural that they be brought within the jurisdiction of one service.

The SAS Regiment remained in Perth and the Black Hawks were operated by the Fifth Aviation Regiment (5 Anv Regt) at Townsville, on the opposite coast. The scope of this wonder machine extended to night operations that would have been once considered impossible. The capacity for night operations appeared to be significantly enhanced by the development of 'Night Vision Goggles', or NVGs, mounted on the helmet, capable of magnifying the residual light at night from the moon or even stars, displaying objects in a green tinge against a black background.

Such developments put higher and higher strains on individuals. It was as though human beings had to adapt themselves to the demands of machines. When flying at night, even using conventional aircraft and without the aid of NVGs, soldiers always had to contend with limitations on vision. NVGs vastly restricted the range of vision, from a normal visual arc of 120 degrees to an arc of 40 degrees, which is virtually tunnel vision. The world was seen as a series of green-tinged outlines. Vision was no longer stereoscopic, so it was much harder to estimate distances or rates of closure with other objects. Visual acuity, that is, the ability to make out objects in precise detail, was so limited that anybody wearing them would not have legally been allowed to drive a car. In conditions of cloud cover they became virtually useless. One pilot, Captain David Burke, was later to say, 'It's like trying to fly while watching a small TV screen. It's obviously a very difficult task. Flying the sorts of missions that we were doing is the most demanding thing we do.' Warrant Officer Bill Mark, who was also part of the Black Hawk Air Crew, was to say on ABC television's *Four Corners*, 'I always used to say . . . that with NVGs, your eyes bled at the end of it because you are looking through that tube for so long.'

Perhaps inevitably, accidents occurred. This was a result of the human factor and the vagaries of unexpected equipment failure. The manufacturer calculated an attrition rate (loss of aircraft, for whatever reason, including accidents and mechanical failure), at 3.4 helicopters per 100000 flying hours. In 1988 a Canadian Black Hawk on night training struck a formation of three other Black Hawks on a separate mission, killing 17 soldiers. In March the same year a Black Hawk crashed in Kentucky, with similar numbers killed. The investigation found human error to blame, as well as limited training and the restrictiveness of NVGs. Between 1980 and 1996 the US Military had reports of 50 service helicopter accidents involving Black Hawks. NVGs were a factor in a huge proportion of these. The US Army Safety Centre found that Black Hawks were involved in 56 of the US Army's 210 non-combat air deaths between 1987 and 1993. There were faults found in the main rotor assembly and in the tail assembly, and adjustments were made. In 1988 shielding was installed in some aircraft to protect them from radio wave interference.

When operated properly Black Hawks were ideal for the types of training being contemplated: CT missions which were regarded as the most important training the military could undertake in peacetime, and Special Recovery Operations (SROs), which were aimed mainly at the rescue of hostages. Two exercises were planned each year: Rotor Dusk in November–December, and Day Rotor in June, in which the SAS and the aviation regiment could work together. The SAS started rotating its troops to coincide with the training and the aviation regiment followed suit, so that over a number of years members of both units would have expertise. For the exercises, the SAS did its planning in Perth, flew to Townsville, and gave its mission plan to the aviators. The units were to work in combination, doing missions by day and by night.

The programming put a heavy demand on organisations, men and equipment. The Australian Army did lose one Black Hawk, in a training accident, at Oakey in Queensland in 1992, when two of the four-man crew were killed and the other two were injured. In 1994, following a rappelling accident in the Rotor Dusk exercise of that year, 5 Avn Regt said that in all future planning of CT exercises, there would be a joint reconnaissance by both the SAS and the aviation representatives to check for dust and any other obstacles that might hinder the success of the mission. This was reiterated for both the SAS and 5 Avn Regt prior to Day Rotor 95.

There were other problems as well, related to the aircraft themselves. The demand for spare parts outstripped supply and a large proportion of Black Hawks in the early to mid-1990s were grounded. At one stage there were only three flying out of the original 39. As a result army pilots missed vital training. Additionally, during this period a significant number of army pilots left the service. This might have been partially due to frustration with the way things were in army aviation, but as with the RAAF, the commercial world with its generous salaries was always looking for aviators. In the 18 months prior to Day Rotor 96, 20 flying instructors had left the services, taking with them their own expertise and the capacity to train others. The remaining flying instructors were under more stress. One of these was David Burke, who was working 16-hour days at the beginning of 1996. Burke, 34, had been flying Black Hawks for six years. He swore by the machines and believed in the value of the training to the security of Australia, but an army psychologist concluded he was pushing things too hard. He pronounced that Burke was suffering from 'chronic fatigue'. It was decided that if possible Burke's responsibilities ought to be shared out. If he was to remain a flying instructor, then he need not always fly 'Flight Lead' in Black Hawk formations, where he had to not only fly his own aircraft but give directions to others.

Day Rotor 96 was planned by the SAS Regiment in Perth in March of that year. One Squadron SAS was to do the exercise. There were no representatives of the aviation regiment there. This was an inevitable consequence of the two elements being on opposite sides of the continent, although not an unprecedented problem in the military, which throughout its history had been obliged to wed disparate arms of one or more services. The Black Hawks at least were ready to go, and the army was anxious to demonstrate them, taking the then Prime Minister, Paul Keating, on a trip in one when he made an electoral visit to North Queensland. It did not impress anybody, least of all Keating, when the helicopter clipped the tops of trees, badly damaging the blades. It was a warning—a minor miscalculation with potentially lethal consequences.

For Day Rotor 96, an advance SAS party including Captain Sean Bellis, who had formerly been an army aviator and had himself flown Black Hawks, travelled to Townsville. Bellis and another SAS officer, Captain J.M. Gardener, did a reconnaissance of the High Range Training Area 40 kilometres to the north-west of the city from April 22 to 26. There were to be heliborne assaults by day and by night on 12

June to extract 'Australian hostages' who were theoretically being held by terrorists in the High Range Training Area. The assaults were to be accompanied by live mortar fire, the mortar rounds falling ahead of the assaulting helicopters. The assaulting helicopters would be accompanied by helicopter gunships on the flanks to provide covering fire ahead of the attack. When the assault helicopters arrived the troops would slither down the ropes and assault the position.

In early May Bellis and a Sergeant A.B. Rowland of the SAS had a look at an artillery base, Fire Support Base (FSB) Barbara, in the training area and decided that it was a suitable venue for the exercises. A more discerning look might have picked out some problems. It was small, but it also had very few vertical features, the sort of things that could be picked out by a helicopter to orientate itself when coming in at night. The gun emplacements were flat against the ground, like all battlefield installations should be, easy enough to see from the air by day, but a much more difficult proposition in the dark.

'A' Squadron, 5 Avn Regt, was assigned to Day Rotor and did a two-week work-up period, from 27 May to 7 June, to bring themselves to a pinnacle of efficiency. It was presumed that Black Hawk crews retained some of the expertise they had picked up in Rotor Dusk 95, but that in itself was a dangerous assumption. As Burke said later, efficiency depended on frequency as much as anything else. Pilots who did not practice such missions for months on end became rusty. There were also deficiencies in the work-up exercise itself. There was no training in firing through aircraft doors, no familiarisation with mortars, no night-flying on NVG with three aircraft line-abreast. There was some line-abreast flying by day, but this was only for short periods, not for the extended period envisaged for Day Rotor 96. The squadron did not receive detailed advice on the mission until the SAS sent a copy of orders on 6 June.

Bellis did a reconnaissance of FSB Barbara on Saturday 8 June, but at no stage, contrary to earlier directives, was there a combined reconnaissance of the SAS and aviators, nor was there a reconnaissance by the aviators at all. Bellis was looking at the lie of the land, but by then the line-abreast formation for the aircraft had already been decided. Even then the estimates of distances were wrong. The reconnaissance party estimated that FSB Barbara was 250 metres across, with 150 metres between the westernmost and easternmost installations. In fact, the distances were shorter. FSB Barbara was only 210 metres across and 96 metres in length between east and west installations. The 96 metres gave just enough space for three aircraft to come in line-abreast and retain minimal separation. The 210 metres allowed the two flanking fire support aircraft to participate. There was not an inch to spare, and no margin for error should someone fall out of line on a dark night.

In keeping with the undertaking to take stress off Burke Major Chris Jameson, the Officer Commanding 'A' Squadron, 5 Avn Regt, directed that a more junior pilot, Captain Kel Hales, be trained up for the Flight Lead job. Hales accepted the job and liaised with Bellis. Some 18 months before Bellis had flown as an army aviator with Hales as his co-pilot, so he had no trouble telling him what should be done, though by then Bellis was an SAS man. In all probability, though they were the same rank, Bellis was acting as Hales' superior, and Hales was not making independent judgements. Bellis assured Hales there was nothing to worry about.

The main body of One Squadron SAS arrived at the RAAF base Garbutt in Townsville by Hercules C-130 transport on

10 June. The official two-week exercise began on 11 June. That day, SAS safety officers did their own reconnaissance of FSB Barbara and fire support personnel in Black Hawks did a firing practice over FSB Barbara. At Townsville's Lavarack Barracks, SAS soldiers practiced rappelling and assaults. Bellis realised that the photographs he had requested a month before had not arrived. He sent a request to Three Brigade headquarters for photographs and got facsimiles of photographs in reply. He ordered SAS intelligence Sergeant M.V. Williams to make a video of FSB Barbara. Williams did so, but the vibration of the aircraft and poor light combined to make the video of such poor quality that it was virtually unusable.

That night Bellis held a briefing to members of the SAS Regiment in the aviation squadron headquarters. The orders were given according to the standard SMEAC ('situation', 'mission', 'execution', 'administration', 'command and signals') formula. For 'situation', the orders segment given by Sergeant Williams, a whiteboard was produced that had a diagram of the layout of FSB Barbara, put together by SAS Warrant Officer Class 2 M.J. Woods. The diagram was wrong in one critical detail. It showed six gun emplacements, but on the western side of the base there was one more than there should have been, and on the eastern side one less. For troops who were to come down by rope and then attack on the ground, it hardly mattered, but for the aviators, who had to find the right points at which to let the troops down, it was vitally important. Nobody at the briefing picked up the error. They were hardly in a position to.

Hales gave a briefing separately to the aviation squadron. As was pointed out later, he himself had not gone on a reconnaissance of FSB Barbara. Neither had anyone from the aviation regiment. They were depending on information that had been given to them by the SAS. They were even using the same whiteboard sketch, with its incorrect detail. The aviators took the briefing seriously. Some even took down their own sketches of the layout of the fire support base and were ready to take them with them on the mission. Those who were not making notes would have been forming mental models of what they expected to see. When Jameson questioned Hales on the dimensions of the target area, Hales replied, 'Sean has checked it out, it's OK.' Jameson knew that at least Bellis was a former aviator and he believed he would have looked at FSB Barbara from an aviation perspective.

A dreadful, potentially fatal, weakness was developing. Though aviators from 5 Avn Regt would be expected to have some knowledge of FSB Barbara, having done gun-lifts there, there was no detailed reconnaissance or familiarisation with the area by pilots who, when it came to the crunch, had the responsibility for success of the entire exercise in their hands. It was so desperately crucial that they should have had a look for themselves. Flying to the base in fading sunlight, with mortars landing to the north and flanking aircraft firing into the area, they were carrying out a precise mission. A practice run during the day certainly would have had value, but light conditions would be different. If there were any other variations the complexity, and the risk, of the exercise would be multiplied.

There were a number of aspects of the mission that were most disturbing, at least in retrospect. There was some uncertainty as to how many Black Hawks would be available. At first it was said there would only be one, then two, but on 12 June it was decided that there would be six available, enough to carry three loads of assault troops with another in reserve

and two aircraft in fire support. Jameson only discovered at
final orders that nobody from his squadron had actually done
a reconnaissance themselves of FSB Barbara, so he decided he
would go on a dry run over Barbara and check the area out
for himself.

The decision was made to send the assault aircraft in with
three line-abreast, the flanking helicopters getting ahead to
lay down fire support, and another assault helicopter behind
the first three. Hales would be piloting Black One, the left
helicopter in the assault line of three. Burke would be piloting
the middle helicopter, Black Two, and the Air Element Commander (AEC), Major Jameson, in Black Three on the right.
Each helicopter would have a co-pilot and a left and right
loadmaster, who would be looking out of the left and right
doors respectively. They could look ahead, but their main
responsibility in formation flying was to ensure that separation distances were maintained. The Black Hawk coming
up the rear, Black Four, would be behind Black Two and had
only that one aircraft to keep in its sights.

There was a problem with line-abreast flying. It required
far greater attention to the other aircraft and if a problem
developed there were issues with manoeuvrability. It did have
the advantage of launching a large number of troops quickly
into an assault, confronting an enemy at once instead of by
the planeload. If there was some danger in the way the assault
was to be conducted, it had to be measured against the directive to make training as realistic as possible.

Hales was addressing his duties as Flight Lead. When Burke
tried to exert some supervision over Hales, Jameson told him
to 'back off'. There was no decision that because Hales was
now Flight Lead, he should fly his aircraft at the centre of the
formation instead of on the left. From a commonsense point

of view, it was always going to be more difficult giving orders from the flank. It was also noted that Jameson, being the senior officer, could have chosen not to fly a helicopter himself but to have undertaken the role of overall supervision, which was sorely needed. There had been no detailed consideration of 'abort procedures'—what the aircraft should do if something went wrong and they had to pull out. To fly over the base would have been to fly into the range of the mortars. The dimensions of the mortar target area were unknown to the pilots.

These were the conditions under which the helicopters took off from RAAF Garbutt at 1 pm on 12 June to run through the day assault. The 24 aviation and 43 SAS troops represented the cream of the Australian Army. David Frost, 29, from Fairfield in Sydney, had been in the army for 12 years. He had initially been rejected for service in the SAS, but had worked on his fitness and won approval. Corporal Darren Smith, 23, had been in the army for five years, had qualified for promotion to sergeant and was engaged to be married. He had served eight months with the SAS in Somalia. Captain John Berrigan, 27, had been a bricklayer after leaving school but had joined the Army Reserve, met his future wife who was a Reserve Army pay clerk, then signed up for the Regular Army at the age of 22. From there he had gone first into officer training and then the Aviation Corps. His wife, Anna, was later to say, 'It was always Black Hawks with John. They were his life. First were his Black Hawks, then his crew, then his family.' The family at that stage included a son, Benjamin. These soldiers were all to die.

The Black Hawks flew in tight formation over the Stuart Range to the High Range Training Area going through the various stages of preparation: the '18-minute call', the

'15-minute call' and the 'three-minute call', in which the troops were to put themselves in higher and higher stages of readiness prior to leaving the aircraft. Their initial pass over FSB Barbara was a 'dry run' in which there would be no live firing and the troops would not rappel to the ground. The pilots discovered that Barbara was not as big as they had expected it to be from the briefing. It was not possible to go in in perfect line-abreast. They would have to go in in a slight 'V' formation, with the middle helicopter slightly behind the other two. That coincided with the layout of the gun emplacements which were the roping points, which was quite logical, but Jameson, in Black Three on the eastern flank of the three assault aircraft, asked Black Six, giving fire support on his right, to move further to the east to give him room. This meant that Black Six had to go beyond the boundaries of FSB Barbara.

Then they returned and did the real thing. The Mortar Fire Controller had been late getting to his position, so live mortar fire was not included in the day mission. The troops descended by rope from four Black Hawks and successfully attacked the objective. The soldiers and aircraft returned to Garbutt at 3 pm. At the debrief, there appeared to be some differences between Hales and Burke. Burke accused Hales of having gone to the wrong roping point. There was no satisfactory resolution to this. Jameson overhead the conversation but did not use his capacity as AEC to resolve the conflict. Nothing had gone amiss and Burke and Hales agreed that they would go to the same roping points as they had during the day.

Hales did at one stage have a radical idea about how the approach should be made. He suggested that they fly in line along a creek to the west of FSB Barbara, then turn and go in line-abreast from that direction. Jameson was unimpressed. His reported words were: 'Get f——! That is crazy, mate! It would take a month to practice. We will do it exactly as we did this afternoon.' Hales, from all accounts, abandoned any idea of varying the approach by night, but there were strong indications that he had the wrong mental map, and that even in the day mission he had been converging on the point Burke was making for. The SAS, acting on the recommendation of Bellis, believed that to make the exercise more valuable, the helicopters during the night mission should come in at a lower altitude, so as to mask their approach. This was standard enough tactics: hugging contours in order to reduce the chance of being hit by enemy fire and creating a greater chance of surprise. It was also decided that the fire support aircraft, Blacks Five and Six, should be released from the formation at an earlier stage than during the day, so that they could have more time over the target to fire at it before the assault helicopters arrived.

The release of the fire support aircraft was always signalled by the '30-second call'. This was taken to be the time Flight Lead had sighted the target and was thereby inviting the other pilots to sight the target as well. This was the final stage. The helicopters would adopt their final assault formation, the troops would be ready to go down the ropes, and from that moment the aircraft were expected to maintain formation but track towards their individual targets. If the formation was heading in the right direction there was no conflict between these objectives, but the 30-second call had, over time, come to take on a new meaning. It was meant to signal the release of the fire support aircraft and the adopting of the final formation with assault troops at ready. It no longer necessarily signalled that the Flight Lead had seen the target and it need not be given 30 seconds from the time the formation would arrive over the target.

These were two significant changes, an alteration to the pattern of the day mission, that created in effect new conditions that the pilots would have to confront in the dark, wearing NVGs. They were changed contrary to Jameson's directive that the approach should be done exactly as it had been during the day. There had been a rehearsal of the day mission. There was none for the night counterpart. There was a feeling that the day mission had been a rehearsal for the night, but two things would be different that night: they would be flying lower, meaning that the field of view would differ from the day; and they would be releasing the fire support aircraft earlier, when the target need not necessarily be in view.

The sun set at 5.42 pm. The weather was fine and there was no moon. The flight took off at 6.30 pm and went to the 'initiation point', a designated point from which the assault would be launched. At the initiation point they adopted a lower altitude, rising over hills and going down valleys. They flew between 30 and 70 metres above the ground. The 18- and 15-minute calls were made and the troops started preparing themselves. Somewhere in this process, Hales went off track, perhaps because of the downward slope of the hills to the west. Each time the formation went over a hill it was possible they might have inadvertently been going further and further off track. Hales had a navigation system that would have shown him that. It would also have been apparent to the other aircraft that he was going off track, but nobody thought to warn him.

The 30-second call came when the formation was a minute and 25 seconds from the target. It was later estimated that the formation was between 300 and 400 metres off the track it had flown during the day, and between 3.5 and four kilometres south-west of FSB Barbara. There was a ridgeline between the formation and the fire support base, so it could not be seen from where the call was made. Blacks Five and Six accelerated, aiming to arrive at FSB 15 seconds ahead of the assault aircraft so that they could get more practice in laying down a pattern of fire cover. Black Six's crew saw a distinctive line of trees that they knew they should be heading towards. It was at 'one o'clock', or 15 degrees to the direction they were heading. Black Six turned right and made for it. Had the formation been on track, it would not have had to make such a deviation. Black Five had more difficulty identifying where it had to go but made for it in the right direction, over unfamiliar terrain.

Blacks One, Two and Three followed, having gone line-abreast at the 30-second call. They were two rotor diameters, or 67 metres, apart. Having decelerated to give them more time to get their bearings, the pilots were looking for landmarks. The crew in the assault formation saw nothing of FSB Barbara until they were about 1500 metres from it, and then, with some sense of urgency, the pilots started looking for their roping points. They were coming at the fire support base at a bearing of between 48 and 62 degrees instead of 15 degrees as they should have been. The frontage available to them was restricted by the angle and the new direction presented a different picture than had been presented during the day.

The difficulty of making things out on the ground was made worse by the fact that the sun was still setting and a hill was casting a huge shadow over the base. The problem with NVGs is that they are not suited to making things out when there are different light intensities in the same field of view.

The NVGs adjusted to the brightest intensity, denying the air crew the ability to make out things in deeper shade. It was, Burke said later, 'an NVG trap'. The problems experienced when trying to find out where they were going probably distracted the pilots, in particular Hales, forcing them to pay more attention to the navigation problem than such other matters, like aircraft separation.

Hales knew that according to the whiteboard diagram there was a gun emplacement on the extreme left near where Black Five would be hovering to lay down its pattern of fire. He was to go to the one to the right of it. When he approached he saw Black Five in the position he thought was over the extreme left embankment. In fact, Black Five was still between 50 and 100 metres south of its intended position. It was in fact near the gun emplacement where Hales should have been heading. Hales made two course alterations to the east. He was heading for what he thought was the correct gun emplacement that indicated his roping point. In fact it was the gun emplacement that Burke was heading to. On Hales' second change to the right, Bill Mark, doing loadmaster duties on Black Two, saw him converging and called a warning. Black One turned back towards the left. During the approach, Black Two had moved slightly ahead of and above Black One. Burke said later, 'Simon Edwards, my co-pilot, said, 'We have left the track'. As we came in, there were a number of turns back to the right where Kel turned back towards me, and I just assumed that was fixing up the track.'

Then, at 6.53 pm, Black One, apparently thinking that Black Two was turning to the right towards his own target, made another turn. This time Black One was moving rapidly and dangerously in on Black Two from below and behind. Mark yelled another warning, calling on Burke to, 'Come right! Come right! Come right!' The right-side loadmaster, Staff Sergeant G.N. 'Squizzy' Taylor, with his eye on Black Three, said, 'Don't come right.' Burke said later, 'I knew I was boxed in. I had an aircraft on my left, an aircraft on my right and one behind.' Mark realised Burke was not responding to his warning. He could see Black One through the back door. 'I noticed that we had begun to flare, which put the nose of the aircraft up, and I said to Dave Burke, 'Come up! Come up!'

Black One was lurching towards Black Two at a closing speed of between 39 and 86 metres per second. Black Two, travelling at about 110 kmh, was between 30 and 50 metres above the ground. Because of the angle of approach of Black One, there were difficulties seeing it. In the last few seconds Mark saw someone in Black One, wearing NVGs, look towards Black Two. Both aircraft started turning away from each other, but it was too late. To bank left, Black One needed to tilt to the left, bringing its blades up on the right, into the body of Black Two. The first blade strike by Black One severed the tail boom of Black Two. The second ruptured the fuel tank, causing fuel to spill and quickly ignite, exploding in mid air. The third and fourth blades struck the body of Black Two and the first blade struck another glancing blow. The entire contact had lasted less than half a second, but Mark feared the worst.

Whether the explosion was caused by the heat of the blade striking through the metal, or whether it was ignited by the hot exhaust of Black One became a matter of contention. But the fire spread quickly in Black One and started in the rear of Black Two. Black One lost its blades, one of which remained stuck on the body of Black Two. Black One, having started its left banking motion, continued to turn until it was upside down. It travelled perhaps 35 metres and hit the ground nose-first, with such impact the that cockpit and cabin were crushed into a space of about 1.5 metres. Because it was upside down, none of the crash-attenuation features came into effect. It burst into flame, lighting up the area as though floodlights had come on. The crash killed nine crewmembers instantly, including Hales and co-pilot Berrigan, and two died soon after. Right-hand loadmaster Corporal J.J. Fraser, 5 Avn Regt, survived, but suffered a fractured pelvis, multiple facial and body abrasions and thigh burns. Trooper G. Bampton, SASR, also survived, but suffered multiple trauma, fractured pelvis, thoracic spinal injuries that rendered him paraplegic, and other fractures and burns.

Black Two, having lost its tail boom and tail motor, started revolving in a horizontal arc, having no horizontal stabiliser. Burke, his plane on fire and crashing, called out, 'Sorry fellows, we're dead.' Corporal Gary Proctor, SAS, told Four Corners later, 'I looked over my shoulder and the tail motor fell off the aircraft. At that stage, I decided it was probably worth getting back inside the aircraft because I was hanging out there on the outside . . . the aircraft was on fire and we were rotating quite violently.' Burke struggled to keep the plane upright. Burke said, 'The main motor just went berserk, I mean. Because it was fighting nothing, it had a free run on it, I cannot describe it to you, but I can hear it now quite easily. It was just unbelievable. I think we spun about three times and during the second time, while there was a massive pitching because of what we had lost, and the centre of gravity had moved, so the aircraft was pitching as we rotated and I actually thought we had gone upside down, and when that happened, that was it. I thought we were dead.' Burke managed to keep Black Two upright, but it landed very heavily.

Because Black One's blades had destroyed structural supports within the aircraft, the roof collapsed, but other crash-attenuation features lessened the impact.

Black Five, to the front, had quickly banked away. So had Black Four, coming behind. It had flown up and to the right, continuing over FSB Barbara in a north-easterly direction and linking with up Black Five. A Mayday signal was sent at 6.54 pm. Black Three landed immediately ahead of its roping point and crew and passengers scrambled out to do what they could. Black Six stopped its firing and landed at a point north-east of FSB Barbara. A message went to the mortar platoon to stop firing.

Burke, having suffered six broken ribs, struggled out of the aircraft and made to a point in front of him. Corporals Dominic Boyle and Gary Proctor, also suffering fractures, went up to him. Black Two was now well on fire. Flames emanating from the left rear were starting to envelope the aircraft. Boyle and Proctor knew there were SAS men still strapped to their seats. The two wanted to know what the chance was of the aircraft exploding. Burke could not tell them. The two turned and rushed back into the flames, and fought, amid explosions and flames, to free as many of their comrades as they could. Proctor pulled Mark out, but there was no hope of saving anyone else.

The other helicopters landed and their crews rushed to the stricken aircraft. Some of the SAS men who got out of Black Two rushed back into the flames to save their comrades. The rescue operation was conducted speedily and professionally. The first casualties arrived at Townsville Hospital at 7.15 pm and all were at the hospital by 8.30 pm, with ten soldiers being admitted. Of the 13 crewmen on board Black One, 11 died, comprising three of the air crew and eight of the SAS.

Of the 15 on Black Two, seven died, the survivors comprising all four air crew and four SAS.

A Military Court of Inquiry, presided over by Brigadier Paul O'Sullivan, sat for three months and heard from 144 witnesses. It released its report in March 1997, finding there had been a chain of failures, including poor and rushed planning, that had combined to make the accident 'inevitable'. A number of officers, including the then Lieutenant Colonel Michael Silverstone Commanding Officer of the SASR and Lieutenant Colonel Tony Fraser, Commanding Officer of the 5 Avn Regt, faced internal reprimand on the grounds that as commanding officers they had to accept executive responsibility. Also facing disciplinary action were Major W.R.M., the Officer Commanding One Squadron, SAS Regiment, Hunter, and Major Jameson and Captain Bellis.

As was pointed out by the commentators at the time, despite what culpability might have been laid at their feet, those who were disciplined were really just pawns in a larger game. A service charged with the responsibility of Australia's security had been pushed by cost, equipment and manpower restrictions into a program that was too much for them. They had taken on a task for which they were not prepared and had pushed themselves, for fear of being perceived as failures, to achieve it. The only real lesson from the entire tragedy was that if Australia was prepared to invest a finite amount of money, equipment and personnel in its defence, then the defence force would have to adjust itself and the scale and ambition of its exercises to accommodate those limitations.

7

The Granville Rail Smash, 1977

I was surrounded by dead bodies and I could not move forward or back. To get me out, police had to crawl in behind me and pull me out by my feet.

John Wilson, NSW Police Rescue Squad

On the morning of 18 January 1977 Robert James Ryan, 34, was running late when he reached the platform at Emu Plains railway station, at the foot of the Blue Mountains west of Sydney. A computer software engineer, four years out of the Royal Australian Air Force, he had been driven by his wife, Trish, from Mt Riverview, a lovely piece of urban development just up the escarpment. He made it in time and climbed aboard the first of the eight carriages of Passenger Train No 108, the 6.09 from Mt Victoria, and sat back to read the computer section of *The Australian*, which always came out on a Tuesday. Les Mitchell, 29, also a computer software engineer, was already in that carriage. Married to Robyn, with an infant son, Simon, Mitchell had boarded the train at Blaxland. The train, on a 126 kilometre journey, was due at Sydney Terminal at 8.32 am. The passengers had accommodated that fact into their schedules, timing their arrival at work and making appointments to suit.

Towns in the Blue Mountains and places like Emu Plains,

hugging the foothills, are virtual dormitory suburbs of Sydney. They have regarded rail travel as part of their lives since the time trains first crossed the mountains in 1867. The Blue Mountains Express had been hauled by an electric locomotive since 5 March 1956, and electrification had vastly reduced travel times, making the Blue Mountains more and more part of the metropolitan area.

Locomotive 4620 was a robust machine. Weighing 112 tonnes and measuring 16.5 metres long, it was one of 40 engines that Metropolitan Vickers Ltd had built at Stockton-on-Tees in England, to New South Wales specifications, between 1955 and 1957. 4620 had entered service in New South Wales on 27 March 1957 and had been well-used. By 11 December 1976 it had travelled more than two million kilometres. At the time there were 38 46-class locomotives in service. Drivers liked the 46-class because of their power, cleanliness and quietness. These locomotives had not had an entirely untroubled history. One had suffered a braking failure and had become derailed at Wentworth Falls in the Blue Mountains on 17 June 1965. Another had been derailed again at Valley Heights on 20 September 1976. In terms of propensity to derail, however, the 46-class did well compared with other classes.

The real problem was that the trains, along with the other rolling stock and the Permanent Way, or 'Perway'—the track system—were being pushed to their limits. The cost of replacing a rolling stock was huge. Everything about the railways costs money, and at the same time demand on them was incessant. Therein lay the seeds of the disaster to come.

Like all such equipment, trains have moving parts that are subject to wear. Rails wear. Wheels wear. Wheel flanges, which run along the insides of the rails, wear thin. Fittings

wear. Electrical equipment wears out. Anything and everything has a 'life'. Sometimes minor things such as springs and
locking pins are broken or missing. On the ground, sleepers
deteriorate, rails get thinner and spikes become less effective,
but engineers did not have the luxury of making frequent
replacements. Shortages of replacement parts as well as costs
forced them to drain every bit of equipment of its value.

The Imperial gauge—four feet eight and a half inches
between rails—needs to be exact, for obvious reasons. It was
recognised that the gauge could be distorted. A tolerance of
2.5 centimetres is allowed between rails to allow for wear on
the rails, provided that all the fastenings are firm. Deviation
of more than 2.5 centimetres has to be attended to.

At the western approach to Granville station, which took
trains under the Bold Street bridge, railway traffic was obliged
to go around a left curve. When any track curves the rail on
the outside needs to be higher than the one on the inside,
allowing trains to maintain proper balance. The higher the
speeds to be catered for, the greater that difference in elevation needs to be. For a train travelling at around 80 kmh,
such as inter-urban services that bypassed Granville station
and continued to Strathfield, the difference in elevation
should be 15.25 centimetres, but on this section of track in
1977 there was a complication. Some trains needed to branch
off the main track and turn into Granville station. To do that
they had to be travelling at much slower speeds. To cater for
them, the difference in elevation had to be reduced, so there
was a compromise between the needs of the high-speed and
low-speed trains.

The compromise in the section of track west of the Bold
Street bridge was very much in favour of the slower trains.
At that curve, the difference between the low rail (the left

rail for a train travelling east) was 3.75 centimetres lower than the high, or right, rail. It was stated later in evidence that for such a difference in elevation between the two rails, 80 kmh was simply too fast for a train going around that curve. At that speed, the train was not sufficiently tilted and it would impose high lateral stresses on the high rail, which had the job of forcing the locomotive and all the carriages to veer left. Those lateral pressures increased with speed. It was later found that the curve itself had over time become uneven. These factors relating to the curve, the so-called 'track geometry', became critical.

If there were problems on this trip, they did not lie with those operating the train. In the driver's seat of the 4620 on 18 January 1977 was a Class Five engineman, Edward Olencewicz, 51. With him was fireman William McCrossin, 26, a Class Two engineman with five years experience. In the early hours Olencewicz had shunted the empty 4620 into position for its morning journey and carried out normal checks of the engine, including a visual inspection. Emigrating from Poland in 1948, Olencewicz had been a public transport employee for 27 years. He had driven trains for 17 years and for 15 of those had driven all 40 of the 46-class locomotives in service, including trips on the Mt Victoria–Sydney route. He had an unblemished record and his Class Five status put him well up the scale of efficiency. A tall man, Olencewicz was regarded by his colleagues as a gentleman. Leslie Thomas, who was guard on the train that day, said later, 'He is one of those drivers that no matter what sort of train you put in front of him he will give you a smooth ride and smooth stop.'

But by the time 4620 set out from Emu Plains that morning, with Bob Ryan and Les Mitchell settling back for the journey and Olencewicz driving, the history of the railway service had been anything but smooth. In order to properly understand the events of that fateful day, it is necessary to delve briefly into the history of the NSW rail service.

From the time the first rail service left Redfern station in the inner city bound for Parramatta on 26 September 1855 the conflicts that plagued the rail service in 1977 had existed. The railway was expensive. People wanted to use it, but they did not want to pay too much. There was no point in telling the public to pay up or walk, because from the outset there was competition. The Sydney Railway Company had only been operating three months when it decided to reduce fares between Newtown and Redfern because of competition from buses. In the rural regions horse-drawn traffic was doing quite nicely, providing the flexibility and convenience railways could not match. When motor cars arrived, powerful bodies such as the National Roads and Motorists Association were influential in diverting funds to roads.

The problem with railways was that they needed continual, substantial funding and constant vigilance. The weights and speeds involved, and the consequences for life and limb when things went wrong, meant that any deviation from the highest standards would create danger. Joe Beecroft, the great rescue policeman of the 1970s, said, 'Wherever there is movement there is the possibility of accident', a simplistic statement, but so profound. There had been a road toll with horses and carriages. A tree stands at the site of Old Government House in Parramatta where Lady Fitzroy, wife of the governor, Augustus Fitzroy, was thrown from her carriage and killed. Ironically, Governor Fitzroy had turned the first sod to mark the beginning of the Sydney Railway Company's operations. By then railways had already established a sad history of accident, beginning in 1830 at the opening of the first-ever intercity railway service in the world, between Liverpool and Manchester service in the United Kingdom when a parliamentarian standing on the track, not appreciating how fast the engine could move, was struck and fatally injured.

The NSW railway system inevitably compiled its own record of tragedy. On 10 July 1858 carriages left the Great Southern Line south of Sydney and plunged over an embankment, killing two—an event written off by a coroner's inquest to equipment failure. In the 122 years of railway operations in Australia up until 1977 there were 22 rail accidents involving deaths of five people or more. Of these 11 were in New South Wales, five in Victoria and six in Queensland. A washed-away embankment at Cootamundra caused a crash on 27 January 1885 that killed eight. Thirteen died on 31 October 1894 when a departing train at Redfern station collided with an arriving train; 14 in a collision during a fog at Exeter on the state's southern highlands; five on 10 June 1926 when the Brisbane Limited Express was derailed while crossing the Hunter River. On the northern line near Murrurundi on 13 September 1926, runaway rail trucks hit an oncoming passenger train, killing 27 and injuring 36 in what the *Bulletin* described as 'the most complete and disastrous railway smash in New South Wales'. The government ordered a royal commission, after which there was 22-year period with no fatalities. That came to an end with the death of four in the derailment of the South West Mail on 30 June 1948.

Decline in maintenance of the railways was always a problem. It was a feature of the war years, when men were sent overseas to serve in the war and the rail system had to keep operating. In May 1951 the NSW Government pleaded with the Federal Government to facilitate the migration of 8000 workers to service the NSW transport system.

Equipment needed to be replaced, but as long as it could work it kept going. In his history of the NSW railway system, *Along Parallel Lines*, John Gunn quotes one critic who said in 1956, 'Of the 1187 locomotives on the NSW railways, 980 or 80 percent are contemporaries of the T-model Ford. These locomotives, some of them 60 or 70 years old, are absorbing hundreds of thousands of dollars annually in rebuilding and maintenance.'

Governments, however, had many demands on their money and preferred to sit it out. In 1960–1, the railway took up 38.49 percent of the state budget. In 15 years that share would drop by more than half. In 1972 the NSW State Government, in an effort to upgrade the entire public transport system, announced the appointment of a Public Transport Commission with an Englishman, Phillip Shirley, in charge. He had some ideas, but the task was Herculean. In his report for the 1972–3 financial year, Shirley announced that for the first time ever, gross revenue had fallen short of operating cost, to the tune of $79.6 million. Huge pressures were being brought to bear, not the least being union militancy. In 1972–3 wages per employee rose by 38 percent. If there were to be pay rises of that magnitude there had to be a revenue base, but the revenue was not coming in. The rise in freight for wheat rose in the same period by less than two percent a tonne.

In 1973–4, the total deficit rose by 58 percent on the previous year to $125.7 million. In 1975 the state's rail system was losing the state a million dollars a week. The then Minister for Transport, Wal Fife, embattled in his portfolio, said that unless there was an increase in fares and freights, the deficit for the 1975–6 financial year would be $270 million. Fife resigned from the ministry and Shirley announced his retirement as PTC commissioner two years before the expiry of his term. The only solutions were traditional ones: raise the charge for services and slash uneconomic services. That was, naturally enough, manna for the then Labor Opposition, whose transport spokesman Peter Cox referred to 'the great attack on the public transport system of New South Wales'. In a desperate effort to keep the railways operating, maintenance programs suffered. This was reflected in the number of malfunctions, including an increasing incidence of derailments.

Eleven senior PTC engineers were motivated to send a submission to the government. On 27 November 1975 a group of them wrote to the State Government saying, 'We the undersigned Division Engineers of the Way and Works Branch do hereby claim that those policies of the Public Transport Commission which determine track and bridge maintenance resources are in need of urgent major reassessment. We advise that maintenance requirements needed for track and bridges have been severely reduced as a result of a staff freeze, non-approval of critical staff submissions . . . track safety in some locations can no longer be guaranteed. This means that track failures . . . will cause an increasing number of derailments.'

Cox moved an urgency motion on transport on 24 March 1976. The next day the State Government announced the appointment of Alan Reiher, a senior Commonwealth public servant, as PTC commissioner. But the Opposition, led by Neville Wran, was on a winner on the transport issue. It triumphed in the State Election of 1 May that year. With PTC losses amounting to $350 million a year, the new government had a priority to get the system back on track. It stood by its pre-election pledge to reduce fares by 20 percent. It set up a PTC joint council to improve relations with the unions. It

made improvements to rolling stock, ordering 362 new carriages and allocating \$26 million for railway facilities. The
financial situation did not improve, however, and the 20 percent fare cut had failed to increase patronage.

It was in this context that locomotive 4620 glided down
the rails to Sydney, strained and tired, but steadfast. Its last
bogie change had been on 27 December 1972. Bogies were
normally changed every three or four years, depending on
wear, but there had been a problem with supply of new
bogies to 46-class locomotives. 4620 was being used a 'bit
more' beyond its scheduled change of bogie. The front wheels
were worn to the point where there was insufficient metal in
them for them to be machined again to restore their profile. A
46-class wheel was 112.5 centimetres in diameter when new.
It could reach 103.75 centimetres before it was condemned.
In August 1976, when the wheels of 4620 were measured, the
right front wheel was found to be right on the limit of 103.75
centimetres, but the left front wheel was found to be 103.65
centimetres. Not only were the wheels worn down there was
also too much of a difference in diameter between the wheels
themselves. The maximum allowable difference was 0.08
millimetres. The difference between the front wheels of 4620
was one millimetre.

Engineers were doing their best. They had requested
second-hand wheels to replace the worn ones on 4620, but
none were available. The wheels continued to be used after
the flanges were judged to be satisfactory. The flanges were
vital—if one became too thin it would simply break off.
Despite this the left front wheel was later found to have a
visibly narrower flange than the right wheel. Herbert Croft,
then superintendent in the running maintenance section of
the PTC, said in later evidence that he was prepared to let

a condemned wheel continue to operate until a replacement became available, but the last inspection of 4620 had been in August 1976. It was decided back then that there needed to be new wheels and axle sets and that the left front wheel should be condemned as unusable. From then until 18 January, the condemned wheel had travelled another 43 000 kilometres, though a further check on the flanges had found that they remained satisfactory.

On the day in question a poorly designed, poorly maintained track was being ridden on by an overstressed locomotive. The question now is: on that particular section of track, in the approach to Bold Street bridge, were there indications of any problems there?

There had, in fact, been signs of trouble. In October 1976 drivers had reported that the Granville section was 'running rough' at a point west of the Bold Street bridge. This meant that the ride was bumpy or rocky. If that was happening, there was something wrong and it should be attended to. In November 1976 the then state president of the Australian Federated Union of Locomotive Enginemen, Joe Booth, had telephoned Douglas Neil, principal engineer, maintenance, in the Ways and Works Branch of the PTC, saying there was a problem with the section of track west of the Bold Street bridge. Neil had passed instructions on that that section was to be checked. It was, and a subsidence was found in the ballast, which was remedied, but, quite literally, there was rot.

Sleepers have a life of 15 to 25 years, but being wood they can deteriorate at different rates. From the surface, the sleepers near the bridge looked in good condition, but as it turned out a relatively small section of track in the western approach were in poor condition. One was partially eaten away by white ants and in fact broke into halves when it was later roughly handled. Despite the fact that in June 1976 the lines around the Bold Street bridge had been removed and reassembled, none of the sleepers in that section had been marked for replacement. James Nicholson, the track supervisor based at Granville, said later that he had got timber from a job at Auburn for replacement of six timbers in the western approach to the Bold Street bridge. More timber would have been put in, he said, had it been available.

When spikes were later removed from that section of track, some were found to be worn, possibly also allowing for movement of the rail. Their use had been tolerated. New spikes were being introduced into the system and old ones were being allowed to wear out. Was this safe? Of all the components of the Perway system, the spikes and lugs hugging the rails and binding them to the plates and sleepers were the most vital. If they failed, everything failed.

There was another safety mechanism: the diligence and competence of the track inspection staff. It was a grinding job, however, and there were many kilometres of track. Physical checking was difficult because the area being inspected was even cluttered with debris. There was danger from passing trains. Formal training in track inspection was conducted at a school at Valley Heights, west of Sydney, but at the time the railways were suffering a dearth of experienced inspection staff. A great deal of evidence was to reveal how thoroughly the track was checked. Wilbur Mann, who was an assistant track supervisor from 29 November 1976 to 19 December 1976 said he had done regular inspections and had seen no defects. He had not seen instances of lifted spikes, but agreed that those sections might have been covered by ballast. Gerard Michael Sheehan, an assistant track supervisor from 5 October 1976 to 15 October 1976 said he walked the track at Granville three times a week and had seen nothing unusual. Earl Thomas Lansley, who had been acting track supervisor from 26 December 1976 to 7 January 1977, also said he had seen nothing unusual. James Nicholson, track supervisor, said later he had urged repair work on the track and it had been done in November–December 1976. At one stage he had recommended a speed restriction for that section but had encountered resistance to the proposal.

If any of the inspectors could ever have been accused of complacency, which is at best arguable, the situation was hardly helped by the mechanical aids, such as the RVX2 Matisa machine or the RVX3 Plasser cars that checked for evenness and gauge. There were certain assumptions about them that were not warranted. The Plasser machine did not measure the track at points and crossings, where there were various lines at angles to each other, so there were limits on how they could be used. The Matisa machine could perform such measurements, and on 22 November 1976 a Matisa went through the area, measuring gauge and elevation, and revealed that the greatest deviation from the gauge was ten millimetres, well within the allowable limit. On 11 November 1976 Douglas Neil personally went over the section of track in a 46-class locomotive from Lithgow and he felt the train had negotiated that section of track well. He did similar checks on 30 November and 17 December and had found the track satisfactory.

It was never conclusive as to whether any individuals were at fault in the checking of the track. Things always look different in hindsight. According to later evidence, the rails in the section on the western approach to the Bold Street bridge had developed an irregular wear pattern. This could only have happened if the rails were moving. According to further evidence there were also sections on the plates below the rails that were shiny—an indication that the rails were moving across them. Ronald Wise, chief inspector of Perway for the PTC, later found shiny marks on plates holding the high rail. The 'dog-spikes', as the spike, meant to hold this rail firmly in position were called, were 'ineffective'. The high rail on the curve had been moving. In August, 1976, the track at that point, on the approach to the Bold Street bridge, was found to be 1.25 centimetres wide of gauge, but that was within acceptable limits.

Ahead of Train 108 was the Bold Street bridge, 33 metres long and 18 metres wide, a large but rather innocuous structure that had been there since 1956. It had been built in three sections, with heavy concrete canopies, steel superstructure and two sets of steel trestles. Each trestle had eight stanchions embedded in concrete footings, but the stanchions were not themselves encased in brick or concrete, as they might have been and as they would be if the bridge were built today. From the day the bridge was built, any engineer could have seen that these unreinforced steel structures would have been brushed aside by any locomotive that came off the rails and ploughed into them.

The bridge was capable of taking heavy vehicular loads and complied with the construction requirements of the time. At that time there were 152 bridges of similar construction in New South Wales. None of those bridges had anything fastening them to the concrete abutments at each side of the track. The ends of the canopies merely sat on mountings in the abutments. As long as nothing disturbed them, the mountings and the trestles would keep the bridge up. The Bold Street bridge had never been designed to be as massive as it was. When the road approaches were built, they were found to be a different height to the bridge, so engineers put an extra layer of concrete onto the canopy to bring the height up. This made the weight twice what it should have been. The engineers calculated, correctly, that the bridge's supporting structure could tolerate that.

Did the bridge designers, or for that matter the state rail authorities, give any thought at all to the question of what would happen should the trestles be destroyed or damaged by a rail vehicle? There is some evidence that they did. Ross Best, a PTC engineer, said in later evidence that though the bridges had not been designed to withstand the removal of a trestle, they did have some inbuilt resistance to impact. Two stanchions in an eight-stanchion trestle could be removed and the remaining six could retain the integrity of the bridge. By 1977 the vulnerability of steel trestles to impacts from rail traffic had been addressed internationally. In 1970 the New South Wales Government made it mandatory for all new railway bridges to have concrete casing to a height of 1.5 metres along each trestle. This concrete had the ability to deflect runaway rail vehicles. On the face of it there is no reason why such concrete walls could not have been built around the trestles of existing bridges.

There had been warnings that the Bold Street bridge itself was susceptible to impacts from runaway rolling stock. In 1967 a derailed wheat wagon had done exactly that, damaging a stanchion that was later repaired, apparently without raising any question as to what would have happened if the situation had the offending vehicle had not been a wagon but an entire train. There had been a derailment on that section in 1975 in which a stanchion had been struck by a loaded coal wagon. When inspected later, the stability of the bridge was unaffected. Surely on each of these occasions the question should have been raised about more serious impacts. Of course, one way of getting over the whole problem was to build a single-span bridge. But that became a matter of economics. Single-span bridges cost more, Best said. It was cheaper to put up bridges on trestles and to bank on the fact that the trains gliding past year after year would never derail at a critical point. Had there been a single-span bridge there that morning, then all the rail system would have experienced would have been a derailment, possibly with no serious injuries at all.

On the morning of 18 January Train 108 stopped at 20 stations and made one unscheduled stop because of signals near Wentworthville. It arrived at Parramatta at 8.08 am, three minutes behind schedule. It waited for two minutes for passengers to alight and to board, then moved off at 8.10 pm. The train had at least 469 passengers. Because it was school holidays, it was not as full as it would otherwise have been. Normally it would have had around 600 passengers and there would have been standing room only. From Parramatta the train increased speed over a kilometre to the maximum of 80 kmh, maintained that for 600 metres, then dropped back to 78 kmh and approached the left bend, which would take the train under the bridge and past Granville station, two kilometres east of Parramatta. Olencewicz, whose next scheduled stop was Strathfield, shut off the throttle and prepared to reduce speed for a section of track at Clyde, where there were restrictions.

Train 108 was to move round the left bend and bypass Granville station on the main line for through trains. Just over 70 metres west of the Bold Street bridge, 4620 approached point 73. From all the evidence gathered afterwards it appears that as 4620 rounded the bend it came to a point where the gauge had deviated too far from the standard gauge. The deviation might have been less than five centimetres, or two inches—twice the maximum deviation that could be tolerated, possibly not enough to cause the left front wheel to drop off the rail, but enough to create a very dangerous situation. It is possible that at this point the deviation of the gauge and the speed of the train combined critically. A slightly higher or lower speed might have made all the difference. Whatever the exact cause, the fact is that the left wheel dropped off the rail.

'I passed the signal in the clear position and soon after that, approximately at the diverging of points, I heard a very loud crack,' Olencewicz said later. Bob Ryan heard a thud, and a violent rocking, and he knew, in the seconds he had to think about it at all, that something had gone wrong.

The train continued for 13 metres. The left front wheel, hard up against the side of the low rail, collided with a check rail that took out a chunk of metal. The right wheel continued on the top of its rail, but the section of the flange pushed hard against the side of the rail. The track had precious little room to accommodate the dropped-in wheel on the left as well as the right wheel on its rail, especially when the gauge reverted to its normal dimensions. The pressure on the right wheel became impossible and, on a section of the high rail later found to have been heavily worn, the flange rose up, mounted the rail and dropped onto the other side. The other wheels followed, those to the left between the tracks, bumping along the sleepers, those on the right completely outside the rails. The engine was out of control.

Olencewicz went for the emergency brake, which acted on the entire train, but there was great momentum and the engine rocked violently in its rampage over the 46 metres between the point of derailment and the northern trestle. At the point of impact the train was travelling at 70 kmh. The engine brushed the eight stanchions aside like matchsticks and continued onward, tearing apart a power pylon that left a jagged edge, tore up the adjacent track and toppled onto its side, 67 metres beyond the bridge. Olencewicz was pinned to his seat, McCrossin beneath him. Olencewicz called out to McCrossin to see that the brakes and throttle were off, and then to switch off the train's power. It was the last thing Olencewicz was able to do that contributed positively to the situation.

The first carriage, containing 73 passengers, including Bob Ryan and Les Mitchell, had remained attached to the engine and had caught the jagged edge of the power pylon six metres east of the bridge. The stump of the pylon ripped through the carriage above window level, separating the roof. Ryan and seven others ended up in a tangle in the hollow of the roof. 'I don't remember exactly what happened,' Ryan said years later. 'The top of the carriage came away from the base and it toppled over. A lot of people were still sitting in the seats because of the base of the carriage had not turned over. Everyone were stunned. They were trying to come to grips with what had happened. We saw plenty of people who needed help and we did not want people to go wandering onto the other tracks.'

Les Mitchell had not made it. The stump of the power pylon had hit him in the head, killing him instantly. Seven others in the carriage were dead. Thirty-four were badly injured. Behind them the second carriage, having become uncoupled from the first carriage, had gone off the rails and, largely intact, had glided into the wall at the northern side of the tracks, clear of the bridge, its 64 passengers shaken but none seriously injured. Behind them the massive bridge was tottering. The northern span was unsupported. Christian Dupressoir, from Valley Heights, sitting in the third carriage from the front, said to Ted Foster beside him, 'I have travelled for 17 years and this is my first derailment.' Then Dupressoir heard a crack and a scream. He heard Foster calling out for calm. He saw Jack Maddock, from Warrimoo, rise from his seat.

The northern segment of the bridge, with an estimated weight of 250 tonnes, began to tilt, then slipped from its mounting on the northern abutment and fell flat, hitting almost all of the third carriage and half of the fourth. The 320-tonne central span, its southern end still supported by a trestle, remained partially suspended but in a precarious position, almost off its mountings. The northern span missed Dupressoir and Foster, but forced Maddock back into his seat. Dupressoir saw people in the next three seats trapped. Maddock and a couple from the fourth seat scrambled out. Derek Bates, from Glenbrook, was in the fifth seat, suffering back injuries. Dupressoir and others moved debris to get him out.

There was turmoil on the track. One commuter, Bill Ludwig, thrown from a door, was suffering from a fractured leg and concussion. For scores of others still in the third and fourth carriages, there was no hope. The carriages had no chance of withstanding the force, nor did the people inside them. The carriages had burst outwards and the concrete canopy had pushed everything beneath it into a space as small as 20 centimetres above the floor. Some passengers, flung through windows, had a chance. Most of those remaining were crushed to death.

In the immediate aftermath, as the bewildered occupants of the four automobiles that had gone down with the bridge emerged relatively unscathed; surviving passengers, shaking themselves out of their shock, looked around for something they could do. Some pulled off ties and belts to use as makeshift tourniquets, including Ryan, who made use of the first-aid knowledge he had picked up in the air force. The first ambulance was there two minutes after the accident. A total of 85 ambulances were sent to the scene. The fire brigade had its first vehicle there at 8.25 am and firemen helped 10 of the injured. Several firemen, at great risk to themselves, plunged into the wreckage. Police rescue personnel were also plunging along tunnels in the wreckage. Ambulanceman Michael McInally reached Bryan Gordon, who was trapped by the thighs, conscious and in great pain. 'I squeezed in beside him and we talked for 11 hours on and off as the layers of steel pinning him down were slowly cut away,' he said in an interview years later. 'He was a lovely guy and told me all about his wife and four-year-old daughter. I just held his hand and gave him orange juice.' They got Gordon out, but other would-be rescuers realised despairingly that they could do little. Dr Bruce Jeffery, from Parramatta, realised that the best he could do was to give morphia and intravenous fluids to the injured while others worked to free them from the wreckage.

This writer, about to leave his flat in suburban Eastwood at 8.40 am to go to work, got a call from an assistant chief of staff, Reg Holliday. 'There's a train hit a bridge or a bridge hit a train or something, get out there,' he said. By the time I got there emergency operation was under way. Passengers from the last four carriages had got out of the train and most had caught taxis. Premier Wran arrived with his face twisted in a knot, his transport minister Peter Cox, who had led the charge on public transport, beside him.

As news spread to the Blue Mountains towns, there was terror. Everybody, but everybody, knew someone who was on that train. Nobody knew who was dead. In Blaxland, Elisabeth Koch tried to ring her daughter, Ingeborg, who had taken a train to the city. She did not know which train Ingeborg had taken. The telephone lines were clogged. She could not get through for several hours. 'You have no idea how I felt when she answered that phone,' she said. Ingeborg had, by chance, taken the earlier train. Mark Slater, who lived in Katoomba, knew his uncle Bill Ludwig was on the train and spent all day frantically trying to find whether he was alive or dead. Dr Reg Mitchell said later, 'In our case, we were at Port Stephens. We got a message to go to the local post office and ring my father. They told us about Les.'

Constable Richard Lamb and a fellow member of the Police Rescue Squad cut through the roof of carriage three to pull out five people. They could hear people screaming and calling out from within the wreckage. There were people he would have rescued had he not realised that doing it at that time would have injured them further. He looked further down the carriage using a torch. He could see a woman. 'I could see she was still alive,' he said. 'But she was lying in a pool of blood and brain matter.' Joe Beecroft was working his way towards a trapped man, Ian Decker. A doctor amputated the arm of a dead woman to allow rescuers to go further, but there was no way the slab could be easily lifted. By 1 pm on the day of the accident, the public had given 2000 donations of blood. Department of Main Roads personnel went to work with jackhammers over the next 22 hours, often under the spray of hoses because there was danger that low pressure gas in the wreckage would be ignited. Huge cranes were set up on the northern side of the bridge.

I stayed there two days. Heading the operation on the first day, the then Inspector Ray Williams, frantically busy though he was, was liberal in his attitude to the media. Superintendent George Marshall, who took over cracked down. I saw the bodies being taken out to a makeshift morgue, one man carrying them calling out plaintively to bystanders to stand and show respect. When the main slab was lifted, police and other personnel allowed to watch from the top of the track reeled back in unison as the crushed bodies came into view. Joe Beecroft emerged exhausted. A radio reporter crashed in rather boorishly and asked him how he felt. Joe broke down and cried. By 3.20 pm on 19 January, when the last body was removed, the number of dead was 80, comprising 43 men, 36 women and a young girl. A total of 213 people had been injured, 31 of whom were admitted to hospital. Three of those, including Bryan Gordon, were later to die. In the final tally, eight of the 73 passengers in carriage one died, 44 of the 77 in carriage three died and 31 of the 64 in carriage four died.

Peter Cox ordered an immediate departmental inquiry. There was to be the inevitable coroner's inquest, and there would also be a royal commission. There were political bunfights. The deposed Premier Sir Eric Willis lashed out at criticism of his government by trying to blame the tragedy on the Wran Government, a criticism that did not go down well with the public. The Wran Government made an immediate and sustained commitment to heavily invest in rail maintenance, coming to $200 million in the first five years. That commitment has been continued to the present day. Coroner Mr T.M. Weir sat for 14 days. He exonerated Olencewicz and the crew of the train. He found poor maintenance to have been the critical factor, in particular the amount of wear on the flanges of the leading wheels and the amount of wear on the high rail.

A judicial inquiry was conducted by Judge James Staunton, sitting from 21 February 1977 and taking evidence from 75 witnesses. The departmental inquiry that had preceded his became a technical inquiry to assist him. Staunton found that the cause of the derailment had been 'clearly the very unsatisfactory condition of the permanent way in the lead of number 73 points'. The gauge had widened, there was poor track geometry and locomotive 4620, in negotiating the curve at high speed, had brought lateral forces to bear on the high rail which had triggered the derailment. 'While it may be correct to say that in order for a derailment to occur it was necessary for the effects of the various defects to combine at one point on the line and in a space of time reckoned, perhaps, in a thousandth of a second, nevertheless derailment of some vehicle was almost inevitable so long as the poor condition of the track remained uncorrected,' he said. The poor condition of the track, he said, 'was the result of the failure to detect and remedy the defects'. He said the wheat truck collision with one of the trestles in 1967 should have been a warning.

The catastrophe was commemorated by a 'Day of the Roses', at each anniversary, where 83 roses were thrown onto the track from the reconstructed single-span Bold Street bridge. Always present were Mark Slater, former mayor John Hennessey and the priest who had attended on the day, Father Les Campion. On the twentieth anniversary, when a memorial was erected at Granville containing the names of each of the victims, this writer took a trip on the equivalent of the 6.09 from Mt Victoria. There were scores of sections of track which were the subject of maintenance works. I met Bob Ryan, who maintained his faith in the system. As for so many others, it was part of his lifestyle. They held the 25th anniversary in 2002. Michael McInally, by then retired, was there. He had never forgotten Granville. He had visited Bryan Gordon's grave every year.

Sadly, accidents have not ceased. On 6 May 1990 an inter-urban train hit a chartered steam train, the famous 3801, at Cowan, on Sydney's northern outskirts, killing six, including Professor John Ward, the retired vice-chancellor of Sydney University. At Glenbrook in the lower Blue Mountains on 2 December 1999, an inter-urban train rammed into the back of the Indian–Pacific, killing seven and leaving many more injured. There were always inquiries, and they were useful inquiries, and changes were made. Inevitably, the horror of rail calamity had fuelled government resolve. In the upshot, a large amount of money was contributed to fixing things, just as, in the aftermath of Granville, a strong single-span bridge was built where the Bold Street bridge had been. The question is: why did there have to be such tragedy, so many deaths, so many tears shed, to get people in authority to do something?

Part Three:
Collapse

8

The West Gate Bridge Collapse, 1970

Error begat error and events moved with all the inevitability
of a Greek tragedy.

Report from the Royal Commission into the
West Gate Bridge collapse

Carmel Egan, a fine and imaginative journalist, once
described West Gate Bridge as being like a gigantic monitor standing astride the River Yarra. It would be difficult to
improve on that. It stands like a huge petrified lizard, poised
in an elongated 'S', linking Melbourne's western suburbs and
indeed the entire western district of the state with the City of
Melbourne and with the eastern and south-eastern reaches of
Victoria. From whatever angle it is viewed, it is the biggest
structure of any kind in the state and the biggest bridge in
Australia, a remarkable example of engineering imagination
and design. It has been responsible, more than anything else,
for radically altering the demographic as well as the history
of Victoria. Without it, Melbourne would still be a divided
city. There would be no CityLink and no Western Ring Road,
the two multi-billion dollar road systems that have reshaped
the traffic and living patterns of so many suburbs and their
people, but which depend on and are inexorably linked to
that massive bridge. The housing boom that continues to see

tens of thousands of people move to the west would not exist. Nor would places like Sanctuary Lakes, Melbourne's most expensive and exclusive new suburb.

Accordingly, in more than just a physical sense, the West Gate is a Melbourne icon, certainly its most impressive and conspicuous and so probably even its most significant icon. But it also has the unenviable record of having in a few horrifying seconds killed more people during the course of its construction than any other structure in Australia.

Naturally enough, little or nothing of the bridge's precocious fortunes could have been foreseen, although the project to cross the Yarra at that point was born into controversy, specifically in 1964, when the Victorian Government defied the advice of its own committee, the Melbourne Harbour Trust and the wishes of the shipping companies. It announced that the crossing would be by bridge and not tunnel. The tunnel option would have been less disruptive and would have cost less, but there were other factors weighing on the collective mind of the government. Melbourne needed a landmark. A government-backed competition to find one had failed. If a tunnel were to be built, it would hardly qualify as a landmark.

Whether it was a miscalculation or simply a manifestation of parochial pride, the government also invited further cynicism concerning its decision when, after first saying that the bridge would be 170 feet (50 metres) above the river at its highest point, it corrected this to say it would be 176 feet (53 metres). Ostensibly, the difference was to accommodate the height of the ships' funnels and other superstructure but, on closer examination, it was revealed that the extra six feet actually made the West Gate four feet higher than the Sydney Harbour Bridge. Victorian politicians and civic leaders also were quick to point out that as well as Melbourne's height being 176 feet compared with Sydney's 172, Melbourne's total length would be 9000 feet (2700 metres) while Sydney's was just 3000 feet (900 metres). Melbourne's bridge would have 10 lanes, each 12 feet (3.6 metres) wide. Sydney's had eight, each 9ft 10ins (3.4 metres) wide. The West Gate would be the longest, widest and tallest bridge in Australia.

As if to underline its status as Melbourne's greatest man-made achievement, the Victorian Government would later divert their airliners so that visitors could take a closer look as this magnificent structure rose out of the mud of the river. It was even suggested that the Victorian Premier, the ebullient Sir Henry Bolte, ask his old friend Sir Reg Ansett to get his pilots to make passing sweeps over the bridge as they came in and out of Melbourne airport.

As well as the oddities surrounding its beginnings, there were other glitches in the four years it took to plan and make room for such a massive structure. It was, for instance, announced at the outset that 'some' houses would have to go to make way for the bridge approaches; the final number turned out to be 150. The estimated price of the bridge doubled to $44 million. Although the government made most if not all of the announcements, the bridge was actually built by private enterprise, a group of about 60 companies known as the Western Industries Association. These came to comprise the Lower Yarra Crossing Authority, which in turn became the West Gate Bridge Authority. The government passed a special act to allow it to be an incorporated body, but also allowing it to drop the 'Pty Ltd' from its name, thereby constructing the perception that the 'Authority' was a government or quasi-government body.

Oscar Meyer became the authority chairman. Along with his vice-chairman Rupert Vian, he showed an almost

Bolte-ish zest and optimism, moving on to become the driving force behind the bridge's construction, so much so that he often remarked that the bridge was his 'baby'. The authority joined with Maunsell and Partners in becoming joint consulting engineers. It chose probably the world's most reputable and famous company in civil engineering, the London-based Freeman, Fox and Partners as the bridge builder. Freeman Fox had five men on its board who had been knighted for their bridge-building expertise. Its international and royal awards were unsurpassed by any other engineering firm in the world. In the previous five years it had designed 19 highways, 18 bridges, nine railroads, ten tunnels and ten power stations, as well as a series of dams, factories, radio telescopes and cranes. It had done renovations to London's St Paul's Cathedral and the Dome of Discovery that had been built for the 1951 Festival of Britain.

What more could Melbourne want? This brilliant expertise would guide this gigantic project that would take the city into the seventies and beyond in what Meyer described as a 'West Side Success Story' that would give Melbourne a gigantic hand across the river. Soon there were other practical advances as huge tracts of long unused land in the west were transformed into residential estates and industrial centres. These were hectic and hopeful years. Australia's vast mineral wealth was just being fully realised and the irrepressible Sir Henry Bolte continued to surprise and delight his people with schemes to make Victoria great. He had bustled his way through the boardrooms of Europe, selling Victoria to the industrialists, convincing them that their search for raw materials and a deep-water port to ship them were over. Westernport Bay, a few kilometres south of Melbourne, the 'Ruhr of Australia', as he called it, would provide everything they wanted. All that was needed now were the right plans to cope with this enormous growth. The key to everything was the West Gate.

In February 1968 the government announced the major contracts for building the bridge. The biggest, $15 million for foundations and concrete bridgeworks, went to John Holland and Company and to Frankipile (Aust). A further $7 million for the fabrication and erection of the five steel spans went to Werkspoor Services and Construction, later to be known as World Services. The government said the bridge would be finished by March 1971, at a cost of about $60 million, and that toll charges of about 25 cents a car would eventually pay for it. Work started on 9 April 1968, with Sir Henry turning the first sod and cutting a piece of string.

The magnitude of the project soon became evident as the first of what became 1000 men moved on to the sites—at Spotswood on the west, and at the Fishermen's Bend airfield on the east. The contractors brought with them huge cranes. They also brought steel girders, weighing up to 30 tonnes each and with bolt holes big enough for a person to put their fist through, which were initially tipped onto the ground like matchsticks from a box. Viewing areas on each bank of the river became favourite spots for families out for a weekend drive, or for those who just liked to sit and watch as the huge concrete pylons rose more than 50 metres from the ground. As 1968 and 1969 rolled by, the pylons, each containing an average of more than 90 cubic metres of concrete and kilo-metres of reinforcing steel, stood out like sentries across the river, not quite in line so as to allow for the 'S' shape, and not quite level so as to allow for the gentle gradients at the bridge approaches.

Twenty-eight pylons were used as the feet of the mighty bridge that was coming into being. The spectators could visualise the colossus that would tower above them, its peak and centre span more than 330 metres above ground and an overall length greater than the distance from Spring to Spencer Streets—greater than the diameter of the City proper. If the watchers sat and admired long enough, their imagination would also conjure up the sight of the two towers, on which cables thicker than a person's arm would be strung to hold the bridge steady. What the watchers could not see during those heady expectant days was the trouble brewing among the men working amidst the mass of steel, concrete and equipment.

Work on the concrete pylons and concrete approaches to the five main central spans went smoothly, but when it came to the steel to be used for the central spans, things started to go sour. On the one hand the Melbourne executives of Freeman Fox had problems with their head office in London. They also had conflict with the Maunsell. John Holland, which had been well ahead of schedule for the concrete work, was so anxious to get on with the rest of the job that it often gave scant attention to laid-down procedures. The steel contractors, World Services, failed to supervise its men or check disputes before they developed into stoppages. Eventually, while no official announcement was made, World Services handed much of its work over to John Holland. The four firms—Freeman Fox, World Services, John Holland and Maunsell—argued among themselves and within their own organisations so much that procedures laid down for the safe and proper handling of the project were often abandoned altogether.

The unions played their part too. A prolonged demarcation dispute between builders' labourers and ironworkers

over who should work on the steel sections of the bridge led
to strikes, protest meetings and walk-offs. John Holland's
expanded role was to erect the steel sections as well as
complete the concrete work and blacktop for the roadway.
Despite its good record earlier during the concrete work,
John Holland could not solve the spate of union problems
that led to more than half the working hours being lost.
Some of the men, for example, took weekdays off and came
to work at weekends when, after the first four hours, they
were paid double time. Evidence at the later royal commission showed that when the men were confined to their cabin
because of rain they were paid the full rate. There was no
incentive for them to walk a few yards to work under cover
inside the hollow steel box-girders. Other disputes included
a strike over having a first-aid officer on one of the piers;
another for not having been paid for the initial two-day
stoppage; a three-and-a-half day stoppage over a claim for
Saturday pay after the men were sent home because of rain;
a week-long strike because on the one hand the men wanted
a dismissed boilermaker reinstated while on the other they
wanted a hydraulics technician sacked because he worked
10 minutes later than the rest when, they said, it was too
dark to work.

The proud people of Melbourne did not yet know just
how dreadfully sick the bridge was, and there were some
hints available. At one point early in the construction, men
walked off the job because a sag was reported in one of
the bridge spans. The deputy Victorian Opposition Leader,
Frank Wilkes, related the incident to State Parliament in
March 1970. His remarks were dismissed by the Parliament
and denied by the Authority which, though the owner of the
bridge, relied heavily on information from its contractors.

Scene at the top after the Mt Kembla mine explosion (*Town and Country Journal*)

The implosion of the Royal Canberra Hospital (Andrew Meares, *Sydney Morning Herald*)

Harry Hill picks through the wreckage of his home after the Ash Wednesday bushfires (Fairfax Photo Library)

The Granville train disaster (Fairfax Photo Library)

The collapsed West Gate Bridge (Fairfax Photo Library)

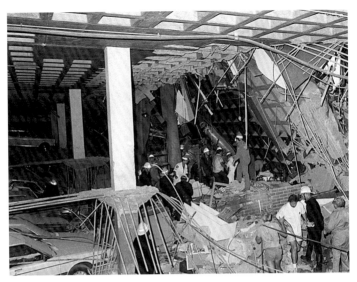

The Newcastle Workers' Club after the earthquake (Alan Jolly; republished courtesy of *The Newcastle Herald*)

Rescue workers carry Stuart Diver out of the wreckage after the Thredbo landslide (Dallas Kilponen, *Sun Herald News*)

The bridge collapses at the Maccabiah Games (Jeremy Feldman/AP/AAP)

An area of Casuarina devastated by Cyclone Tracy (Rick Stevens, *Sydney Morning Herald*)

Tony Hancock and two of his children at their Ashgrove home, swept away by the Brisbane floods (Fairfax Photo Library)

Crew abandon the *Sword of Orion* during the 1998 Sydney–Hobart yacht race (Andrew Taylor, *Sydney Morning Herald*)

Evidence would later emerge that the contractors readily lied about what was happening.

The first outward sign that the West Gate might not be completely safe came not from the bridge itself but from other bridge projects. The Fourth Danube Bridge in Vienna encountered problems in November 1969, when it sagged up to three feet along parts of its length. On 2 June 1970 at Milford Haven in Wales, a bridge under construction collapsed, killing four men. The relevance to the West Gate was that these two bridges were being built on what was known as the 'box-girder' principle, which Freeman Fox had pioneered and used in most of its bridge-building projects. An inquiry into the Milford Haven disaster established that the collapse and consequent fatalities had been the result of human error and lack of attention to safety. Meyer, realising the level of concern in Melbourne, took pains to give assurances that there was nothing to worry about, that the West Gate was completely safe. He even went to far as to say that Milford Haven and West Gate were not even similar, although he said there would be a three-week delay on building for what he described as a 'belt and braces procedure'.

Nevertheless, the Authority appeared to have concluded that it could not fully trust the assurances it was getting from its contractors. At the time of the 'belt and braces' operation in March 1970 it called in a London firm of engineers to check on the bridge structure. The firm, G. Maunsell and Partners (unconnected with the joint consulting engineers of similar name) found there were 14 'inadequacies' in the steel section it inspected. These findings were not to be made known until a long while later. Had they been made known immediately, there might have been a change in construction methods at that point.

At the time of the G. Maunsell inspection John Holland had completed the concrete outer sections leading up to the two opposite banks of the river. This left the 834.6 metre steel section over the river still to be built. This section was made up of five spans—two outer spans and one larger central one. They were to rest on and stretch from piers numbered 10 to 15. Pier 10 was on the west side and pier 15 on the east. The spans therefore were numbered west to east 10–11, 11–12, 12–13 (the main span), 13–14 and 14–15. Their lengths in sequence were 110.25 metres, 141.75 metres, 330.75 metres, 141.75 metres and 110.25 metres, which meant that the two opposing outside spans leading to the middle were identical in length. The lengths of the steel bridge were 112 metres twice, 141 metres twice and 336.4 metres for the central span, making a total of 848.1 metres. The total length, including the concrete approaches, was 2582.57 metres. The overall length, including the approach roads, was 5.6 kilometres.

Once in position and joined together on top of the piers the five steel spans would form what is called a continuous box-girder bridge. The piers numbered 12 and 13, holding up each end of the main central span, were, in fact, extended upwards about 50 metres higher than the others so that they also became towers from which cables would be strung to support the spans. In essence that was what the finished bridge would look like, but to achieve it the builders had to start with a relatively small section known as a box-girder. The box-girder system was favoured because it was cheaper, lighter and easier than other forms of bridge building. The term 'lighter' is of course only comparative because each of the spans weighed more than 1400 tonnes and each box-girder that formed a component part of the span weighed more than 120 tonnes.

The full box-girder, when in place across the full width of the bridge and looked at face on, was shaped a bit like an inverted wedge with the pointed base cut off square and the top rounded to form the camber of what eventually would be the road surface. The 'wedge' was largely hollow, although there were internal braces and cross members to add to its strength. To make lifting more manageable it was decided to divide these box-girders into half-boxes. The erection procedure—chosen by World Services, not Freeman Fox—was to put the two outer spans, 15–14 and 10–11, up first. Then they would cantilever out from the end of these spans towards the centre, starting at pier 14 on the east side and then on pier 11 on the west. The same operation would be repeated on piers 13 and 12 respectively and then beyond these to the middle, where they would join and form the central 12–13 span.

Cantilevering meant lifting each half-box into position and supporting it with trusses at the bottom and cables at the top while it was bolted to the already built section of the bridge behind it. The other half-box would then be brought up alongside it. Cantilevering was a little like having a set of matchboxes, each matchbox representing a half-box girder. One matchbox would be lifted and fixed into place and then the other would be brought up alongside it. A third matchbox would then be lifted into place and fixed to the outer end of Matchbox No 1 and a fourth fixed to the end of Matchbox No 2, and so on, placing them one at a time, end on end and side by side, along a given length. In this case, however, the 'matchboxes' were the size of a modest suburban home—about 15.6 metres long by 12.6 metres wide—and each weighed 120 tonnes.

In order to reach this cantilevering stage, the builders first had to put spans 15–14 and 10–11 in place on top of the piers. This was to be done by an entirely different erection method. Instead of lifting the half-boxes into the air one by one, it was decided to join them together on the ground and lift them into the air in a strip. It meant, in effect, splitting the span down the middle and assembling each half-box end-on-end on the ground. Then each completed half-length would be lifted separately and joined alongside the other half-length above ground and on top of the piers. It was a little like building a stretch of roadway more than 100 metres long and 10 metres thick, dividing it down the middle and lifting each length on to a high-rise building about 50 metres tall. To add to the problem the boxes were not square. They were flat on the bottom and tapered outwards on one side. Their most critical feature as it turned out was that they each had slightly curving top plates to allow for the road camber.

The job of lifting these half-spans to the top of the piers required enormous strength and absolute precision. Huge jacks and trusses were needed to lift each half-span slowly up the side of the pier and then push them across on rolling beams until they were in position and resting on top of the piers. It was the first time this method had been used under these conditions. It was extremely exacting and, according to experts later, the difference in the height of the two joined half-cambers should have been no more than 2.5 centimetres and preferably less than 1.25 centimetres. Constant checks also had to be made to see if sudden weather changes affected the steel. Putting up span 14–15 on the east side of the river began smoothly and simply. A temporary staging was laid and the huge steel panels were rolled into place and joined together—along with internal stiffeners and braces—to form the half-boxes. Each half-box was then bolted to the next until they reached the required length of more than 100 metres. Once this was completed the half-span was lifted a few feet off the staging so that it hung freely on the jacks at each end.

Minutes after the initial lift, however, buckles suddenly began to appear in the steel. The men could see that the whole assembly was unstable. Just as suddenly, the buckling stopped. Instead of lowering the span back to ground level, it was decided to insert a series of braces, beams and other stiffeners to strengthen it. The time lost in lowering the span back to ground level would only have been minimal, but World Services was plagued with union troubles and the arguments of its co-contractors, and was anxious to make as much progress as possible. It approached the engineers for the designers, Freeman Fox, for permission to strengthen the span while it hung in the air. The engineers had already experienced troubles in getting their London office to provide calculations, but fortuitously the company's consultant engineer, Sir Gilbert Roberts, was in Melbourne. He saw the damaged span and took part in the discussions with World Services.

At the later royal commission, Roberts was to say he had based his decision to agree with World Services on calculations worked out by Freeman Fox's relatively young deputy resident engineer, Peter Crossley. He would later say the calculations were 'not too far wrong', but in fact, on the royal commission's findings, there was a significant error of arithmetic. The decision that it was safe to proceed with the lifting was based on a totally inadequate analysis of the situation, and neither Freeman Fox nor World Services had any real idea of the stresses imposed.

As it turned out, the damaged half-span was lifted into place up on top of the piers. It was followed some weeks later by the other considerably strengthened half-span and the two were brought together on the rolling beams. A section around the middle of the span could not be straightened. A splice along the centre line that held the two half-lengths together had been worked on from both ends almost to the middle, but when it came to bolting this small middle section together, it was found that there was no flexibility left. The only solution the engineers could come up with was to undo bolts along a seam on the inner panel and hope that this would allow for a small movement to take out the buckle.

They decided not to attempt this operation until more boxes could be added to the end of the span pointing towards the middle. These were to be added by the cantilever process and it was hoped that their weight, applied at the end of the span, would cause it to stretch and thus reduce the bending around the area of the buckle. The operation proved to be successful and was, in fact, achieved after only two half-boxes had been added to the end of the span, but it was done in the absence of the man in charge of the plan, Freeman Fox's Timothy Burbury, who said later that he was considerably annoyed when he arrived on the site at 9 am to find that work had already started. As it was, some 30 bolts had been undone and it had had the desired effect of flattening out the bulge in the middle of the already erected span between piers 14–15. The movement of the plates was slight and new bolts were put back with only minor reaming of the holes. The royal commission would describe the incident as a regrettable necessity. The added stress almost certainly reduced the safety of the bridge.

Back at the site back then there was no room for warnings or pessimism. A major engineering problem had been solved relatively simply and the completed span was sitting neatly, proudly and safely on the top of the piers. It had been the first operation of its kind and, apart from the bit of bother about the buckles, it had been a huge success. The engineers and men moved on enthusiastically to the west side of the river. The people of Melbourne, though hearing and reading of the frequent walkouts and other union troubles, were blissfully unaware of more profound problems. Industrialists were expanding their old factories or building new ones. The highway from the west side down to Geelong was radically upgraded. Developers and land speculators were gobbling up hundreds of hectares of farmland in anticipation of the land boom they knew would follow the opening of the bridge. The Authority commissioned a public relations firm, International Public Relations (IPR), to tell people all they wanted to know about what was going into 'their bridge'.

As Melbourne eagerly awaited its membership in the Great Bridge Cities of the World Club alongside New York and San Francisco among others, its people read avidly the progress reports and technical data IPR sent out. Now was the time for learning, and watching and admiring as those huge piers—the sides of which were big enough to use for a drive-in movie screen—rose out of the rubbish tips and mud of the Yarra. Certainly the warmest glow of pride came when one noted that Australia's very own John Holland group had been largely responsible for creating this magnificent giant. The fact that more than half the firm's 200 men on-site were foreign-born was a bonus. It all reflected the Australian spirit with migrants and native-borns working side by side to realise a dream.

Besides reading about its amazing progress, people could go down to the Yarra banks and watch the bridge take shape. This they did, arriving in their thousands from all over Victoria and Australia. Almost every evening and on weekends the viewing platforms were packed with audiences who gazed up in awe as first the concrete spans and then the steel spans were slowly put into place. Those with binoculars could even see the proud and confident smiles on the faces of the men, particularly the riggers as they walked briskly along narrow, swinging beams or bounced the bottoms of their rubber-soled boots on spanner handles to tighten up bolts. It was almost as if the men were showing off their bridge and performing for the crowds down below. It was better than any circus.

On 15 May the big cranes and jacks were ready to lift the first of the half-spans onto piers 10 and 11 on the west side. A week later it was in position on top of the beam. By 28 August all that remained was for the two longitudinal halves to be joined together and to be lowered off their temporary rolling beams on to permanent bearings. The more curious of the onlookers might have wondered why a few days later the bridge-builders began lifting huge concrete blocks onto the top of the span. What they did not know was that these blocks—ten of them weighing a total of 80 tonnes—were the builders' way of solving a problem they faced when the two half-spans were brought together. It turned out that the camber of the northern half had ended up 10 centimetres higher than the southern half. They decided to force the northern half down with the weight of concrete, but, just as the last concrete block was put in place, a buckle appeared near the centre line—a big one that stretched in parts for more than three metres. It did not appear much worse than the earlier one on the east side, and it was thought that it could be fixed without anyone knowing about it. It was later claimed later that someone threw sacks over the buckle when the Authority's general manager, Cec Wilson, was due to come up on the span.

The difference between this problem and the earlier buckle on the east side, however, was that this time the two half-spans were still on their temporary bearings. The strain could not be eased by cantilevering boxes out towards the centre and stretching the buckle as they had done on the east side. John Holland's section engineer, William Tracy, his counterpart with Freeman Fox, David Ward, and their overall boss, Freeman Fox's resident engineer, Jack Hindshaw, were in a quandary. Hindshaw was particularly worried and knew he would have to abandon the laid-down procedures to remove the buckle. On the other hand he was already in the middle of a row with John Holland staff over strict adherence to the procedure manual. For days they wondered what they should do. On 13 October Hindshaw decided that bolts would have to be removed around two of the box-girders where the buckle was most severe. He told Freeman Fox's Peter Crossley and David Ward. They were not happy with the suggestion.

Hindshaw said it was the only solution, telling Ward that he would have to implement the operation and assuring him that the bolts would have to be removed only in groups of six or eight at a time. After each group was removed the box-girders would be thoroughly examined before moving on to the next group. Ward told Holland's William Tracy of Hindshaw's decision. Tracy was not happy either. He was so concerned he insisted on a formal written confirmation. Ward agreed and also made it clear he would personally supervise the operation. What both men overlooked was that Hindshaw had not specified whether the bolts should be removed as soon as possible or left until later when the erection had reached a safer stage.

At 8.30 am on Thursday 15 October, Ward and Tracy met on top of the span between piers 10 and 11 and began instructing the men to remove the bolts. A check was made on the first group of eight bolts. When 16 had been removed the men saw that two of the plates had moved so that the bolts were jammed. The Freeman Fox inspector, Ernest Enness, suggested they force the jammed bolts out by over-tightening with the special air-guns. It worked and the holes were cleared. It was not until 30 bolts on one side of the centre splice and seven on the other had been removed that they noticed the bulge begin to flatten. Suddenly the gradual flattening changed dramatically.

A vicious and inexplicable buckle appeared and began to spread throughout the whole length of the two spans. Then the northern half seemed to settle gently. Everyone knew that there was something dreadfully wrong. What they did not know was that the full weight of the northern span was being held up solely by its southern counterpart. Men were summoned to speed up the re-bolting work. Set procedures were forgotten as they tried frantically to get the bolts back into place. At 11 am, Ward tried to contact Hindshaw to tell him to get over to the west side as quickly as possible. The phone on the east side rang. Crossley picked it up. He went out to find Hindshaw. By the time Hindshaw and Crossley had crossed the river and got to the top of the west side span, re-bolting was well under way, and the buckle appeared to be disappearing, but the whole mass of steel had moved. Hindshaw knew instantly what he was looking at. He was horrified.

Whether it was his nature, the lack of communication that had built up between him and the men, or a desire not to transmit to them the frightening possibility he had become aware of, there was no sign of panic in his voice as he urged the men to hurry. He remained outwardly composed for almost 20 minutes. He was still calm when he walked to the phone and contacted World Services' senior representative on the site, Gerit Hardenberg, and asked him to come over. Then shortly before 11.50 am, as if musing to himself, Hindshaw asked, 'Shall I get the bods off?' An eerie pinging noise filled the air. The men standing on top of the span looked down and saw that the noise was being caused by flakes of rust peeling off the steel. The bolts were turning blue.

The bridge fell away beneath their feet.

At precisely 11.51 on the morning of Thursday, 15 October 1970, the red emergency light on the switchboard of Melbourne's ambulance headquarters began to blink. Before the operator could speak a voice blurted out, 'She's gone! The bridge has gone!' At precisely 11.54 am Melbourne's police headquarters received this message: 'Disaster at West Gate. West side. Span collapsed. Send all services.'

For Ian Miller, 39, a father of three and a graduate of Melbourne University, the completion of the bridge would have been the pinnacle of an already outstanding career. He had worked on Canada's great Trans-Canadian Highway and, on returning to Australia, had been appointed project engineer for the Silverwater Bridge in Sydney. In 1965 he had won John Holland the coveted construction achievement award when he built the Captain Cook Bridge over Sydney's Georges River. Two years later he won another award for building a wharf at Bunbury in Western Australia. Now he was John Holland's project engineer for the West Gate Bridge.

Ian and Jack Hindshaw were walking towards each other when suddenly the bridge groaned. Bob West's wife, Pat, and the three kids were in bed when he left for work. He was dead less than five hours later. It was still dark when Bill Harburn, a keen soccer player who once captained Australia shortly after migrating, slipped out of bed from beside his wife, Mavis. It was not until two days later that they were able to identify his body.

Jack Grist and Fred Upsdell had been mates since they met in Middlesex, England, more than 20 years before. On migrating they had become neighbours at Altona, not far from the West Gate Bridge. They became even closer when Jack's daughter, Yvonne, married Fred's son, Gerald. Jack, 54, went on to become a foreman on the bridge and Fred, 66, took a job as storeman because he couldn't stand the thought of retiring. Jack called for Fred on the morning of 15 October 1970. They were on the job early, so they took an early lunch break together in one of the huts which, for some reason, had been put directly beneath the latest span to be lifted into place. Rescuers found their bodies only inches apart. They were later buried alongside each other.

Victor Gerada had tried to speak to his mates about the shudder he felt, but was worried they would call him a coward, so he had told his wife, Doris. Doris heard the sirens. Something inside her told her to start running. As she raced down the slight incline of the street the bridge loomed up in front of her. She could see it was broken. She ducked under a policeman's out-stretched arm and ran blindly towards the ambulances. She saw Victor's shirt and arm jutting out from under the blanket that covered his head.

Ian Miller, Jack Hindshaw, Bill Harburn, Bob West, Jack Grist, Fred Upsdell and Victor Gerada were among the 35 men who died when the West Gate Bridge collapsed. Eighteen men were injured and many of them were crippled for life.

Others had miraculous escapes. When the bridge sagged and dropped away, Charlie Sant simply sat down on a box, fell with it to the bottom and escaped unscathed. John Thwaites got away with two black eyes, 'as if I'd just gone 10 rounds with Lionel Rose'. George Stassoulakos grabbed hold of a metal bar and waited, escaping without a scratch. John Laino bounced around inside the hollow of the bridge like a ping-pong ball. When he surfaced he saw the carnage around him and waded into the mud to try to find his workmates. Ed Halsall thanked the very force of the bridge collapsing for his life. He was on the ground below the span and, on seeing it coming down, he ran as fast as he could. The sheer impact of some 2000 tonnes of steel and concrete hitting the ground created a wind blast that lifted him off his feet and sent him flying through the air, clear of the falling wreckage.

Then there were the heroes. Like John Laino, Bill Snowden survived. He got out from under just in time but went straight back into the mud to dig for mates. He and John Laino later helped identify the dead and unconscious injured. John Dooty, 20, the long-haired larrikin from Ascot Vale, was a bit of a clown and the brunt of many a joke. He too got out but went straight back and refused to stop. The ambulance men, seeing he was exhausted, ordered him off the site but after a cup of tea and a bite to eat he was back digging and searching.

As the news of the crash hit Melbourne, the government immediately activated a state disaster plan and all available firemen, ambulance officers and police were called in. Alongside them stood nurses, doctors, priests, boy scouts and men and women from the Salvation Army. As some semblance of order was pieced together from the chaos, the men of the bridge reluctantly wandered off into the arms of family and friends.

Dave Robson and Kevin Lowe were too shaken to go home yet. They went down to the pub where they used to drink with their mates. This writer happened to join them there. They'd done their share of digging and dragging out bodies and all they wanted was a drink. 'I've never seen so many men cry as I did today,' Kevin said. 'Christ those Salvos are worth every bob they get.' Dave said, 'Jeez I'd like to go home and sleep for a while. But I know if I shut my eyes, I'll see it all again.'

For so many of those who survived the legacy was shattered nerves and nightmares. Desmond Gibson's nightmare lasted almost three years. He was 29 when the bridge went down with him inside it, praying. He turned grey within weeks. He had three heart attacks before his fourth, on 4 August 1973 at the age of 32, brought the number of men the bridge killed to 36. History has it that the toll was 35, but who knows? Like Gibson, the deputy chairman of the Authority, Rupert Vian, died shortly afterwards. It could be said that Meyer, the man whose unshakeable enthusiasm was undoubtedly the main driving force behind the bridge and arguably the one most responsible for it being built, died prematurely.

The bridge was finally opened on 15 November 1978 at a cost of more than $200 million, ten years and seven months after it was started. Sir Henry Bolte was not at the official opening. I telephoned him at his home to ask him why, and he was so genuinely upset I agreed then not to repeat what he told me, but he is now dead and so I feel I can. 'I just couldn't be there,' he said. 'The damn thing has killed too many people.'

The opening date was more than eight years after the collapse. In that time there was even more controversy involving such things as more union problems, disruptive traffic flows into the south eastern suburbs and the sacking of contractors as well as what was probably the bridge's most harmful episode: the walk-out and subsequent bitter dispute between Dr William Fairhurst, the bridge's new designer and builder, and others to the point where people like the then Labor Federal MP Barry Jones were calling for yet another royal commission into the running of West Gate.

Then there was the royal commission into the collapse itself. It was headed by Deputy Chief Justice Sir Esler Barber along with one of the world's finest engineers, Sir Hubert Shirley-Smith, and leading engineering academic Professor Frank Bull. It attracted the very best legal minds in Australia—12 Queen's Counsel no less. Less than a month after its last sitting day, the commission came out with its 8000-word, 300-page report. It was described by the engineering community throughout the world as one of the most searching, thorough and comprehensive of its kind. It was also one of the most scathing documents ever penned.

'This tragic disaster was utterly unnecessary,' it said. 'The bridge collapsed because of acts of inefficiency and omissions by those entrusted with building a bridge.' To varying degrees, the report blamed everyone involved in the project. In turn everyone involved refused to accept blame or blamed someone else. The commission said the removal of the bolts caused the collapse. This had been done to correct a buckle that had been caused by placing the concrete blocks on one of the half spans to reduce its height and camber difference with the other half span. The fault, however, it said, lay further back. Partly at fault was Freeman Fox, who failed to give proper and careful regard to the process of structural design and who failed to check the safety of erections proposals put to it. Also partly at fault was the method used to erect spans 15–14 and subsequently 10–11. This process called for more than the usual care on the part of the contractor and the consultants, but neither World Services nor John Holland had appreciated the need for great care, and Freeman Fox had failed in their duty to prevent the contractor from using procedures liable to be dangerous.

The commissioners painstakingly pieced together a whole catalogue of administrative, design and engineering mistakes in a report that was sold out within five minutes and was to have repercussions around the world.

In the aftermath of West Gate, authorities throughout the world started to close down 61 bridges and restrict traffic flows on 41 others, forcing their builders to strengthen them before they were allowed to reopen. Further evidence to justify doubt in the design came in November 1971—almost exactly a year after the West Gate disaster—when a bridge across the Rhine at Koblenz crashed and killed five men. Modern construction had become faster and neater. Major freeways could sweep through terrain where previous roadways curved and climbed and dipped. Bridges could sweep across valleys on major highways without motorists even noticing the change in terrain. In the brave new technological world, so many things were possible, but what could not be replaced were the age-old ingredients of patience, caution and commonsense.

9

The Newcastle Earthquake, 1989

I was in Fremantle . . . and one of the other wharfies on the
wharf . . . who knew I was from Newcastle, said . . . 'Eddie,
there's been an earthquake in Newcastle.' And I just . . . 'Oh well,
oh yeah, okay, it's a tremor.' You don't worry about those things.

Aftershocks, *Paul Brown and the Workers Cultural
Action Committee*

Before 10.27 am there had been nothing to suggest that
28 December 1989 would be any different in Newcastle
from other days in the week between the Christmas and
New Year holidays. The temperature was approaching
30 degrees Celsius by mid-morning and there were few
people braving the summer heat on the inner city streets.
While the closure of government and professional offices
for the holiday period kept the numbers down, there was
an additional factor on this day. People were aware that
New South Wales State Transit Authority bus drivers were
walking off the job in mid-morning for a meeting on an
industrial issue and there was uncertainty about when bus
services would resume. This led to the cancellation of a lot
of travel plans.

The regular Thursday hoy players at Newcastle Workers
Club, though, were largely undeterred. Mainly middle-aged
women and retirees, many of them caught early buses into
town and, armed with fistfuls of coins, sat down at the

five-cent poker machines on the club's mezzanine floor to have a flutter while waiting for the 11 am game.

As well as the hoy players there was a steady stream of people renewing club memberships. Most of the remaining visitors to the club were roadies—the technical crew—who'd come to set up the main auditorium for a Crowded House, Boom Crash Opera and Split Enz concert that night. In all there were about 300 people in the three-storey club building.

Sixty-two-year-old Norm Duffy left his wife Miriam playing the pokies on the mezzanine while he went to renew his membership. He returned just on 10.27 am and began chatting with Miriam. He had hardly spoken when the floor began to heave. 'What was that? It felt like an earthquake,' Norm said. 'Something like that, yes,' Miriam replied. It was the last thing Norm heard his wife say. The floor collapsed, dropping the Duffys and many others two storeys down into the club basement, with the shattered floor above throwing large pieces of masonry after them. Norm and two women near him were buried in rubble, but their lives were saved by two poker machines that had formed a bridge above their heads. Miriam was not so lucky. She was one of 13 people in Newcastle who became the first recorded earthquake fatalities in Australia.

No other Australian natural disaster has had the impact of the 1989 Newcastle earthquake. Governments and communities were used to bushfires, cyclones and floods. These were predictable events in terms of when and where they would occur. The only question was the degree of severity, and measures had been taken to limit their impact. Earthquakes, however, were a different matter. An earthquake building standard was only introduced in Australia in 1979 and, even then, only two states—Western Australia and South Australia—had made the standard's safety measures mandatory.

The majority of the states could hardly be blamed for their apparent complacency. The earthquake design standard, AS2121, was accompanied by a seismic map that divided Australia into four zones: 0 (no risk), A (low risk), 1 (moderate risk) and 2 (high risk). Eighty-nine percent of Australia, including Newcastle, was put in zone 0. The risk of earthquakes in this zone was considered so low that no measures aimed at reducing the impact of quakes on buildings were required. Western Australia and South Australia had shown caution because they had experienced the bulk of property-damaging earthquakes. Adelaide had suffered an earthquake on 1 March 1954 that measured 5.6 on the Richter scale—the same magnitude as the one that hit Newcastle. The Adelaide quake, however, which struck in the early morning when most people were sleeping, produced no serious injuries and the damage, while widespread, was mainly limited to cracked walls and loosened plaster and chimneys. The Adelaide earthquake was considered to be something of an anomaly until the Newcastle episode 35 years later. Certainly earthquakes had occurred, but generally in unpopulated areas. Australia was not held to be a continent prone to violent seismic activity of the type that saw 60 000 people die in the 1923 Tokyo earthquake (8.3 on the Richter scale), more than 200 000 killed in a 7.8 quake in a rural area of China in 1976, or 10 000 killed in Mexico City (8.1) in 1985.

Nonetheless the 5.6 earthquake that hit Newcastle caused damage that cost $1.5 billion to repair, as well as killing 13 people and injuring 167 others, 20 of them seriously. The majority of the property damage was in and around

Newcastle. More than 30 000 buildings were damaged, with 192 having to be demolished and 178 others partly demolished in the 12 months following the earthquake. The total area shaken was wider than the greater Newcastle zone and its 450 000 people. Hundreds of buildings up to 340 kilometres away, including a hospital at Liverpool, south-west of Sydney, and a police station near Kempsey, on the north coast of New South Wales, were extensively damaged. By the end of 1994 insurance companies had paid out $962 million on 70 000 claims.

The extent of the damage surprised scientists until post-quake surveys showed that the worst damage occurred to structures erected on alluvial soils—those on the banks of rivers and creeks or where lakes and streams had once been found. The 1979 earthquake code had made no allowance for the fact that alluvial soils shook like jelly, amplifying the shockwaves sent through the ground. The building and scientific experts who drew up AS2121 could hardly be blamed for this. University of Newcastle structural engineering expert Professor Rob Melchers told a symposium in the city several months after the tremor that the role of alluvial soils in earthquakes had only become apparent when the damage caused by a strong earthquake in the Californian city of San Francisco was studied, and that earthquake had occurred barely 12 weeks before the Newcastle event.

Investigations after the Newcastle earthquake also revealed that the city had a history of such ground-shaking incidents, with at least two previous quakes believed, from reports of the extent of associated damage, to have been similar in intensity. The Australian Seismological Centre, a division of the Canberra-based Australian Geological Survey Organisation, estimated that an 1868 earthquake that struck the city had had a Richter magnitude of 5.3, while a 1925 quake had had a magnitude of 5. While the earthquakes caused widespread, mainly minor damage, they weren't seen as part of a pattern and, in 1925 at least, Newcastle people were more concerned about persistent problems with the subsidence of shallow coal-mine workings. Instead of 'earthquake', future written references to the two events used words such as 'creep' and 'tremor'.

Although earthquakes have shaken this planet since its rigid outer surface was formed 4500 million years ago, there is still much about them that puzzles scientists. The basics of an earthquake are straightforward. The Earth's surface is made up of rock plates that are slowly pulling apart in some areas and pushing together in others. These movements produce cracks, or fault lines, often at depths of only a few kilometres below the surface. When pieces of the huge rock plates break away, the energy generated by the collapse moves along the fault lines as seismic waves and causes the surface to shake. Seismic waves travel at up to 14 kilometres a second, so the closer an earthquake is to the surface, the greater the risk of injury and structural damage is likely to be even with a moderate earthquake. The point on the Earth's surface directly above the source of an earthquake is known as the epicentre. An earthquake is generally followed by a series of smaller tremors known as aftershocks.

The most intense earthquakes take place at the margins of plates pushing together, such as in the Himalayas and New Zealand. These areas have historically produced massive devastation and large loss of life. Earthquakes in Australia are of a different type. The Australian continent sits in the middle of the Indo-Australian plate, with tremors caused by movements within that plate. One source of stress is the northward movement of the plate at the leisurely pace of seven to ten centimetres a year. Another is the pressure of the oceans on the margins of the plate. Some areas are underlain by rocks which are particularly 'stressed out' and more subject to cracking and shifting. The Hunter Valley in which Newcastle sits, on the deep alluvium at the mouth of its namesake river, is one of these vulnerable areas. Scientists still are not sure why these areas are earthquake-prone. One theory is that the Hunter region suffers because it lies on the margin of two major thrust faults, the Peel and the Hunter-Mooki, which have been caused by the collision of two geological sub-units within the Indo-Australian plate. The rocks of the New England region are moving south, pushing over the top of the newer rocks of the Sydney Basin. The theory suggests that the energy created by this slow movement is stored in smaller faults below the Hunter and eventually released as earthquakes.

The magnitude of earthquakes is generally measured by the Richter scale, which has a logarithmic basis. Each whole number unit represents a tenfold growth in the magnitude of the Earth's shaking over the previous whole number and a release of energy that is 30 times greater. Thus, a Richter scale 5 earthquake is 10 000 times stronger than a scale 1 and releases 810 000 times the energy. There is no upper limit, although the largest earthquakes recorded since the scale was introduced in 1935 have measured 9.5.

Put another way, a Richter scale 5 earthquake releases energy equivalent to a small, 20 kiloton atom bomb—the size used on Hiroshima in World War II. An earthquake like the one that hit Newcastle, with a magnitude of 5.6, has the potential to do horrendous damage provided the right conditions. The structural damage caused in urban areas built on naturally deposited alluvium or on fill that was material dredged from the city's harbour made it clear that the destructive power of earthquakes could no longer be ignored in Australia.

This message was reinforced by subsequent studies. Peter Hughes, a Brisbane consulting engineer and founding member of the Centre for Earthquake Research in Australia (CERA), established in the wake of the earthquake, told a Newcastle conference in October 1991 that the city had been fortunate that the earthquake occurred when it did, in a period when schools, many offices and some industries were closed. Using the data on the damage that had been done to buildings, he estimated that if the earthquake had struck at the same time on a Thursday two months earlier, 900 people could have been killed and 10000 injured. The lives of between 200 and 300 children could have been under threat, as well as those of 300 to 400 people in the streets, with the remaining potential fatalities mainly in technical colleges and factories.

In a 1993 study, CERA director of research Dr Jack Rynn suggested what would happen in Australia's largest city, Sydney, 150 kilometres south of Newcastle, with a population of 3.5 million, if it were hit by a 5.6 earthquake. He put deaths at 3000, serious injuries at 40000 and damage at $40 billion. Like Newcastle, much of the city was built on alluvium and it had many structures of a similar age and type to those which had collapsed or been damaged. Because of Sydney's importance as an economic centre, a moderate earthquake within 50 kilometres of the city centre would have the power to paralyse the whole nation. 'But the apathy towards earthquakes is still there,' he said, 'which is most dangerous because an earthquake is not like a storm or a cyclone which you can see coming and know what to expect.'

This apathy was despite the fact that seismological records show that an earthquake of Richter magnitude 5.6 occurs somewhere in Australia every 18 months to two years, and that earthquakes of larger magnitudes, including one that measured 7.2 in Meeberrie, WA, in 1941, have occurred near townships.

At the time the earthquake struck, Newcastle was adjusting to major changes that were taking place in Australian manufacturing industry. The city began life in 1804 when convicts were sent from Sydney to mine coal that had been discovered a few years earlier. The coal was initially shipped to Sydney or exported, and the city did not boom until Broken Hill Proprietary Co (BHP) opened a steelworks in 1915, with steel processing and manufacturing industries quickly following. At the beginning of the 1980s a global steel industry recession led BHP to begin cutbacks at the Newcastle steelworks that eventually led to the plant's closure in 1999. The initial steel industry retrenchments coincided with a rationalisation in Australian manufacturing that produced company amalgamations and job losses. As it entered the turbulent 1990s, Newcastle, Australia's sixth largest city and heavily reliant on manufacturing, did not need the extra problems associated with a massive disaster of a type new to Australia

The epicentre of the earthquake is believed by the Australian Geological Survey Organisation to have been about 15 kilometres south-west of Newcastle and 11.5 kilometres below the surface. The shockwaves from the underground fracturing and collapse of a large area of rock quickly spread from the epicentre, causing the surface to ripple. Some people working in their gardens reported seeing the ground 'bubble' twice in quick succession and claimed that they heard an accompanying noise like a sonic boom, while surfboard riders in the Pacific Ocean off Newcastle beaches said that two large waves had suddenly appeared in a sea that had been flattened all morning by a westerly wind. When the shockwaves hit soft alluvium, the reverberations intensified and buildings shook violently—violently enough in many cases to cause partial or even total collapse. The earthquake, despite being only moderate in Richter terms, was recorded on seismographs around the world, but due to the failure of authorities in eastern Australia to recognise that earthquakes posed serious risks, the closest recording station to Newcastle was in Canberra, almost 400 kilometres away. While the lack of measuring equipment close to the epicentre made it difficult to estimate the length of the earthquake, it is believed to have lasted no more than seven or eight seconds.

If governments were unprepared for earthquakes, they merely reflected community views. One of the first rumours to spread around inner Newcastle was that there had been a massive explosion at the BHP steelworks, particularly as a large black cloud of smoke could be seen rising above the works. There also were stories that a large aeroplane had crashed and exploded. With electricity cut off for more than an hour and telephone services disrupted for much longer (this was before the establishment of mobile phone networks), it was a long time before most people learned that an earthquake had taken place.

They knew something had happened because their immediate surrounds went eerily quiet for a few minutes after 10.27 am. Pedestrians who had almost been hit by building materials raining down in inner suburban shopping centres quickly came out of their daze to rush to help others who had been struck by the bricks, tiles and timber. Residents of older-style houses, mainly those dating from the 1890s to the 1920s, emerged from the structures to find that chimneys had collapsed. The spire of a historic church fell, heavy gravestones were thrust from the ground alongside the city's Anglican cathedral, and the marble figure of a soldier with head bowed toppled from a war memorial. Motorists drove slowly to avoid the debris from damaged buildings and there was remarkable politeness at dozens of blacked-out traffic signals within a 14 kilometre radius of the city centre. Railway services were brought to a halt immediately so that tracks could be inspected, but the ground, while it had shaken severely, had not been deformed or opened up. The earthquake's jolt, however, had damaged about 50 percent of the commercial buildings in the Newcastle CBD and 80 percent in nearby suburban Hamilton, the two worst-affected areas. A motorist who was driving along Beaumont Street, Hamilton's main business artery, when the quake struck said that it 'looked like a plane had come down and smashed through the top of all the buildings.' One in ten buildings along the street had collapsed or been extensively damaged and three elderly pedestrians had died, hit by falling awnings and walls. The death toll was even greater at the Newcastle Workers Club, two kilometres away. Nine people, again mainly elderly, either lay dead beneath rubble from the collapsed three floors or died soon after being rescued. The earthquake's other fatality—the thirteenth—was a woman who collapsed from shock when the earthquake struck while she was in a doctor's waiting room. New South Wales Coroner Kevin Waller, at his inquiry into the earthquake deaths in July 1990, ruled that the woman's death on the day after the tremor could be attributed to the disaster.

When the earthquake hit the Workers Club, cleaner Howard Gibson was in the auditorium which collapsed. Hoy caller Stan Gill had just asked him to replace some light-globes when the floor and walls began to shake. Gibson fled to one side of the auditorium, fell, and was pinned beneath falling chairs. The floor collapsed under Gill and he rode down it like a child on a slippery dip, ending up covered by chairs and rubble and calling for help while he could hear screams near by. A pair of roadies elsewhere in the auditorium also went down with the floor. One died. The other, Patrick Murray, survived when a chair fell on him and broke the fall of a potentially crushing block of concrete. Murray's trunk and legs were trapped and he waited for rescue for more than four hours, initially calling out for help, then singing 'every song I've ever heard with the word "help" in it,' as he said later in hospital.

The city's fire brigade headquarters at Cooks Hill, just around the corner from the Workers Club, was extensively damaged by the earthquake, but that didn't stop officers from racing swiftly to the club when they heard it had collapsed. The first emergency workers on the scene, they were confronted by a confusion and horror their training had not prepared them for. People were emerging dust-covered and bleeding from what remained of the building. A three-storey wall, weighing 300 tonnes and supporting a disembodied false ceiling, was leaning perilously at an angle of 60 degrees over the section that had collapsed. Cries for help came from people trapped in the debris, but it was obviously going to be difficult and dangerous to dig them out. Within 15 minutes the fire officers were joined by police and other emergency service workers and the slow and desperate task of removing the rubble began. Checks with people who had been in the club suggested that as many as 50 people might be trapped, a figure which fortunately proved to be an overestimate.

At the city's ambulance headquarters, just over a kilometre away in Hamilton, a wall of the building had collapsed in the earthquake, forcing officers to transfer to a generator-powered mobile control unit outside. Four people fielded calls for help and dispatched units without a break for five hours after the quake, trying to sort out which calls were the most urgent. The situation was complicated by the breakdown in communications. The officers staffing the mobile radio kept hearing the BHP explosion rumour, a story that wasn't put to rest until three-and-a-half hours after the earthquake. Like the rest of Newcastle, the steelworks had lost its electric power when the earthquake hit and had to stop production. The gas produced in its coke-making ovens, which was used in smelting iron and steel, had to be burnt off as a safety measure. It was the smoke and flames from this precaution-ary operation that caused panic among nearby residents and prompted the explosion rumour.

While the inner-city rescue effort was focused on the Workers Club, the emergency service workers in the other key damage area, Hamilton, were spread 500 metres along Beau-mont Street.

Near the northern end of the serious damage zone a sus-pended awning on the Kent Hotel collapsed onto the footpath. The hotel was nearing the end of a $300 000 refurbishment and the reaction of co-owner Pauline Stirling when the build-ing began vibrating in the earthquake was, 'Oh, god, what have the builders done?' Looking through a ground floor window, Stirling saw the awning falling slowly and pull-ing part of the wall away. One of the hotel staff rushed out and, seeing the legs of a child sticking out from beneath the rubble, hastily uncovered him. While the eight-year-old boy was able to walk away, a 59-year-old removalist, Cec Abbott, who had stopped outside the hotel for a chat while taking his lawnmower to a repair shop, died from multiple injuries when the awning hit him. Newcastle City Council subsequently amended its building code to require awnings and elevated verandas to be supported by props. Supporting poles had been removed in the 1950s because they were thought to be dangerous if struck by motor vehicles.

The earthquake produced some memorable sights and sounds as people volunteered their services to help the emergency workers. In Hamilton, for example, a bus driver called Eddie King stopped his vehicle in Beaumont St and asked police if they would like him to transport injured people to the then main Newcastle hospital, Royal Newcastle. The police had put a group of about 20 cut and bruised people into an undamaged bottle shop but by the time King stopped all but five had left the building. The quintet were put on to the bus and King drove away, singing at the top of his voice in an effort to cheer them up. Elsewhere, an off-duty policewoman in pink shorts and T-shirt had borrowed a police shirt from a colleague and was helping to control the traffic at a busy, rubble-strewn intersection. Community service groups lived up to their name. Stirling later recalled standing outside the Kent Hotel with dozens of other people involved in the rescue operation and eating 'wonderful spaghetti sandwiches' that the Salvation Army had prepared.

Royal Newcastle Hospital, a sprawling complex of buildings behind the city's main beach, was hastily evacuated when the earthquake struck. Medical Superintendent Brian Masters said that the hospital, like other public institutions, was unprepared for such an event. 'Our disaster planning had simply never contemplated the possibility of an earthquake isolating and disabling the hospital,' he said. A police vehicle was parked in a street outside the hospital executive suite while a policeman delivered a subpoena. Dr Masters, emerging from the hospital to take stock of the situation, noticed a loud-hailer in the car and commandeered it to direct the initial earthquake response. Hundreds of patients were evacuated from the hospital in 30 minutes, many carried on trolleys and stretchers, and put in a clifftop park behind the hospital or on the walkway at South Newcastle Beach, with small marquees erected to shade the most seriously ill. Anaesthetised patients were even taken from the operating theatres for fear that an aftershock would bring down walls that had been cracked by the initial shock. 'One chap having an arthroscopy awoke on a trolley in Fletcher Park gazing at the blue sky above—not quite a near-death experience, but something he won't forget,' Dr Masters said.

By early afternoon more than 300 emergency service personnel were at the Workers Club, searching for people in the rubble of the three collapsed floors. By late afternoon, the local emergency workers had been supplemented by personnel, vehicles and equipment from the NSW Central Coast towns of Gosford and Wyong, 85 kilometres away, and from Sydney. Bus timetables were suspended and the city's bus fleet was used to take workers home early from the city. As the evacuation was taking place, barricades were set up to restrict access to the CBD and adjoining suburbs while buildings were checked and made safe, or, in the most serious cases, demolished. The three-storey Newcastle Returned Services League Club, a central city building erected in 1911, was demolished within hours of the earthquake after one wall collapsed and the structure became unstable. Hundreds of residents were left temporarily homeless when the damage to their houses raised questions about safety.

By early evening several injured people had been rescued from the rubble at the Workers Club, Norm Duffy among them. Duffy became a folk hero in Newcastle for the way he helped to soothe the two scared women buried near him in the masonry and the darkness while they waited for rescuers to find them and get them out. The rescue effort was suspended for fifteen minutes at about midday when the police officer who had assumed command of the Workers Club operation ordered all the rescuers from the building after a high brick wall moved when touched. An engineer warned that it might collapse, particularly if there was an aftershock. Duffy was in agony, his left leg seriously injured, in the hours he was trying to give his companions hope. When he was finally pulled out of the hole, a paramedic realised that he was suffering from potentially fatal crush syndrome and, indeed, his heart did stop beating once he was safely outside the ruins. Paramedics were able to revive him and he spent the next five months in Royal Newcastle Hospital recovering from his ordeal. Others were not so fortunate. The rescue operation continued for 60 hours, coming to an end at 4 am on 31 December when the last bodies, those of two 60-year-old men, a club maintenance man and a friend who had called to see him, were recovered from the Workers Club basement.

Police orders for all the rescue workers to leave the Workers Club about an hour and a half after the earthquake and at several other times later in the day contributed to a prolonged, bitter and very public dispute between the key rescue services. The first few hours were critical to the chances of finding people alive, according to paramedics and to fire officers who were using heat-detecting equipment to try to locate survivors buried in the rubble. Police officers, while acknowledging this, told the coronial inquiry into the earthquake that they had acted on the advice of engineers. In the event, the withdrawal of rescue personnel from the ruins did not contribute to lives being lost. A Sydney-based forensic medicine specialist stated at the inquiry that eight of the victims would have died almost instantly from their injuries, while the ninth had suffered such severe blood loss and shock that he probably had survived for no more than an hour.

Twelve hours after the earthquake, a team of seismologists arrived from the Australian Geological Survey Organisation in Canberra and began setting up seismographs around the city to record the aftershocks that were expected to follow the earthquake. Team leader Kevin McCue contacted Lord Mayor John McNaughton the next morning to warn him that the city could expect an aftershock with a magnitude of 4.5 on the Richter scale between a day and seven days after the earthquake, followed by possibly hundreds of smaller tremors, each of diminishing intensity. This was the standard pattern with earthquakes, with the initial aftershock generally being about one full unit down the Richter scale from the quake's magnitude.

To the surprise of the seismologists and the relief of Novocastrians, the second big shake failed to eventuate. An aftershock with a magnitude of 2.1—strong enough to be recorded by a seismograph but too weak to be noticed by people—occurred at 8.08 pm on 29 December. There was also a stronger but still barely noticeable Richter scale 3 tremor two months later on 23 February 1990. For several years McCue attributed the lack of aftershocks to the comparative depth of the earthquake, but that theory went out the window on 6 August 1994 when a 5.4 magnitude earthquake hit the rural hamlet of Wallaby Gully, 49 kilometres west of Newcastle and 10 kilometres south-west of the city of Cessnock. The eight-second earthquake, which resulted in a $32 million payout on 8200 insurance claims—some in suburban Newcastle—was followed by an aftershock on 27 September with a small 1.3 magnitude. As the Wallaby Gully quake was a shallow one, barely 2 kilometres below the surface, its depth could hardly have been the reason for the size of the aftershock.

The NSW Department of Family and Community Services opened an earthquake disaster recovery centre in a suburban high school hall the morning after the earthquake and by day's end 1000 people had sought aid on accommodation and financial assistance, as well as social security advice. The centre continued to be busy until it closed in December 1991, as did an Earthquake Counselling Service set up by the Hunter Area Health Service that averaged 35 counselling sessions a week in the 12 months after the earthquake. The NSW Government and its federal counterpart were not to be so supportive in other respects, despite visits to Newcastle in the wake of the earthquake by Prime Minister Bob Hawke and Premier Nick Greiner, both of whom promised the full support of their governments for Newcastle's recovery. Once the immediate crisis was over, Novocastrians found that the promised support had qualifications attached to it.

Mayor McNaughton was holidaying at Tea Gardens, an hour's drive north of Newcastle, when the earthquake occurred. He was taken at high speed back to the city in a police wagon and called an immediate meeting of key players to work out who should take charge of the emergency: the lord mayor, town clerk, chief of police or local head of the defence force. No-one knew, but the meeting decided to give the role to the Newcastle Police Superintendent. This, as it turned out, was the right decision under the law as it stood in New South Wales. The meeting ended with the officials confident they would be able to manage the unexpected situation.

After all, the state of emergency they believed the NSW Government to have declared gave the police and Newcastle City Council extraordinary powers to take action such as ordering the demolition of dangerous buildings while the earthquake crisis lasted. The only trouble, as a still angry McNaughton revealed in July 1993 to a Senate committee inquiring into disaster responses, was that nobody in the NSW Government had declared a state of emergency. McNaughton only found that out when he contacted Premier Greiner a week later to seek a renewal of the declaration, as required by law.

The first sign of things to come followed the establishment by John McNaughton of the Lord Mayor's Earthquake Relief Fund on 31 December to handle the donations flowing in from all parts of Australia for earthquake victims. The Federal Government offered a sum of $250 000, but only on the condition that the NSW State Government would match the amount. In turn, Greiner, on the eve of a meeting with the Prime Minister on 3 January 1990 to discuss a post-earthquake restoration program for Newcastle, said the bulk of the money would have to come from the Commonwealth if the NSW Government was to repair its buildings quickly. While Greiner spoke of the need for something similar to the Darwin Reconstruction Commission, set up and financed by the Federal Government after the 1974 Darwin cyclone disaster, he came away from the meeting with Mr Hawke satisfied with an agreement for the two governments to fund the rebuilding on a dollar-for-dollar basis. The governments made it clear that no new organisation would be established to oversee the city's renewal.

The lack of coordination between government authorities soon persuaded Newcastle City Council that it would have to act alone in drawing up an earthquake renewal management plan. The plan, announced on 17 April 1990, gave the council the leadership role in coordinating the activities of organisations responsible for people services, the built environment and planning.

The council's initial approach to the governments to fund the employment of a renewal coordinator met with the response that the money could be taken from the Lord Mayor's Earthquake Relief Fund, even though the trust deed that governed the operation of the fund clearly stated that the money could not be used for such a purpose. The governments later agreed to fund the position, initially for a year, but said the council would have to meet the cost of all other renewal jobs.

On the eve of the second anniversary of the earthquake McNaughton said bluntly that the city was 'on its own', that 'the governments have walked away from us. They promised us the world in assistance immediately after the earthquake, but when it came to getting cash out of them we had to fight every inch of the way.'

This did indeed seem to Novocastrians to be the case. While Newcastle City Council was having difficulties three and four years after the earthquake in getting some owners of commercial buildings to bring them up to new earthquake safety standards, the NSW and Federal Governments, which should have led by example, had left major buildings barricaded and only partly repaired. Similarly, when the council sought a four-year assistance package from the Natural Disaster Relief Fund in 1991, the governments refused to fund costs the council had incurred because of the earthquake. The council was given $7 million, only half what it had sought. About $1.7 million of a $5.2 million claim for wages paid to extra staff taken on to handle the added workload the earthquake

engendered was rejected. A modest $165 000 claim to cover
the income lost when the council deferred sending out rate
notices in January 1990 because of the trauma caused by the
earthquake was also given the flick. The biggest item rejected
was $2 594 000 for the replacement of badly damaged sport-
ing facilities, including grandstands. This could not be paid,
the council was told, because it amounted to improvements
rather than repairs and would put the council in a better position than before the earthquake. The council's argument that
changed fire safety regulations meant that a repair job would
not be enough was ignored.

As the months and years passed after the earthquake,
scientists and others voiced concern that governments
were again paying too little attention to earthquake risks.
An insensitive decision in Canberra saw the removal of a
$20 000 seismograph from a monitoring post in Newcastle
on the eve of the first anniversary of the earthquake. The
recording device, the last of eight that had been brought to
the city straight after the tremor, was taken away despite
calls by geologists throughout Australia for Newcastle to
have a permanent seismograph in view of its history of earthquakes. A voluntary service organisation, the Kiwanis Club
of Newcastle, put forward $8000 to help buy the city its own
seismograph. Newcastle City Council matched the sum and
the Bureau of Mineral Resources, which owned the unit that
was removed, contributed $16 000. In 1992 the Federal Gov-
ernment allocated $1 500 000 over the next three years to
set up monitoring stations in other cities, hoping the states
would contribute. They did not.

While Newcastle City Council and business groups had
initially sought a Darwin-style reconstruction authority, the
city's recovery probably benefited from the absence of such a

bureaucratic body. The council took the lead from the outset and after a meeting with police and other emergency services on 31 December announced that efforts were being made to re-open the CBD on Monday 8 January—just 11 days after the earthquake. This was much earlier than the four to six weeks disaster experts had suggested to John McNaughton as the time that would be needed to make the extensively damaged area safe. Some adjacent suburbs in the exclusion zone had the barricades removed on 4 January—the residents were getting testy about the lack of services such as mail deliveries and having to show identification to get through the guarded barriers. The 8 January target was met, although speed restrictions and extra parking limits were placed on motor vehicles. Hamilton's Beaumont Street, on the other hand, was not fully re-opened to traffic for six weeks.

The post-earthquake period brought inevitable traumas and arguments. One of the hottest issues was the demolition of buildings held to have architectural and historical value. Heritage groups asserted that owners had taken advantage of the concern about aftershocks and further damage to win approval for the demolition of significant late 19th- and early 20th-century structures that could have been restored. While council officers denied that this was the case, the council took an increasingly more critical stance on demolition applications. Some buildings that were earmarked for demolition were eventually redeveloped as high-priced inner-city apartments in the late 1990s.

There were problems with under-insurance, and the timing of the earthquake—falling in the busy post-Christmas sale period—affected the viability of some businesses. The earthquake proved to be a boon for Newcastle in at least one respect, with the repair and reconstruction work on thousands of houses and commercial premises giving a healthy boost to the city's ailing building industry. While the Newcastle CBD continued to battle for shoppers' dollars throughout the 1990s, this was due more to competition from suburban shopping complexes than from the earthquake. Beaumont Street, by contrast, boomed once the scaffolding was down. Known as Newcastle's 'Eat Street' before the earthquake, it strengthened its hold on that name, with a greater variety of restaurants being opened. The City Council's post-earthquake planning guidelines also ensured that the street retained its appealing 1920s character. Newcastle Workers Club, for its part, was back in business in an all-new $20 million building on the same site, opened by Prime Minister Paul Keating on 3 July 1992.

The council was labelled as hard-hearted by some people over the rules it applied to disbursement of funds from the Lord Mayor's Earthquake Relief Fund, but the fund trustees correctly followed procedures that ensured that account-ability was visible. By the time the fund was wound up in December 1994 and its remaining assets transferred to a new Newcastle Region Natural Disaster Relief Fund Trust, it had disbursed $9.9 million in grants and loans to earthquake victims and still had $1.3 million in cash and investments—evidence of its careful management, given that $7.9 million had been donated to the fund. The deed of the replacement trust allowed 50 percent of its funds to be donated to any disaster-hit area in Australia.

The Council also became embroiled in a series of legal actions arising from the collapse of the Workers Club and claims about approvals the Council had given for a series of extensions to the club in the two decades before the earth-quake. At one stage 13 people injured when the club collapsed were suing the Council and the Club, and the Council and the Club were suing each other, but also jointly suing the architect, engineer and builder of the extensions. Soon after, the Council was suing the insurer it had when the earthquake occurred. Most of the actions were eventually settled out of court. The most serious casualty of the legal imbroglio was an official history of the earthquake, a project the Council shelved in 1992 on the legal advice of its insurer because the information in the document might have posed what a town clerk's minute to the council called 'unacceptable risks' to the organisation.

The 1989 Newcastle earthquake led to many changes in disaster management in Australia. Rescue operations were hampered by the incompatibility of mobile radio and computer systems operated by the emergency services, as well as by rivalries between the services. Clear lines of command were subsequently established and more compatible communications equipment was introduced. Newcastle City Council, community organisations and emergency services jointly produced a local disaster management plan (Displan), which has been used as a model by other towns and cities in Australia and overseas. Adopted in March 1994, Displan provides a clear picture of what must be done in an emergency and who is responsible for getting the things done. The plan is constantly updated by a management committee.

The most significant changes, however, have been to the national building code. A new earthquake building design standard, AS1170, was introduced in 1993 to ensure that the damage caused in earthquakes was minimised and sustainable. Under the code, the former no-earthquake-risk zone 0 was abolished and towns and areas were rated on a new earthquake hazard map according to their risk of experiencing an earthquake. The ratings were based on the expected ground acceleration rates of seismic waves. Newcastle, with an acceleration coefficient of 0.11, has the highest risk rating of a major urban centre. The rating means that Newcastle has a ten percent chance in a 50-year period of experiencing an earthquake with an acceleration coefficient of 0.11. The risk ratings for other major urban centres are: 0.10 for Adelaide and Geelong ; 0.09 for Perth; 0.08 for Sydney, Wollongong, Canberra, Melbourne, Darwin and Rockhampton; and 0.06 for Brisbane, Cairns and the Gold Coast. The code applies to new domestic construction as well as to commercial buildings, although only one type of domestic construction is affected: double cavity brickwork on soft soil. Buildings used by essential services require more stringent designs. The new national code is tougher than an interim one implemented by Newcastle City Council in 1990, which introduced A and 1 zone ratings from the 1979 code.

Having experienced three earthquakes with a Richter magnitude of 5 or more in 150 years, most Novocastrians expect there will be a similar quake within half a century of 1989. The Australian Geological Survey Organisation's Kevin McCue told the 1990 coronial inquiry into the earthquake deaths that there was a 65 percent chance of such a quake taking place near Newcastle within 55 years. The Wallaby Gully earthquake four years later proved him right, but whether there will be other moderate earthquakes is anyone's guess. Certainly a lot of research has been done in the area around Newcastle since 1989 to try to learn more about why the earthquake occurred and to predict the damage of further such events, but none of the mysteries associated with the earthquake have been resolved.

In August 2000 a geological team from Queensland University of Technology reported the finding of a 40-kilometre long fault beneath the Pacific Ocean, about 20 kilometres south-east of Newcastle. This fault, they claimed, was the source of the 1989 earthquake. The finding was greeted cautiously by other seismic researchers who said more information was needed before such a claim could be considered.

The vast and troubling gaps in knowledge about earthquakes are reflected in the powerful final scene of *Aftershocks*, a play by Paul Brown and the Newcastle Workers Cultural Action Committee that looks at the 1989 Newcastle earthquake through the eyes and words of people who were associated with Newcastle Workers Club. The play, first staged in Newcastle in 1991, ends with John Constable, a young Workers Club cleaner who has daringly rescued two of his fellow workers with no recognition until the play was staged, telling of a recurring nightmare in which he finds the core of the earthquake. It is below the club's basement, but when he opens a door in the tunnel he finds himself on the street outside the club. The mystery hasn't been solved. The threat of the earthquake is still there, somewhere in the rocks below Newcastle. It is a conclusion that leaves audiences stunned and silent.

10

The Thredbo Landslide, 1997

Carinya Lodge was gone.

Manos Ellard, Thredbo resident

On the metal path up the slope to the summit of Australia's highest mountain, Mt Kosciuszko, a summer tour guide might point to a rock with a low-lying shrub clinging to it, a Mountain Plum Pine, *Podocarpus lawrencei*, growing at 1800 metres, far above where other trees can survive. It survives, as it has since it sprouted some 400 years ago, on heat stored in the rock. Within it, if the searcher is patient enough, might be found a Pygmy Possum, *Barramyidae parvus*, a mouse-sized mammal thought to have been extinct until the fresh remains of one were discovered. This tiny mammal survives by hibernating during the winter, otherwise moving in the space between snow and ground. In the summer period it only comes out at night. In fact, too much sunlight can kill it. Wary of foxes, it has survived because it has adapted precisely to the conditions, responding to every change, sensing every danger.

It is a harsh environment, one that has developed over millions of years of extremes. Ground moss holds up to seven times its weight in water, releasing a steady trickle that spills down the mountainside, ensuring that the lower reaches have moisture. It is extremely fragile, taking 30 years to recover at any place where a traveller treads on it.

All through the Snowy Mountains there is one clear message: these conditions need to be treated with respect. If they do not get that respect, they hit back. Skiers get lost and die, snowboarders dig caves during snowstorms and die there and buses topple off roads never intended for such vehicles. People have indeed survived, many because they have been careful and knowledgeable, but most, in modern times, because nothing has happened to put them to a serious test. Because of the attractiveness of the snow and all its opportunities for enjoyment, the lure of cabins and taverns and food, such traits as humility, canniness and caution are often discarded or forgotten.

When the Snowy Mountains Hydro-Electricity Authority (SMHEA) bulldozed a road through the mountains in about 1955 to assist with its magnificent engineering scheme, its directors had clearly shown how people, in specified circumstances, can master nature. To get from one point to another, it was necessary just to do a rough grade, pushing uncompacted earth, rocks and trees to one side. SMHEA, which had initial responsibility for maintaining the road, was not averse to the idea of tourists coming to look at its works. Over time, the road, though it was only ever a rough construction road with an anticipated life of 20 years, was to become a fixture known as the Alpine Way, 108 kilometres between Jindabyne in the east and Khancoban in the west.

In 1955 Tony Sponar found what he thought was a suitable site in Crackenback Valley for a resort area and four people formed a syndicate called the Kosciusko Chairlift and Thredbo Hotel. In 1958, Kosciusko Thredbo Ltd was floated as a public company. The SMHEA commissioner, Sir William Hudson, asked a senior engineering geologist, Mr D.G. Moye, to do an inspection. Moye identified two areas below the Alpine Way in Crackenback Valley that he thought were unstable. One had a creek flowing through it, which made him think that development, such as cutting into the hillside, should be done with great caution. The other area was swampy ground between two creeks. The Alpine Way was upgraded in 1958, but nothing could compensate for the slipshod nature of the original construction. There were slumps or slides along its length in 1958 and 1959. It should have been apparent that the road needed to be reconstructed from its foundations. Instead the maintenance authorities depended on what really amounted to band-aid work.

In November 1961 Lend Lease Corporation bought the shares in the Kosciusko Thredbo Ltd, forming a new company, Kosciusko Thredbo Pty Ltd (KT1). In doing so, it leased the village area from the Kosciuszko State Park Trust. With Lend Lease joining the party, development was set to take off. The following month a surveyor completed a plan for the first subdivision. The sites considered suitable for building, beneath 1.3 kilometres of embankment holding up the Alpine Way, were given lot numbers. Significantly, some areas were not given numbers, including one area that had two streams running through it and an area of bog grass. The area, which would have been 'Lot 61' on the survey had a lot number been allocated, was adjacent to the Alpine Way and coincided with the area that Moye had pointed out.

On a measure of steepness comparing horizontal and vertical distances, a ratio of more than 1:1 horizontally to vertically gives some promise of stability, increasing as the ratio increased. When it gets towards 1:1 it becomes a sheer cliff. Less than 1:1 represents a concave cliff. The slope above Lot 61 was 1:2, which meant, because the embankment was comprised only of uncompacted road fill, that it was only of marginal stability. Control of excess water was vital to maintain the embankment. With proper drainage, the slope had at least a chance of being maintained indefinitely, but even without human intervention there were signs of gradual movement in the hillside, a natural creep later estimated to be anything from one to ten millimetres, but on the best estimate perhaps two millimetres per year. A closer examination would have shown that trees on the upper slope were leaning, or had 'pistol' shapes, consistent with the ground moving while they were growing, then stabilising, to allow the trees to resume vertical growth.

The area below the Alpine Way at this point, including Lot 61, was in fact the site of an ancient landslide that had occurred hundreds, possibly thousands, of years before. There was nothing from a superficial point of view to stop development, though proper engineering works would be needed to ensure stability. The then village manager at Thredbo said, 'This lot is extinguished, but the so-called unbuildable slip area is not necessarily unbuildable'.

The road continued to provide warnings. A major landslide occurred on 2 October 1964, barely missing Winterhaus Lodge and causing considerable consternation. The slide cut off Thredbo, at least in one direction for several weeks. There had been cracks in the pavement, unusual flows of water and distortion of the road surface. An engineer said the slide had been caused by water saturation of uncompacted fill, and added, 'The steep underslip below the road and the proximity of guest houses made it difficult to provide any additional support for the fill'. The owners of the Winterhaus Lodge complained that no remedial work was being done despite the warning. The SMHEA drafted a letter saying the park trust had allowed the development to continue 'without reference to the needs for maintenance of the road along the steep terrain where slips have not been infrequent'. The authority decided not to send the letter. Instead it sent a note promising work would be done.

The road was repaired, but no long-term plan was prepared. The NSW State Coroner, Derrick Hand, was later to note that Gerarduz Dusseldorp, chairman of Lend Lease and KT1, agitated that the Alpine Way be upgraded to give better access to Thredbo. The focus, however, was not on the section above the village. The impression in hindsight is that the business executives were more interested in getting people to Thredbo than protecting them on arrival, but there would have been no conscious decision to expose people to risk.

Who was to do the work on the road was subject of an ongoing squabble between the shire, the SMHEA and the park trust, all of whom pleaded lack of funds. The squabble was sufficient enough to be the subject of an article in the *Sydney Morning Herald* on 13 June 1965.

In January that year KT1 designated Lot 61 on its plans as suitable for building. This site coincided with what Moye had singled out as an unstable area. Adjacent lots were developed. The park superintendent, Neville Gare, decided that Lot 61, now renumbered as 'Lot 78/79', or 'Lot 78', could also be built on subject to examination of the ramifications of building so close to the road. He warned that if development was crowded in the vicinity of the embankment, it would restrict the ability to work on the road. He suggested that the NSW Department of Main Roads (DMR) should be consulted, but the DMR replied that it was not in a position to give advice as it did not control the Alpine Way. In October 1965 the park trust approved Lend Lease's development proposal, but said that no development should go over the lease boundaries closer to the road embankment than the plans allowed.

No architect or engineer missed completely the dangers of the road. John James, an architect retained by Lend Lease, warned Dusseldorp in August 1965 that there should be close attention to drainage. He suggested redirection of water away from what he thought was a particularly vulnerable part of the road, but KT1 said it was not responsible for the Alpine Way, which it was under the control of the SMHEA. In effect, road maintenance was being shrugged off while development proceeded. In November that year engineer and then village manager Albert van der Lee prepared a plan on which he put the word 'slide' on the space representing Lot 78. The inclusion of the word did not appear to trouble anyone. As development continued, boundaries became more refined and the area marked 'slide' became a reserve.

In April 1968, the YMCA Ski Club (Canberra) took an option to build a lodge on Lot 78. The plans referred to the site as an 'old creek bed'. Van der Lee's initial advice to the architect was that the builder needed to check whether the subsoil and fill batter required drainage. He said building on the old creek bed was 'probably possible' once drainage factors were dealt with. He assumed the architect would take these things into account and design a building to suit the conditions. The lodge was built by volunteer labour between October 1968 and mid-1969. Van der Lee allowed an increase in the width of Carinya Lodge—as the lodge came to be named—by six metres, taking it into the area of swamp grass. If Van der Lee was justified in at least some of his assumptions, there were clear lapses in others. The National Parks and Wildlife Service (NPWS) did not give its approval until October 1969, well after work had started. The Snowy River Shire Council did not give approval to any building application at the time. Eventually it was given retrospectively on 9 December 1971.

1968 saw another landslide along the Alpine Way. That year the SMHEA handed over responsibility for the park roads, including the Alpine Way, to the NPWS. The NPWS in turn asked the DMR to act as its maintenance agent, with the SMHEA, which still made some use of the roads, agreeing to contribute $200 000 a year for the next 10 years, $150 000 a year for the following five years, and $100 000 a year for five years after that.

It was not hard to see that things needed to be done. On 1 April 1968 the DMR undertook an inspection and its engineer noted that the road was 'tending to slip down onto the village'. Attempts were made to have Alpine Way declared a main road, which would have made it the direct responsibility of the DMR, but the DMR resisted, saying it did not have the money. Nobody took the health of the road to heart as a personal mission. The DMR said it acted on NPWS direction, but the NPWS relied on the DMR for advice.

Early in the history of Carinya, residents noted there was plenty of water around. In *Christie*, the YMCA's journal, there was an item in 1970 under the heading, 'Did You Hear?'. It said, 'Try standing outside the drying room door and listening to the sound of trickling water coming from under the stairs. You have heard about the car that floats on fluid. Now we have a lodge that does the same thing!' The YMCA's interest in Carinya was taken over by the Brindabella Ski Club. In 1973–4 the four-storey Bimbadeen Ski Lodge was constructed further to the north, on the other side of Bobuck Lane. This was the ground that Moye had noted as the swampy ground between two streams, but many good and fruitful ski seasons were enjoyed by all members, going out into the snow by day, living it up in the village and sleeping snugly in their apartments.

Warning voices continued. In 1971 a NPWS engineer called Isberg wrote, 'The general impression of the area is that development close to the road batter should never have been allowed'. More slides occurred on the Alpine Way in 1973 and 1974. In October 1978 fifty metres of the Alpine Way broke away three kilometres east of the village. Hundreds of tonnes of rock, mud and trees slipped 200 metres into the Thredbo River. There had been heavy rains for a week and several springs had been flowing into the batter. Warning cracks had appeared on the road. Such was the concern that the NPWS declined to approve a proposal by KT1 that a new subdivision be created below the Alpine Way. This was known as the 'Western Subdivision'. The NPWS retained a consulting firm, Coffey and Partners, to do a study and the firm said that at this point the Alpine Way was of 'marginal stability'. The DMR said that the Western Subdivision should not go ahead until the Alpine Way was reconstructed, but added that repair of slip areas on the Alpine Way was usually very expensive and not terribly efficient, and that it was 'not economically feasible' to undertake these particular major reconstruction works.

Bill Dagger, a building surveyor with the NPWS, instituted a system that required a preliminary geotechnical report for all new buildings or major alterations in Thredbo, but still the question of whether there was imminent danger to the existing village was not addressed. Other developments were occurring that in retrospect had further safety implications.

In November 1978 consulting engineers Judell Platt were retained to do a major upgrade of the water reticulation system in Thredbo. They used asbestos cement piping with Supertite joints, reinforcing the pipe at every turn and bend with 'thrust blocks' and 'anchor blocks' that—in accordance with James Hardie and Company Pty Ltd, manufacturers of the pipe—needed to be installed adjacent to the turns and bends to counter the tendency of rushing water to push the pipe out of alignment. The size of these blocks needed to be precisely calculated. The pipes themselves, though widely used, were quite brittle. If they were to be used, the manufacturers instructions had to be strictly adhered to.

Dagger was also one of those conscientious enough to notice the landslide menace. He had written in 1979 that for years he had had ongoing concerns about the stability of the Alpine Way. Had the 1978 landslide occurred above Thredbo Village, he said, there would have been considerable damage, and there were three or four locations on the road above the village that required special precautions. He had insisted on proper footings for new buildings and retaining walls. Such precautions, together with attention to drainage, might have sufficed, but proper preparation, according to a consultant geotechnical engineer, Tim Sullivan's observation, years later, necessitated making the site impregnable against fill subsistence.

The countdown to tragedy began when a water main was proposed that would run along the northern shoulder of the Alpine Way. This installation was undertaken to satisfy the NSW Board of Fire Commissioners, who wanted a source of water to fight fires in lodges or bushfires in that area. In 1983 van der Lee told the NPWS of the plans to install the water main. Water was to be pumped uphill from the Thredbo

River, kept in two storage tanks, each with a capacity to hold 90 000 litres, and then released along the main, which was to run east along the Alpine Way, then dive downhill in a northerly direction between Carinya and Schuss Lodges. It was to be built through the very area that had been marked 'slide' by van der Lee so many years before, and then it would join the town water main at Bobuck Lane, near Bimbadeen Lodge.

Jim Smith, a DMR foreman, walked the proposed route of the water main along the Alpine Way in company with Peter Wright, a KT1 supervisor, and Philip Rye, a contractor. Smith said the main should be set back from the road and buried at a depth of 60 centimetres. KT1 started work without getting approval from the NPWS. When the work was brought to Dagger's attention he ordered it to stop. On 4 May 1984 KT1 resort engineer Michael McConnell sent a development/building application to the NPWS, saying construction was 'rather urgent'. The next day Dagger gave his approval, but in doing so said that 'particular emphasis shall be placed on the consolidation of back fill along the top bank of the road'. He also said, 'The area below is a slip zone and the build-up of water in a soft trench could increase the risk of movement.' Dagger said the DMR should give a letter of approval for the proposed route. No such letter was ever, apparently, obtained, and when it came to actually ensuring that the road batter was compacted, Dagger assumed that would be the job of the KT1 engineer. Three days later Dagger approved an application for extensions to Schuss Lodge, in an adjoining lot to Carinya, saying as he did that there should be a geotechnical report to take into account factors of site stability.

The ten centimetre pipe was made of asbestos cement with Supertite joints and had the same requirement for thrust and anchor blocks. The construction, between April and June

1984, was undertake by a work team from KT1 supervised by Andy Griffiths, who received no detailed plans but instead relied on his earlier experience upgrading the Thredbo reticulation system. He decided the one way to counter the water pressures and their distorting effects was to encase at least some couplings and joints in concrete, rather than put the thrust and anchor blocks adjacent to the bends and turns as the James Hardie construction manual recommended. The effect of this was to make the pipe less flexible.

Lend Lease saw the construction as a minor work. McConnell did not provide any design documentation and contented himself with driving past to ensure that work was in progress. Dagger did not think there should be any greater engineering involvement. He said later that he only referred matters to NPWS engineers if they related to major capital works. In effect the construction team was left to decide for itself which thrust and anchor blocks, if any, were to be built. In all probability the 90 to 100 degrees north turn downhill to Bobuck Lane was done in one bend, creating a huge amount of water pressure at that point. In all probability, Hand found later, the 'Schuss bend', as it was later referred to, was totally encased in concrete. The turn could have been done in two 45-degree bends, which would have lessened the pressure on those points, but there is no evidence that that was done.

What was lacking was any ready means of checking the pipe. Had it been laid along the ground, the pipe might have been subject to damage from general exposure or things falling on it. It would have been unsightly, although it might have been camouflaged by rock facing. It could have been laid along a concrete drain that would take away any water that leaked. If it was exposed it could have been checked at any time. Instead it was underground, deep enough for leaking water to get into the fill without even showing itself at the surface. So concealed was the pipe that its presence might not even have been taken into account in further calculations about road repairs, development or stability. If the original pipe layers were prepared to swear by the efficiency of Super-tite joints, they were wrong. The pipes had not been designed to withstand the 'pullout' forces produced by ground creep.

In 1984 the DMR decided to reconstruct a lot of the Alpine Way, but it did not include the section above Thredbo because of the cost, enhanced by the awkwardness of such close-up development. The people in greatest danger were not to suffer large-scale inconvenience. The seasons came and went and so did the visitors, trundling up to the mountains with their skis and snowboards. There was the odd tragedy. In August 1985 Stephen Crean, a Commonwealth public servant and son of the former Federal minister Frank Crean, left Charlotte pass on a pair of skis, telling friends he would be back for lunch. He apparently got lost, and after perhaps days in the wilderness made it to a point 60 metres from the Alpine Way, only three kilometres from Thredbo. His skeletal remains were found in January 1987.

That year Lend Lease sold its shares to Greenfields Pty Ltd, which changed its name to Kosciusko Thredbo Pty Ltd (KT2). Shares were held by Amalgamated Holdings. A year later the SMHEA, as per agreement, withdrew from any involvement in funding the Alpine Way. The NPWS had total responsibility for funding the maintenance, drawing from its own budget with occasional injections of cash from special grants by the NSW State Government. The NPWS retained the Snowy Mountains Shire Council to do maintenance. In April 1988 the shire engineer, Robert Bright, warned about the state of the Alpine Way and said the section above Thredbo was 'in poor condition and requiring remedial work'. In 1989 a 20-metre wide section of road broke away and dropped 200 metres two kilometres east of Thredbo. KT2 initiated a study of the possibility of Thredbo being isolated by a landslide and concluded that if there were to be any slide, there would be sufficient warning from cracks in the road.

From late 1990 Tony Sullivan, a district engineer with the NPWS, joined the list of people who had expressed concern about Alpine Way. In 1991 the consulting firm Sinclair Knight and Partners warned that the Alpine Way was in bad shape and needed urgent remedial work, warning that a road failure had the capacity to 'damage property and subsequently endanger human life'. That report was used by the NPWS to get more funding for work on the Alpine Way, but the funds were not directed to the road above the village. The creep continued imperceptibly and the water main, undetected and undetectable, suffered in silence.

The Roads and Traffic Authority (RTA), which had by then replaced the DMR, did make inspections. In August, 1991 Sullivan took David Warren-Gash, an RTA geotechnical expert, on a tour and pointed out the problems of the road. Warren-Gash noted the place in the village area with two watercourses running through it and, looking uphill, saw that the trees were distorted, indicating continuing earth movements. He told Sullivan there was 'nothing of immediate concern' and that inclinometres—instruments that measure earth movements—should be installed at strategic points on the road: two of them at culverts above the village, to give adequate warning of movement. Warren-Gash had said the inclinometers would give 'peace of mind' and recommended that steeper fills be supported 'as the need arises and funds become available'. The pipeline was not mentioned.

In February 1992 inclinometres were installed at three places above Thredbo Village. In January 1993 Warren-Gash told the NPWS he had done inclinometer readings above Thredbo and had detected movement in one of them that was only slight and associated with normal earth movements. At the other one (which happened to be at the western end of what was later the landslide site), there was 'nothing to worry about', but the road elsewhere continued to sound its warnings elsewhere, suffering washouts in early 1993 and 1994. If the Alpine Way water main was out of site and mind, there were plenty of other warnings that pipes anywhere could suffer problems.

Steven Vassallo, a plumber and chief operator of the Thredbo water supply and water main system at the time, repaired a number of pipes. One he believed had been damaged by ground movement, another by traffic, and yet another by general development. A 20 centimetre asbestos cement pipe running up the side of Bimbadeen Lodge failed in 1993. Vassallo noticed a steady flow of water coming from the ground and when he excavated the pipe next day he found a small fracture—enough to send water spurting out, thereby bringing it quickly to notice. At another breakage Vassallo had noticed water pooling on the ground, on a straight section of the water main on the Alpine Way, about 100 metres from the Schuss car park. If that had been allowed to leak, he said, the fill would have become saturated. Vassallo reported the fractures to his superiors who had told him that the system of reticulation was under review. The assistant village engineer, Euan Diver, was concerned that if water pipes leaked in the vicinity of Bobuck Lane, well below the Alpine Way, that a large section of Bobuck Lane would wash out.

On the Alpine Way front, Warren-Gash continued to do surveys until his term ended in 1996. He did not express concern or make recommendations about reconstructing the road above the village, but the NPWS did attend to general upgrade of the road, including sealing the Alpine Way along its course, particularly on its western end towards Khancoban. Above Thredbo, attention was paid to the 'Winterhaus Corner' because it was a traffic hazard. The NPWS decided that the hillside should be cut into in order to widen the road, and that a retaining wall be built to keep the soil back. The wall was designed in 1995 and, delayed by the eternal problem of funding, constructed between 5 February and 27 March 1997.

Had someone been looking for them, they would have seen signs that something was already wrong. There had been an increase in water around Carinya Lodge since early 1996. Evidence was later to be presented, though it remained contentious, that dampness was found in the surface of the Schuss Lodge car park. The lodge manager, Ron O'Reilly, said later that in June that year that he had wanted to move a post that had been embedded 45 centimetres and that it had come out easily and that it had been wet. In July 1997 water was seen on the basement floor of Carinya, when there was no rainfall to account for it. A ski club member, Terry Gee, said, 'Every bit of ground was holding water as opposed to water running through the area.' From 25–7 July, resident Jacqueline Vicki Dunstan noticed water running through the lodge's garbage enclosure.

On the night of 29 July occupants of several lodges heard strange sounds around them. Frederick Law, a visitor from Gosford NSW, heard a 'creaking, like a tension type of noises, like something being twisted . . . the actual sound itself was something I have never heard before. It reminds me of something you would expect to hear in a boat, with flexing and twisting'. At 10.30 pm David Eager, a resident of Schuss Lodge, heard what he described as 'a low, rumbling noise'. On the evening of 30 July, between 12.30 am and 6 am, residents of Gunyang Lodge heard noises which one described as 'a major cracking or groaning' and a 'scraping sound'. Between 9 and 10.30 pm that night, residents of Schuss and Gunyang Lodges heard 'loud, unusual cracking or squelching noises'. The tortured earth appeared to be fighting back, giving way only grudgingly, but in fact, on later expert evidence, that it was an initial slide. Nobody thought to really question what these odd sounds meant.

On the night of 30 July William Reeve, of Roseville in Sydney, went to clean his teeth in Gunyang Lodge and found that the water he turned on was 'totally black'. He went back to his room and then heard 'a loud roar, followed by a crack and a whoosh'. It was 11.40 pm. The main slide had started. The first collapse was from the south-west corner, near the Schuss car park. Earth and mud broke away and slid, carrying off trees, removing the support of another mass of earth, which began sliding north-east towards Carinya. Eager heard the same low rumble he had heard the night before. The mass, comprising about 1300 tonnes of earth and rock, hit Carinya, killing its one occupant, John Cameron. Carinya toppled forward and slid with the mass across Bobuck Lane onto Bimbadeen, which collapsed, the concrete slabs of its four floors crushing everything that was inside. Refrigerators, washing machines, driers, beds, mattresses, filing cabinets and computers were squashed, sometimes into mere centimetres of space. Among the chaos, intermixed with water and mud, trapped in their beds or knocked down in the few seconds they tried to flee, were 18 people.

Within minutes emergency services had been called. Residents ventured onto the site. One man stepped into what appeared to be quicksand, coming up to his thighs, and quickly retreated. He saw water gushing downhill. Another would-be rescuer, William Reeve, heard what he believed was 'a call for help'. 'I heard this while at the side entrance,' he said. Manos Ellard, at the time a Thredbo pizza parlour employee, heard people calling for survivors. 'There was no verbal response, there was scratching,' he said. 'Carinya was gone yet it seemed to be coming from the back of where Carinya had been. We walked to an area near the centre of the slide site, what was later termed the A-shape due to the appearance of some concrete slabs. On the downside of the slide the mud in sections came up to my knees and a lot of water was still running down the slope in a stream-like fashion. When we got within the A-shape structure, I could hear the voices of a male and a female person. The voices were faint but the male appeared to be saying, "Help!"'

Martin Thomas, a ski instructor, moved towards the voices. He heard a female voice saying in a calm, controlled way, 'Hello?' He also heard a man calling out in an American accent: 'Help me, I don't want to die!' An ambulance officer, John Bartley, crawled under that A-shape, or 'A-frame' and came within a metre of trapped people. 'The only word I could hear was 'help!', he said. 'It was said repeatedly.' He could hear the sound of gurgling, he said, consistent with someone drowning. He continued crawling, until he was on his stomach, but then a station officer grabbed him by the ankle, fearing for his safety, and hauled him out. Other people said they heard voices coming from the rubble on the night. Two people, later identified as skiing instructors

Michael and Miriam Sodergren, 46 and 41 respectively, were heard trapped beneath the A-frame.

People, stumbling round in the darkness and wet and cold, were limited in their ability to do anything. They were also in danger from further sliding. Nobody knew how the slide was going to behave, certainly not in the darkness. No responsible authority would have exposed anybody to further risk. It was certainly too dangerous for anybody to go tunnelling. Police evacuated the site. Forty minutes after the slide the water stopped flowing. The water storage tanks at the top had drained through the fractured pipe. On August 1 Senior Constable Peter Stephen, an expert in closed spaces rescue, went tunnelling beneath the A-frame and found the bodies of the Sodergrens. The parents of Michael Sodergren later questioned whether they might have been saved had people gone straight in. Medical evidence later suggested that the Sodergrens might have survived up to three hours, but whether a rescue was feasible in such a time-frame and in such circumstances was another matter. State Coroner Hand was to find that he was satisfied the decision not to do immediate tunnelling was 'a correct one'.

The emergency services and the media descended upon the site over the next few days: police, State Emergency Service volunteers, ambulance officers, fire brigade officers, consultant engineers and NPWS officers. Profiles of the victims indicated that they had been for the most part employees at the resort, youthful, vigorous and full of fun. All of them had been caught in the disaster, as most victims are, purely by chance. There was predictable pathos in what was written about the incident. Journalist Paul McGeough described Oscar Luhn and Aino Sensburn as, 'two lonely people who had wandered the snow country for 30 years before discovering that they loved each other only 12 months before their death.'

As the cranes got to work, the pathetic personal belongings of the victims could be seen: books, shirts still on hangars, bedding, piles of clothes neatly folded. Journalist James Woodford wrote, 'Through binoculars from a vantage point at the other side of the valley other personal items remained tantalisingly visible but out of reach—a pillow, coloured blankets and perhaps, most bizarrely, a poster-sized Vodka advertisement, which because of its bright colour was prominent throughout most of the day.'

Despite the huge effort, involving 600 rescuers working in shifts round the clock, only one survivor, Stuart Diver, was located. He had been lying in pitch blackness, holding the hand of his dead wife, Sally. A reservations manager at the Thredbo Alpine Resort, Sally had been pinned down by a concrete block. Stuart had tried to lift her head above the water but she had died instantly. Freezing, covered in mud and propping himself on his elbows to keep his own head above water, not knowing whether he would ever be released from his tomb, he had hallucinated at times, but had eventually heard the rescuers coming for him. He was brought to the surface in the late afternoon of Saturday, 2 August, having been buried nearly 66 hours, and suffering frostbitten toes. The last body, that of Tony Weaver, who had died of head and chest injuries, was removed at 2 am on 7 August, nine days after the landslide, in pelting rain that was whipped through the trees by a fierce wind.

Memorial services were held. The parents of Stephen Urosevic, 32, who had been front office manager at the Thredbo Alpine Hotel and was killed at Bimbadeen, sobbed and said, 'Where is our Steve? Where is our Steve?' There were immediately questions as to who was responsible. In hindsight the warnings had been screaming out for years. Tom Gallard, a former ranger, exclaimed, 'It is not as though everyone didn't know about this!'

Most of the water main had been carried away in the land-slide, but some remained. It was found in that section that at least two joints had been separated sufficiently to allow leaking. One joint was found to have pulled out 52 milli-metres. Another had pulled out 13 millimetres. The largest separation was at a bend of 11.25 degrees where there was no thrust block. According to expert evidence, a bend of this magnitude without thrust block support would have resulted in the pipe developing a rocking motion as water flowed. It was possible that the separations had been caused by the landslide itself, but there were other indications that the pipe had indeed been leaking: the fact that the south-western corner of what was then the scarp, which extended 30 metres along the Alpine Way, was wet and the rest was mostly dry; the saturation of ground in the Shuss car park; the apparent scouring pattern in the ground indicating that there had been water running.

An inquest was held by Derrick Hand in 1999 and 2000. Lend Lease, the RTA, the NPWS, shire council, individual witnesses and families of the victims were all represented. Altogether there were 16 parties involved in the inquest which, assisted by Ruth McColl SC, went through the history of the Alpine Way and the village development. It quickly became apparent that the many, many warnings about land-slide over the years had been lost or ignored. Some parties were naturally concerned about liability. Lend Lease, whose period at Thredbo had seen the construction of the water pipe, and the NPWS, which had approved the construction, the DMR (represented by its successor the RTA), which had approved the route, and KT2, which had taken over the village and with it the responsibility for maintenance, were all keenly interested in what would ultimately be found to have triggered the slide.

Lend Lease presented a theory that the construction of the Winterhaus retaining wall, which had been an initiative of the NPWS, had inadvertently triggered the landslide because its construction had provided a passage for water to get from above the road through an aquifer to the other side of the road and into the fill. A particular 'I-beam', used in the construction and dug into the bottom of the culvert on the south side of the Alpine Way, was singled out as the likely culprit, its hole providing a possible channel for the water to get into the aquifer. Some highly qualified experts supported the theory. One, Andrew Shirley, argued that five holes drilled into the surface of the road for poles supporting the retaining wall had provided a pathway for the water.

Heavy machinery, including a ten-tonne vibrating roller, had been used on the road, close to the water main, which possibly brought further stresses to bear. Nobody was thinking about the pipe, and the vibrations through the soil might have had an impact on it, though how much is difficult to say. Michael John Polin, a civil engineer, gave evidence that it was not uncommon for asbestos cement water pipes to break as a result of heavy traffic loads imposed on top of the trench. 'I would have thought that wheel loads, a truck, anything could have dislodged that joint at that time,' he said.

Dr Laurence de Ambrosis, a geomechanical engineer, said the soil creep was the critical factor. By his calculations, it would have been three millimetres a year. 'The soil will grip the pipe and take it with it,' he said. 'I believe that changes in the creep would have induced gradual bending of the pipeline within its fracture limits.' The pipeline was particularly vulnerable to stresses when it moved between stable areas and unstable ones. Once stresses were transferred to the pipe, there was a risk of the pipe fracturing or a joint pulling out. De Ambrosis believed that the water had eventually started leaking, and that the leak had increased with increasing pressure. He believed that eventually water had forced its way to the surface of Schuss car park, forming pipe holes in the ground where it spurted and leaving a layer of silt. Other evidence of leaking including washed gravel in the northern part of the water main trench and differential wetting of the scarp. De Ambrosis believed that the pipe had been leaking for 'some time', but how long he could not say.

Once the leak started, the water build-up would have been quick enough. Michael Polin said that a pipe leaking at a tenth of a litre per second would give the equivalent volume of a running tap, and in a very short time deliver 120 cubic metres, the equivalent of a backyard swimming pool. A slow leak over a long period of time, he said, would create saturation conditions, and because of the rate it would not have been detectable in a drop in water pressure in the lodges. In normal circumstances the water would not have reached the surface.

The coroner's inquest was exhaustive, sitting for 158 days and hearing from 103 witnesses. Ultimately Hand, who was particularly impressed by the arguments of geological engineer Tim Sullivan, retained to assist the inquest, found that 'in all probability' a leak from the water pipe had produced the critical saturation which triggered the catastrophe. He was critical of the NPWS, which had approved the construction of the pipeline and which had had responsibility for the road and the safety of the village. He also criticised the DMR/RTA, which had approved the pipeline route.

Many things happened in the aftermath. In September 1997 more than 1600 people, including rescue volunteers and their families, attending a Government House function designed to thank them for their efforts. An outbreak of food poisoning affected dozens, if not hundreds, who attended. The same month, Amalgamated Holdings announced that trading in Thredbo had slumped after the landslide, but had since returned to normal. In June 1998 Amalgamated Holdings launched a $2 million advertising campaign to promote the resort for a ski season that was expected to see 470 000 visitors there.

Another consequence of the disaster was that the road above the village was reconstructed. A gabion wall replaced the old fill, using blocks of granite encased in wire cages, layered one against the other in such a way they seemed to have the permanence of the pyramids. The steepness factor had gone from 1.2 to 1.5 to one. Special drainage systems were installed. From the time of the landslide until June 2001 a total of $69 million was spent. That sum, or its equivalent in contemporary values, could have been spent at any time in the four decades since the first syndicate put together plans to develop the resort. It took 18 deaths to finally loosen the purse-strings.

This writer visited Thredbo in April 1999 and saw the foundations of Carinya Lodge, as well as the gap across Bobuck Lane created by the landslide. I also saw areas of earth slumping due to moisture, including part of Banjo Drive. It appeared that the slump was threatening a lodge. The overwhelming impression was one of moisture. Everything at the bottom of this massive mountain was wet, as it had always been.

There had been recommendations, causing great consternation, that some lodges should be closed down for safety reasons. Naturally they were resisted. In June 1999 almost a kilometre of the Alpine Way above Thredbo was reopened in time for the ski season. At the chalets there would be heaters and refrigeration and telephones, carports and carpets and continental quilts. The environment remained as extreme, and as before, if the holidaymakers thought at all about larger issues of safety, they would assume that 'they'—other people, somewhere else, with designated responsibilities—would be looking after it. The trouble is that throughout the history of Thredbo, people with designated responsibilities had made exactly the same assumption.

11

The Maccabiah Bridge Collapse, 1997

Suddenly Egyptian jet fighters, MiGs and Soukhois, appeared in the sky . . . the ground shook with the bombardment. I quickly took off my helmet and handed it to Dayan; I was more concerned for the safety of this worldwide symbol of Israeli courage than for myself. But he refused my offer with a smile, saying, 'In this war, every man takes care of himself.'

Uri Dan, To the Promised Land: the Birth of Israel

Israel and its people had always had a precarious existence, from biblical times, and life got no easier for anybody moving to The Promised Land from the time Viennese journalist Theodor Herzl instigated the Zionist movement in 1896. The occupation of Israel encountered opposition. The British, pressured by the Arabs, decided, in one of their less glorious episodes, to send intending immigrants to concentration camps. The Arab opposition was relentless. The declaration of the State of Israel by David Ben-Gurion in 1948 was done in the midst of virtual warfare. Ben-Gurion confided to his diary that the state had been established, but 'its fate lies in the hands of the defence forces. Around the country there was great joy and happiness, and once again I was a mourner . . .

The warfare continued, ranging from terrorist sorties to armed invasions, seemingly culminating in the Six Day and Yom Kippur Wars. The outrages continued and passions defied restraints. The Munich Massacre was followed in 1974 by the slaughter of 24 children in the northern town of Ma'alot. Egyptian president Anwar Sadat tried to make peace and was assassinated. Israel's Yitzhak Rabin moved in that direction and paid with his life. The grave of the fanatic Baruch Goldstein who cut loose on Muslims at prayer became a shrine to his sympathisers. Israel's military actions were normally swift and violent, but had a darker side, such as in the 1982 massacre of Palestinians when Israelis apparently let Lebanese Christian Phalangist militiamen get at them.

The environment in which the Israelis found themselves bred toughness, self-reliance, dedication to perceived historic destiny. It also bred a certain fatalism and, once the duty had been done for the security of the state, a certain selfishness. Visitors repeatedly remarked on the contradictory traits displayed by Israelis who were so careful and productive in many areas of endeavour, yet so nonchalant and uncaring in others. In 1997 American athlete Michael Wender remarked, 'I have been surprised how beautiful the country is, and it's remarkable what the Israeli people have accomplished here in such a short period of time. [But] I am so intrigued by the contrasts of the country. The people fought so hard for freedom, yet there is litter and pollution everywhere. The people are grateful and gracious, but when you get into a car, it is like being in a war zone.'

The Maccabiah Games, beginning in the city of Carlsbad, Czechoslovakia, in 1921, had become an institution in Israel, symbolising the survival of a people. The initial Maccabians had been fighters who had defeated their rulers and regained the Holy Land. Australian Maccabi competitor Elaine Smaller said, 'Most awful things have been done to us but two or three thousand years later, we are still here.'

The Maccabi World Union was a federation of Maccabi organisations in Australia, North America, South America,

Europe and Israel. Australia's Jews, great contributors to the nation who have been present since European colonisation, were staunchly supportive of Israel and the Maccabiah Games. In 1993, in the Ramat Gan Stadium outside Tel Aviv, 320 Australians had competed and had brought home 52 medals. For the 1997 games it was to assemble a team of 300 adults and 71 juniors—the third-biggest team after Israel and the United States. The turmoil that beset so many aspects of Israeli life gave no particular exemption to sport. If visitors to Israel were full of nostalgia, their experiences were not totally positive. Australian Maccabi competitor Peter Scott said that incidents in 1993 had left a 'nasty taste'. In July 1997 the 15th Maccabiah Games were to bring together 5500 athletes from all over the world, but these competitors would not enjoy an event unencumbered by the emotional and administrative baggage of Israel.

The Maccabi World Union appointed an organising committee for the 15th Maccabiah Games. Comprising 35 members, the committee was headed by Yoram Eyal, a ninth-generation Israeli born in the town of Rehovot in 1950. The games had been good to Eyal. As a child he had competed in the gymnastics display at an opening ceremony. He had become an executive member of the World Maccabi Union and though the Maccabi positions were honorary, he relished the perks, attending regional Maccabiah Games in the Americas and Europe. 'I love the sportspeople, welcoming them at the airport, organising them, transporting them,' he said. For 13 years, he had been manager of the hotel in the Kfar Maccabiah hotel and sporting complex, which were owned by the Maccabi World Union. With his new appointment, some of his relatives had key appointments, helping with the promotion, which included the opening ceremony, up to 50 000 spectators and the presence of the President of Israel, Ezer Weizman, and the Prime Minister, Benjamin Netanyahu.

Between the assembly area of the athletes and the stadium was an inconvenient waterway, the Yarkon River. A wooden footbridge spanned it, which was quite sturdy but of limited capacity. After the opening ceremony at the 1981 Maccabiah Games, thousands had tried to get across the river to the car park and had been caught in the crush on the bridge. Elaine Smaller said later, 'There were thousands of people trying to get across. We were jam-packed like sardines.' A fireman felt obliged to turn a hose on the crowd. The problem was not addressed and it recurred at the 1985 games. Thereafter the Israeli Defence Force, using its well-practiced engineering skills, provided a temporary bridge for the games in 1989 and 1993.

In 1997 the Israel Defence Force said it would build a bridge for the games, but only in return for 330 000 shekels, which, calculated from the prevailing exchange rate, was about $83 000. The Maccabi World Union had a budget of $12–16 million, but it felt that the asking price was too much. Negotiations were protracted, and finally the organising committee decided to have a bridge built for a cheaper price than the military was asking. By then it was late May, and the organising committee had precious little time left.

In Eyal's eyes, and those of his committee, the bridge was a mere detail, a temporary affair to serve for a single day. Surely, in Eyal's mind, it should not cost a fortune. He said later, 'I did not want a massive bridge or a concrete overpass. We were after a footbridge for athletes for one day. Call it a bridge or a temporary footway.' The requirement was for a bridge with a load capacity to accommodate 'thousands of athletes who could cross the bridge in a short space of time',

and there would have to be an engineer's approval that the
structure was fit for public use.

Eyal turned to a man he had worked with, Adam Mishori,
whose company, Irgunit, had put up stages and sets for the
opening ceremony. Mishori's assurances were normally all
the organising committee needed. In his later account, Eyal
said, 'Adam, can you put up a bridge?' Mishori said, 'Yes.'
Eyal was confident that if Mishori had felt unsure of Irgunit's
ability to put up a bridge, he would have said so. He felt that,
as with any such construction, the contractor would retain an
engineer as a matter of course, but Eyal could have checked
that Irgunit was a registered building contractor. Any layman
could have done that.

Mishori offered a price of 120 000 shekels, or $40 000,
but then dropped the price to 90 000 shekels, about $22 500.
Then he dropped it to 85 500 shekels, which came to a bit
over $21 050. Eyal accepted the lower price. He said later, 'I
think before the amount was 90 [thousand shekels] but our
financial controller managed to be a little more creative, paying part in cash, so it cost us less. I was very happy I had
managed to cut the cost of the bridge.'

Mishori had no experience or qualifications in building
bridges, and intended from the outset to subcontract the
work, but take a large share of the money. On the day he
accepted the contract, Mishori turned to a company run by
two contractors he had worked with before, Baruch Ben-Ezra
and Joshua Karagula, whom he said later were 'good friends'.
The two were principals of Ben-Ezra Karagula Metal Factory
Ltd, which had an impressive track record building sheds
and roofs for structures such as petrol stations. They had
built footings for buildings before, and believed that that
was enough to qualify them for designing and constructing

foundations for a bridge. Bridges themselves were a new item, though Ben-Ezra later recalled that he had once put up a small bridge in Jerusalem.

Ben-Ezra and Karagula assessed the project and realised that they had manufacturing components that could easily be adapted to building a bridge. The fact that the loads they would be seeking to accommodate would be at least ten times the loads their previous structures had had to accommodate did not concern them. They agreed to build the bridge for 42 500 shekels, or a little over $10 000—half the price that Mishori had given to Eyal.

Mishori, from all appearances, was ripping them off, despite his protestations of friendship. He could have been just a middleman and introduced the organising committee to Ben-Ezra and Karagula. Questioned later on why he did not do this, he replied directly, 'I wanted to make money at the same time. Is it such a terrible thing?' Eyal said later that the retention of the subcontractors was made known to him. As far as he was concerned, he had put the project in the hands of Mishori and then got on with organising the rest of the games. Quite frankly, he said, he would not have been interested even if he had been told that the construction had been subcontracted out.

Ben-Ezra sat down with his computer and in ten minutes had produced a design. In theory it was designed to take a maximum load of 250 kilograms per square metre. He and Karagula contacted an engineer, Micha Bar-Ilan, who had his own engineering company and with whom they had worked with previously. Bar-Ilan agreed to play a small role, but he would have known he was the only engineer to be involved, and might have assumed total responsibility from the outset. He did not. Instead he agreed to their request that his plan incorporate the manufactured components they already had in stock. Bar-Ilan confined his attention to building the truss, a combination of bars and beams to form a rigid framework, and overlooked the question of foundations and other appendages such as decking and rails. He claimed later he was not offered much money—enough, in fact, for just one day's work, and that, essentially, was all he put in. 'Did they expect me to be site supervisor for $400?' he asked later. He did not regard himself as having a general responsibility for the whole bridge.

Even if he had assumed responsibility for the entire bridge, Bar-Ilan was being outpaced by Ben-Ezra and Karagula, who started constructing the bridge even before he had finished his plan. In fact, on 23 June 1997 Ben-Ezra and Karagula oversaw their workers putting up the bridge in the space of nine hours. They had no blueprint, and certainly no approval by any local government authority, though on this last point no Maccabi Games had ever submitted an application for a building licence in accordance with the legislation, the Israel Planning and Building Law. There was a grey area in the requirements of the law relating to a 'temporary' structure.

Mishori, who never regarded himself as the head contractor, had not supervised any planning or manufacturing. Irgunit did become involved, however, to the extent of putting up the walkway, which comprised beams with plywood planks screwed on, decking wired to the truss, and handrails made of metal tubing. Mishori believed that he had competence to do this because Irgunit had a good track record in putting up staging.

Bar-Ilan did have a look and said that some parts of the construction were not adequate and should be rebuilt to give the bridge a higher load capacity. Changing the construction in this way was naturally awkward, imposing difficult working conditions. Ben-Ezra and Karagula undertook the rectification work on the basis of oral instructions from Ben-Ezra, but Bar-Ilan did not go further with his inspections. He did not check the quality of the welding.

Eyal had no concerns about the way the bridge was built, but was sufficiently interested to at least look at it. 'On Saturday, ten days before the opening, I went there in the morning, moved the barbed wire, went up onto the bridge,' he said later. 'I jumped up and down on it, shook the handrails, and when I came back down I had the feeling that on a humid day, maybe it would be slippery. I asked them to speak to Adam so he would paint the bridge with non-slip paint and add some more strips to prevent slip. Two or three days later I visited the bridge again and saw it had all been done.'

Eyal agreed that he was not doing a searching technical examination. He was doing the inspection of an interested layman. 'You hit a wall with your fist to see if it is strong— that was the kind of test I did, not an engineering test . . . the bridge seemed completely reasonable to me, it seemed OK,' he said. 'On my three visits, I did not have even the slightest possible fear about it, nor did any of the headquarters people who visited it. Nobody made any remarks not to me or anyone else; there was no comment that on the face of it the bridge might be weak, badly built or anything like that.'

Eyal elaborated, 'I came to look at the bridge as I looked at any product we had hired or purchased. It was exactly like I went to the stadium and went up to the main stage and jumped down on it, and looked up to see how the lighting equipment appeared . . . [On the bridge] I jumped on [the decking]. I saw the handrail, I shook it. Just because I wanted to see what was there, that is all.' He had relied on the engineer just as he relied on the producer, Moshe Yanni, who had run the stadium on three consecutive Maccabiah Games.

What Eyal did not appreciate was that no engineer had taken responsibility for the bridge. Nor did he appreciate that even if the bridge could withstand the forces he was exerting on it, it might not be able to withstand those forces multiplied a hundred-fold. What he did not know was that below him were struts and trusses that were poorly welded, columns that were not properly centred on foundation plates that were badly placed and too small anyway—supports that would start bending at far less than 250 kilograms per square metre.

In fact, as it turned out, even if the welding and connections had been executed properly, the maximum load on at least parts of the bridge was 50 kilograms per square metre. The way in which the walkway had been placed on the truss put too much weight on the upper structure, part of which was found later to comprise piping that was crooked and rusty. It was later judged that even if the rest of the bridge had been capable of withstanding the load, the walkway itself would have failed. The maximum load of some parts was as low as 35 kilograms per square metre. Even the bridge railing was subject to later criticism, having been so improperly placed that it constituted a safety hazard.

Nevertheless, the bridge was completed. On 2 July 1997, 12 days before the opening ceremony of the Games, Bar-Ilan handwrote an approval: 'On this day July 2 1997, I examined the bridge and authorise that its implementation corresponds with the plans.' The statement conveyed to other authorities the wrong impression: that Bar-Ilan had approved of the whole bridge, but he had not included the foundations, walkway or railings in his authorisation. It was possible that incidental use of the bridge before the opening day could have disclosed a flaw, such as a heavy truck driving across, but that chance passed. The ramp was left off the southern end so that the bridge would not be used until the opening of the games.

Rising in an arc-like shape, the 16-metre bridge was eight metres above the Yarkon River at its highest point. The river itself, flowing silently and unobtrusively, was like any waterway in a heavily populated stretch of semi-desert with low rainfall and frequent use of waterways for disposal of effluent, whether that effluent was agricultural chemicals or sewage. It had once been a good waterway, carrying 25 500 cubic metres of spring water an hour, but that time had long passed.

Fish had once swum freely in the Yarkon, but had since disappeared, apart from the hardiest fish in isolated pockets. There had been efforts to clean the river up. A Yarkon River Authority had been created in 1988, bringing together 19 official bodies ranging from regional ministries to municipalities, but the authority had a limited budget and its work was hampered by a tug-of-war between rival authorities. If the Interior Ministry and the Ministry of Housing and Construction had their own agendas, nothing much could work. The authority was receiving only two million shekels, or $500 000, a year—two-thirds of what its budget required—and there were only two inspectors were appointed to cope with the entire 27-kilometre length of the river.

Within the waters of that river, there was a virtual cocktail of pollutants including mercury and other heavy metals. Don Bursill, director of Sydney's Cooperative Research Centre for Water Quality, said later the water was 'highly contaminated from a microbacteriological point of view', similar to sewage that had had the solids taken out. The river also had a deadly fungus, *P. Boydii*, which when cultivated appeared as a grey mould. When it invades the human body, it attacks the lungs and central nervous system. Almost everyone who had ever ingested water polluted by it had died. The survival rate was about three percent. Whatever else mattered, it was most important to get people over that bridge without falling into the water; the health of people falling from the bridge was not an obvious thing to think about.

The Australian team were excited and Australia's Jewish community was right behind them. Industrialist Joseph Gutnick had donated $250 000 to get the team there. There were 300 adults and 71 juniors competing. They were going to run, swim and jump, bowl on lawns and tenpin alleys and play bridge. It was costing from $4000 to $6000 each to go there. But what an experience! They were going to see sights of the Jewish State and, in the Jewish firmament, they would be Olympians. Competitor Rod Davies later said that he could hardly wait for the plane.

Yetty Bennett, 50, widowed three years earlier when her husband, Barry, had suffered a heart attack, had three children, Mark, 25, Jeff, 22, and Ilana, 15. She was going to manage the tenpin bowling team. With her was Frank Gaensler, who had gone to his first Maccabiah 14 years before. The two had worked together for 19 months, fallen in love, and looked on the visit to Israel as a virtual honeymoon. 'Greg [Small] became part of the team, he basically became one of us,' Gaensler said. 'We socialised together. We practised together. We spoke about nothing but tenpin bowling.' Elizabeth Sawicki, 47, mother of four, had gone to Israel alone, leaving her husband Henry in Melbourne to look after their four children.

Greg Small, 37, was an accountant. He had been saving for four years to go to the games. Three years earlier he had finished building the family home. He and his wife, Suzanne, 34, also a Maccabiah competitor, had been childhood sweethearts. They had had the same dreams and aspirations, which included a trip to Israel and the Maccabiah Games. They decided not to furnish the lounge room immediately, but to dedicate the money to the trip and complete the furnishing later. They had two children, Joshua, seven, and Rebecca, five, and had decided it would be better for them to stay with relatives in Queensland.

Warren Zines, 56, a highly-regarded resident of Sydney's eastern suburbs, had for two decades played at the Dover Heights Bowling Club. He was known by various nicknames, including Wally, Barney, Herbie, Zinesy and 'mate'. He had a wife, Lynne, a son, Adam, and two daughters, Lisa, and Shelley Jackson. Lynne would have gone to Israel with Warren, but Shelley was expecting her first baby—a baby Warren was destined never to see.

Sasha Elterman, 15, only child of Colin and Rose Elterman, would be playing tennis. Gifted academically, Sasha had taken to sports with enormous enthusiasm, excelling at both tennis and swimming. She was swimming five kilometres three times a week. The Eltermans decided to go with Sasha. 'Rose and I had never been to Israel,' Colin Elterman said. 'This was a great opportunity to be there at the same time.'

The games organising committee attended to final details, including having insecticide poured into the Yarkon River days before the opening ceremony, getting rid of mosquitos but adding to the lethal cocktail. If there was any hint of the trouble that was to follow, it was in the ceremony to light the Maccabiah torch. The torch handle caught fire, causing its carrier to drop it, amusing onlookers but perhaps conveying something more ominous.

On 14 July the southern ramp was put onto the bridge. Several pedestrians walked on the bridge and a number of mini-tractors drove across without apparent ill effect. Police sappers inspected the bridge, but their focus was on terrorism—they were on the lookout for bombs rather than shoddy welding. It was a hot mid-summer day and people were waiting for the cool of the evening. The athletes were screened at 4 pm. The last bridge inspection by police took place at 5.30 pm.

That evening, the athletes, from more than 50 countries, assembled on the side of the river across from the stadium. They would be walking in ranks of six, in national teams some ten metres apart, each preceded by a flag-bearer. The countries would go in alphabetical order. Austria, with 51 members, would go first, followed by Australia. At 7.30 the Games organisers were notified that the athletes were assembled. Eyal said later, 'As far as we were concerned, we had got 5500 athletes to the entrance of the stadium. Then we could say, "Let the games begin!"' In the stadium, Colin and Rose Elterman waited excitedly to see their beloved daughter. Elsewhere in the stands, Joshua Karagula was settling down for a relaxed evening. 'I came to the opening ceremony to enjoy it,' he said. 'I had no suspicions that anything was wrong.'

The teams started moving at 7.45 pm. Austria crossed without incident, then Australia came on. Frank Gaensler said, 'We were basically not quite at the front but four or five rows back and we started to march up this bridge. I had turned around to take photographs of the green hats. Yetty made some comment about the bridge. It was a bit slippery because it was just plywood. We were basically walking arm-in-arm up the bridge. Yetty was slightly in front of me.' They agreed they were reaching the culmination of everything they had worked for. Suzanne Small said later, 'I remember standing on the bridge and feeling with excitement that Greg's dream had come true.' Up to 160 people came to a halt on the bridge. Rod Davies had been concerned about the slipperiness, but said, 'I was at the top of the bridge. We were fairly well packed in and the atmosphere was just absolutely electric.'

Steve Trgo, who was making a film about the Australian team's participation, filmed the Australians walking onto the bridge. Between ten and 15 Australians passed him before he turned to go to the other side to get different footage. 'I walked maybe two or three steps and then I noticed the bridge move and heard screaming behind me,' he said. 'I started running off the bridge.' People further back, blocked by fellow marchers, heard the crack and felt the bridge start to shake. 'I think most of us froze,' Rod Davies said. Suzanne Small heard someone call out, 'I hope this bridge is strong enough!' It was not strong enough, and as the bridge started to give way, Warren Zines was heard saying: 'Oh, shit!'

The load on the upper pillars of the bridge had simply been too great. A key stress pole in the upper portion had bent and placed huge strain on other bridge components. The pressure on the interior columns of the bridge at the northern bank was beyond their tolerance. The foundations could not take much strain. The force on two outside poles of the bridge was four to five times their tolerance. Within seconds the bridge collapsed, the two sides of the walkway, still joined, forcing everyone into the bottom of a 'V' shape. 'It was as though a trapdoor opened and we went straight into the water,' Rod

Davies said. Frank Gaensler said, 'The bridge just opened up. We just went in and other people just fell on top of us.' Steve Trgo said, 'When I turned round, I saw the entire middle of the bridge was gone and that people were in the water struggling for their lives. There are no other words to describe it except to say it was a nightmare.'

More than 100 people were caught in the collapse, mostly members of the Australian team, plus a handful of Austrians. People ended up on top of people and those at the bottom were under water. 'I could hear the screaming and panic and I thought I was going to drown,' said Rod Davies. 'I remember being able to gasp for air for two or three occasions and then being pushed under,' he said. 'I thought, "What a disappointing way to die!"' There were people on top of him and there was nothing on the sloping remains of the decking to grab onto. Opening his eyes underwater, Davies could see someone else's head. Suzanne Small said later, 'I was under the water and basically drowning and telling myself I was going to die.'

Sasha Elterman, also underwater with a broken leg, said later, 'I remember falling in the water and taking five huge gulps. I thought the world has come to an end. I felt I was drowning. People who have near-death experiences say they think about God or their family. I thought, "I am 16 and this is really a shit way to have to die!" Occasionally I would remember to get myself level with the surface of the water and take a breath and look round me at the bank. People were thrashing round but were not really getting anywhere because there was nowhere to go. I must have swallowed a lot of water.'

Rescuers started pulling people out. Rod Davies said later, 'I cannot remember how I got out of the water but I was finally pulled into the bank and then I realised I could not move because my arm was out of joint and was just lying in the mud. There was a lot of action going on around me. A lady was pulled out of the water one-and-a-half metres to my left, her face was very blue. I formed the view that she was dead.'

Greg Small had drowned. Suzanne Small, pulled out, saw people on the bank trying to revive her husband. 'People were holding me back, I could not get to him,' she said. 'Then I was up next to him. And that is when I realised my life had changed in an instant, that it was just all gone.' Yetty Bennett and Frank Gaensler were pulled out unconscious. Yetty Bennett survived four hours. Frank Gaensler, who was initially classified as clinically dead, survived.

Inside the stadium, it quickly became apparent that something was wrong. Yoram Eyal got out and made it to the wooden bridge. He tried to reassure himself that what he saw in front of him was only a hiccup. 'The scene was difficult but I could see that the river was not very deep,' he said. 'There was a feeling that this was a catastrophe, but nobody could have drowned.'

The disaster, even if it was not immediately apparent to Eyal how serious it was, naturally enough placed a dampener on proceedings. It was felt immediately that the wisest course would be to proceed with the opening ceremony. 'We went into the office of the manager,' Eyal said. 'The president [Mr Weizman] asked what was to be done. I said this was a ceremony celebrating a hundred years of Zionism. I suggested that we do the ceremony and that is what happened. At the end of the ceremony, I went onto the stage, and then I described the tragedy briefly, and the audience left and it was all over.'

Continuing with the program and thereby averting a mass exit from the stadium, with the possible result of hampering the rescue effort and clogging roads, was probably justified, however it might have appeared. As it turned out, the opening ceremony, which was scheduled to last two-and-a-half hours, only lasted 50 minutes. It had some of the planned spectacle, on the theme that the future was 'already here'. The television news felt obliged to show scenes of dancing and singing before crossing over to the rescue effort in the Yarkon. People on the riverbank heard the sounds from the stadium. The then chairman of the World Jewish Congress, Isi Liebler, said the switching of scenes was 'surrealistic'. 'I was outraged when I saw Australians being fished out of the water and Israeli dancing going on simultaneously,' he said.

Suzanne Small suffered five fractures in one ankle, injury to the spine and a twisted pelvis. She was to suffer nightmares and stress problems for years afterwards. Sasha Elterman was taken to the Schneider Children's Hospital in a critical condition. Her parents received a call that she was there. 'When we got there, we were told Sasha had drowned,' he said. 'There were seven on the critical list and two were dead.' Some 100 people were taken to hospital. There were more than 60 injured. Yetty Bennett survived for four hours, but succumbed to the effects of almost drowning.

Lynne Zines was on a plane to Israel with her son, Adam, less than three hours after she received the news. She went to Warren's bedside. 'His breathing was very, very distressed,' she said. 'He was regaining consciousness. We could speak to him.' His consciousness did not last.

At 3 am on 15 July, Henry Sawicki in Melbourne received a telephone call telling him that Elizabeth was among the casualties. 'I actually heard myself scream!' he said. He took off for Israel the next day. When he saw her, she said she was 'OK', but there was a tube in her mouth. She had inhaled and probably ingested the polluted water, and she died the following Saturday from lung and kidney failure.

Warren Zines did not come out of his coma and his condition declined. Days became weeks. Doctors were baffled as to what was killing him. After four weeks he died of a stroke. Traces of *P. Boydii* fungus were found in his body. Sasha Elterman remained at Schneider Children's Hospital for six weeks, and her condition was also baffling. Then a sample of the Yarkon River's water was taken and the *P. Boydii* fungus was cultivated from it.

On the initiative of Moshe Peled, Israel's deputy minister for Education, Culture and Sport, the first day's events were cancelled. Then the games continued, complete with organisational blemishes, particularly for soccer teams facing a program without sufficient referees and linesmen. Because of program changes, some soccer teams hardly got a chance to play at all. The Israeli Government was obliged to launch an inquiry, and from the outset there were accusations of cover-up and failure to address responsibilities. The Maccabi World Union went into damage control. A day before the games closed, the director of the games, Ronnie Bakalarz, said, 'I am pleased that there is no responsibility on Maccabi.' It was noted that Bakalarz did not visit the injured or the families of the deceased, and made no inquiry as to their well-being.

A committee of inquiry, chaired by military engineer Brigadier-General Yishai Dotan was called together to make an immediate inquiry. It was noted that one of the seven members, Rami Horovitz, was from the Maccabiah World-wide Administration. Architect Itaman Levitin, one of the inquiry members, said later that Horovitz would not agree with any criticism of the organisation. There was also every chance that everything that transpired in the inquiry was getting straight back to the Maccabiah administration.

On 30 July the inquiry reported that there had been a chain of failures in the planning and construction of the bridge. It said, 'It should be noted that not one of the agencies involved saw itself as overall responsible for the construction and proper execution of the bridge project. Each agent relied on the others to guarantee that the bridge would be fairly suited to its purpose.' The committee did not specify that anybody was responsible, and the chairman of the Maccabi World Union, Uni Netanel, said, 'The report showed that we had no hand whatsoever in this failure.'

Both Netanel and Bakalarz resisted calls for them to resign. Bakalarz said he had been 'party to the whole process' of deliberations over the bridge and believed the organising committee had taken a serious attitude and made the right decision to build the bridge. 'I saw absolutely no fault in their work,' he said. 'The report has come to the same conclusion.' He felt it would be cowardly just to walk away and leave the troubles to his successor. He said he was 'fully confident' that Eyal would be found innocent of any charges that arose as a result of inquiries. He said, 'It was a tragic accident, but it was an accident. Accidents occur; in this country many incidents occur, but I don't see people resigning or stepping down all over the place.'

Australia's Maccabiah teams managed to accumulate 60 medals, compared with 52 in the previous Maccabiah Games, but there was not much joy. Sasha Elterman was flown back to Australia. A $500000 loan was made available for families of the deceased, an amount that was repayable when final compensation was calculated. In the meantime, Sasha

Elterman was forced to undergo more than 20 operations to save her life. The fungus had attacked her brain and back. At Sydney Children's Hospital, Professor Richard Henry said, 'I saw a terrified 15-year-old girl in front of me. It was impossible to know how sick she was.'

Sasha suffered unbearable pain at times. Three times over a period of nine months doctors thought she would die. Colin Elterman never left her side, sleeping for months on end at the hospital. Her eventual survival came about because of an experimental medicine that she was given. She would never properly get over the effects of the illness, or of the invasive surgery to her brain and back. She said later, 'It would have been one of the best experiences of my life but it ended up being the worst experience.'

Suzanne Small, who did not fully recover from her injuries, was afflicted with bouts of deep depression. She suffered panic attacks and nightmares, heard screaming and had to fight off going in her mind back to the horrors of the bridge collapse. She took Panadeine to deal with the pain. She said, 'It all boils down to this: If I did not have two young children totally dependent on me, there would be no reason for me to stick around. I can understand how people can swallow a bottle of pills!'

Eyal, Mishori, Ben-Ezra, Karagula and Bar-Ilan were all charged with causing death through negligence and negligently causing injury. Specifically, Eyal was accused of having approved the job going to a contractor not licensed to build a bridge, Mishori of having allowed an unregistered contractor to do the construction, Ben-Ezra and Karagula of having had the bridge built by their employees but without a foreman or supervisor on site, and Bar-Ilan of having designed a bridge for an unlicensed contractor and of having authorised the constructed bridge despite the negligent way it had been built.

A Knesset committee of inquiry, headed by Misha Goldman, looked at various issues, such as pollution of the Yarkon. But its work was disrupted by elections. On 28 October 1998 the Knesset committee appointed another commissioner of inquiry, to be chaired by Knesset member, Eliezer Sandberg, to take over the Goldman committee's work. In the meantime there were wretched attempts to divert blame. In 1999 the then Honorary President of the World Maccabi Union, Fred Worms, said in a letter to the president of the Board of Deputies of British Jews: 'None of the athletes died from falling off the bridge. The four who unfortunately passed away were poisoned by the water.' The Executive Council of Australian Jewry said in a joint letter of the Zionist Federation that it was 'outrageous' to make such a suggestion. Two of the deceased had died immediately. And anyway, they said, no-one from the Australian team was in the Yarkon River for 'a recreational dip!'

The trial of the five accused began in the Tel Aviv Magistrate's Court on 20 January 1998. In March they pleaded not guilty. The court heard from more than 80 witnesses. Lawyer Peter Redlich, representing many of the injured, said the collapse of the bridge had been a 'gross example of negligence', the worst negligence he had seen in 40 years of dealing with such cases. The judgement, announced on 17 April 2000, found all guilty, and deemed them to have used the time-honoured Israeli approach which was to say 'trust me' and then bypass procedures and regulations. The three judges said that, had the bridge been built according to regulations, it would have been ten times stronger than it was. They said, 'The experts who testified before us expressed shock at the insufferable recklessness these defendants showed as they discovered the actions they took in erecting the bridge intended for significant public events involving many participants.'

After the verdicts the then prime minister's wife, Nava Barak, made a personal call to Colin Elterman. Several hours after the verdicts were announced, Netanel announced his resignation.

When the sentences were announced on 5 June 2000 Eyal received six months jail, with a year suspended, for causing death by negligence, and four months jail, with six months suspended, for negligently causing injury. He agreed to do six months community service instead, on the condition that he begin it immediately, without appealing. He thought reading books for the blind would not trouble him too much, but he confessed to heartache. 'The public will remember me as a symbol of amateurism and incompetence and over time that symbol will become even stronger,' he said. 'It hurts and saddens me, but that's my fate.' In fact he did appeal, and four years later the victims were still awaiting the results of his appeal and those of the co-accused. Colin Elterman noted in 2001 that Eyal remained general manager of the Kfar Maccabiah hotel and sporting complex, on an annual salary of $US 120 000.

Mishori received nine months jail with another nine months suspended for negligence causing death, and four months imprisonment with another six months suspended for negligence causing injury. Ben-Ezra and Karagula each got 15 months jail, with another 15 months suspended for negligence causing death, six months, with six suspended, for negligently causing injury, and three months, with three suspended, for carrying out an engineering operation in contravention of the law. Bar-Ilan received 21 months, with another sentence suspended for causing death by negligence, and six months, with another six suspended, for negligence causing injury. The sentences for each of the accused were to be served concurrently.

Bakalarz held defiantly onto his position, but he was confronted by a recommendation from a Knesset committee that State funding for the Maccabiah Games should be refused unless he resigned. The Australian Maccabi delegation had also announced that it would not send a team to the 2001 games unless he resigned. Bakalarz stepped down on the weekend of August 5–6 2000, saying in his letter of resignation, 'I have always said that if the time comes that my presidency might negatively impact in any way on our youngsters, I would resign from my office.'

For the injured athletes, recovery was slow. The Israeli authorities were not astute in keeping in touch. Lynne Zines said she had received no letter of condolence for the death of her husband. 'As far as they are concerned, we are on the other side of the world and we are forgotten,' she said. 'But they don't know who they are dealing with and this will not be forgotten.' In November 2000 Monique Licenblat, 24, daughter of Elizabeth Sawicki, died at home. Her siblings Michael and Rosyln said she had suffered bouts of depression, had never come to terms with her mother's death and had struggled to find stability in her life. Fifty Australians and two Austrians made a total of 66 claims for compensation in the Haifa District Court in Israel against 19 parties, including the State of Israel, the police, Ramat Gan Municipality, the Ramat Gan municipal engineer, the Bar-Ilan Engineering Company, the Maccabi World Union, Maccabi Israel, and the Phoenix and Magen Insurance Companies.

The attitude of Israelis remained equivocal. Yetty Bennett's brother-in-law, Andrew Simons, said he felt from the reaction of Israelis he met that everyone in the country was touched by a sense of guilt. Negotiations for compensation for the injured dragged on for years. At all times Israel and the Maccabi World Union had to be pushed. Pressure was applied both by the Australian Jewish community and internationally.

On 9 February 2000 three major compensation payments totalling nearly $14 million were approved for Sasha Elterman and the families of Warren Zines and Greg Small. The overall compensation paid out came to $25 million. In July 2001 a much smaller Australian Maccabiah team went to Israel, at a time when Israel was beset by violent revolt and bombing outrages. There was no crossing of the Yarkon this time—the venue had been changed, but other catastrophes, such as the collapse of a wedding hall in Jerusalem, were again driving home the lesson that Israelis really could do better.

Part Four:
Tempest

12

Cyclone Tracy, 1974

Not only didn't it go back south, it even turned north-east. And that's when we had to make serious decisions about what we were going to tell the citizens of Darwin.

Meteorologist Geoff Crane

Originally called Palmerston when it was settled in 1869, Darwin was a backwater until the Second World War, when its strategic value soared as the expanding Japanese 'Sphere of Influence' came closer. Once large deposits of minerals were discovered, Darwin began to boom. Land prices began skyrocketing and the cost of living was one of the highest in Australia. It was a cosmopolitan town with a strong Asian influence—salty plums were the kids' currency in the school playgrounds. Long-term residents were only numbered in the thousands among some 43 000 residents of Darwin in 1974. There were large Chinese and Greek communities. Everyone enjoyed a casual, laid-back lifestyle in what one female resident described as 'man's town'. Not a pretty place, Darwin was a bit ramshackle in parts with a mix of typical British-inspired colonial architecture in town, and a mushrooming conglomeration of mainly high-level fibrous-cement-clad, corrugated-iron-roofed government-rented and private houses in the suburbs. Former Chief Minister Marshall Perron repeated a description, that it was 'not the concrete jungle but the fibro bungle'.

The Dry season from May to October is easy to endure, with warm sunny days, relatively low humidity and cooling sea breezes at night. The Wet season is enervating with high stifling heat and choking humidity. Daily rainstorms dump hundreds of millimetres in less than a few hours, causing minor flooding. The Wet is also tropical cyclone time. These revolving storms breed at an indeterminate rate, but the region averages three or four per season, one in 1937 scoring a direct hit on Darwin and causing an estimated $100 000 in damage—a large sum for the day. There had been one previous encounter, in January 1897, when a 'disastrous hurricane and phenomenal rainfall' virtually destroyed the place. Since 1937 four more cyclones had brought minor flooding, uprooting some trees and causing moderate building damage on Bathurst and Melville Islands, 100 kilometres north-west of Darwin.

Cyclone Tracy was discovered as a potential tropical disturbance on Friday 21 December 1974 and tracked until it arrived at the coast of Bathurst and Melville Islands on Monday 23 December. There were no indications that it was going to produce anything more than winds of 120 kmh and gusts up to 150 kmh. It was dumping enormous amounts of rain, lashed by gale-force winds, but it remained in the Timor and Arafura seas. Most cyclones born off the side of the monsoonal trough in this part of the world tend to move parallel to the coastline and then move south-west to fade away as they run out of speed, hitting cooler ocean water or crossing the Western Australian coastline. As a large low pressure system, Tracy would dump megalitres of rain on the sparsely inhabited inland. Tropical Cyclone Selma had passed through only three weeks before Tracy and had followed the script, eventually petering out as an inland rain depression some 1100 kilometres west of Darwin. It had produced torrential rain and winds of up to 90 kmh on Melville Island, cutting roads and saturating the ground so much that some trees simply just fell over, a rather predictable event in the Wet. There had been no significant wind in Darwin as a result of Selma. When Tracy was spotted, residents heard alerts for three days and then warnings as it approached the coastline, but it was still 110 kilometres or more out at sea.

By midnight on 23 December the radar image showed that Tracy was at the tip of Bathurst Island. The meteorologists, or 'mets' as they were known, released a weather balloon at 7.30 am to check the upper winds. They did not get another radar image until 9.15 am—one that showed a surprisingly different pattern of movement. It had turned sharp left and was heading east. Predicting cyclone paths was not a science in 1974, more of a black art done by extrapolating data and looking at associated weather systems. The mets were hoping that Tracy's sudden irregular movement was a glitch and that it would return to a southerly path, cyclones being known to experience short-term anomalies. Not this time. Defying expectation, Tracy changed direction once more and started to head north-east, straight for Darwin.

The mets tried to work out why Tracy had turned east. They looked at weather systems up to 1000 kilometres from the cyclone to get a clue as to what would happen next, but there were no clues. The cyclone was now only 115 kilometres west-north-west of Darwin. The next set of radar images, taken between 9.15 am and 11.30 am, were not what the mets wanted to see. Tracy appeared to be 'loitering with intent'. It actually moved back towards Bathurst Island for a short period, but then resumed a south-easterly course. Between 10 and 10.30 am, Crane slipped out to do some last minute shopping and banking. He met a tennis colleague, Tony Pickering, and told him what was really happening. Pickering said later, 'We had had Cyclone Selma only a few weeks before and suffered ten days of cyclonic weather. Everyone was sick of talking about cyclones and besides, Christmas was here. I went back to work!' One of the mets was rostered to go on ABC radio and give a live weather forecast. Just as he was about to go to air the cyclone dramatically changed its path. Darwin got its warning. Tracy was coming to town.

In response, most businesses pulled their shutters down. People who had been gathering at Christmas work parties from noon switched their conversation to weather. Most had last heard of the storm being out near Melville Island. They were expecting 'a bit of a blow' and some heavy rain, probably 'just like Selma'. In Darwin's suburbs, people continued preparing for Christmas Eve parties and barbecues, but things were no longer quite normal. Those looking out to sea might have noticed that the blue sky was somehow brooding and malevolent. As the rain became heavier and the sky increasingly dark, most people cancelled their evening activities. At places like the Darwin Hospital, police and fire crews followed well-practised storm procedures. Some householders began taping their windowpanes, but the bulk of the public did not take any special precautions. They cleared their backyards of any loose items.

Darwin harbour is a long stretch of water about twenty kilometres long and ten kilometres across, containing reefs and shallow soundings. On Christmas Eve 1974 there were at least 27 vessels in its immediate vicinity or inside the port area. Another 50 vessels of various sizes were inside the harbour, away from the port precinct. The four Royal Australian Navy Attack Class patrol boats, HMAS Assail, Advance, Attack and Arrow, were designed to handle rough weather. Each was 33 metres long, weighed 146 tonnes when fully loaded, and was crewed by two officers and 16 ratings. Powerful craft, each with two V-16 diesel motors that produced 4000 hp through two propeller shafts and could drive them at 24 knots, they nevertheless had to be looked after. In the early afternoon they were sent to their pre-designated storm moorings in the harbour.

Nick Paspaley's family, who had started a pearling business, decided to leave their boats anchored in the creeks that ran off the harbour, a wise enough decision as it turned out. The harbour master gave the word that all seaworthy vessels were to leave the port area and shelter elsewhere in the harbour. One person who had to move on that order was Rob Perkins, a cadet seaman who had joined shipmates for a session at the pub. His boat, *Clipper Bird*, one of six prawn trawlers in a fleet of a combined Australian–Japanese business venture, had undergone a refit and been back in Darwin for less than a day. The harbour master and his staff lashed unmanned trawlers to the wharves.

At 5 pm the low cloud and heavy rain were darkening the sky. Tracy was now only 70 kilometres offshore and heavy winds were buffeting the coastline. Not yet gale force, they were nevertheless strong enough to bend trees and tip over garbage tins. At 6 pm it was dark enough for headlights. Tracy was only 50 kilometres from Darwin and the wind and rain were intensifying, the rain blowing in gusts that lasted for 30–60 seconds. Temperatures were plummeting and wind noise increased dramatically. At 7 pm a Flash Warning was broadcast predicting winds of 120 kmh and gusts of up to

150 kmh. There was now no doubt that Darwin was smack in the path of the storm. At 8 pm Milton Drew was driving home along largely deserted streets and felt his car buffeted by the wind. 'It took some effort to keep it on the road,' he said.

The suburbs Drew drove through, as well as all the others, were going to be put to the test. The oldest suburbs, such as Fannie Bay and Nightcliff, were only minutes from the city centre, located along the shoreline. The other main area of population was the northern suburbs. Here there were mainly government-built houses, built for public servants—mostly high-set fibrous cement clad houses on piers or brick low-set Housing Commission homes. There had been a surge in building as part of a drive by the Commonwealth to get people to stay in Darwin, making low-cost and low-interest home loans available. There was little doubt that, when conditions were good, Darwin was a nice place to live. The high-set homes had breezeways underneath for ventilation and protection from minor flooding during the Wet season. They had beautifully lush and well-established gardens with the normal clusters of frangipani, bougainvillea and tropical plants and bushes. Some have said that you could stick a garden stake in the ground in Darwin and it would grow, so good was the soil and climate.

How well had these houses been built to withstand the climatic extremes which, at some time or other, were bound to beset the city? In tornado country in the United States, householders had long built underground bunkers. What preparations had ever been made in Darwin? Many houses had a predominance of metal and glass louvres set in banks on all of the major walls to aid airflow, at the cost of weakening the walls.

The leading edge of the real winds—from 120 to 150 kmh—struck the harbour between 11 pm and midnight and created chaos. Winds and enormous amounts of seawater struck the vessels. The high-sided trawlers had no chance against the crashing foam-whipped waves and quickly turned turtle. *Clipper Bird* was on the far side of Darwin harbour, facing into the storm and trying to stay out of trouble. Perkins watched the huge angry swells approaching. 'There was about a metre of foam on the waves,' he said later. 'The spotlights were on but I could only see to the next wave . . . The skipper had the engines going flat out just to steam onto the anchor. But at full pelt we would only manage about 10 knots.' Perkins' skipper asked him to fetch the engineer. Perkins was aghast as it meant leaving the safety of the wheelhouse, crossing a heaving slippery deck in wind that would 'pull the dog off a chain', the deck area strewn with 200-litre drums and heavy trawling chains. In the pitch black, the wind and icy rain was tearing at his skin, his heart was pounding and he had 'eyes like a wild cat'. He got to the engine room and told the engineer to get out there on the deck as well, he was needed. All radar and navigation instruments were destroyed.

Tracy made landfall at about midnight. The Catholic Midnight Mass was interrupted. Those listening to a live broadcast heard the mass drowned out by the wind, which picked up the bells and made them peal madly. Then the mass went off the air. In the next hour Tracy moved into suburbia. At Judith and Gary Watson's cancelled party in the northern suburb of Wagaman, the wind became so strong that a friend called Stephen, whom they had not been able to notify about the cancellation, called a cab. He tried to walk out but the wind pushed him off his feet and he had to crawl to the waiting taxi. In Nightcliff Peter Collins saw vehicles in trouble negotiating the roadways. Heavy torrential rain was coming down at about a 30-degree angle to the ground. A brave motorist in a Holden FB station wagon was trying to drive up his street, coming level with his house and then being blown back.

Water pushed through the metal and glass louvres and loose objects, such as rubbish tins and tricycles became airborne, smashing into walls and cars. Power failed. Lightning struck dramatically, providing the only illumination. Some residents suffered little, but others lost their roofs or louvres, letting in wind and rain, which created havoc. Some homes along the shoreline were destroyed and survivors huddled in cars or in concrete block laundries and storerooms. Cars were overturned. Corrugated iron ripped off roofs and sliced through trees and walls. Trees and shrubs were totally stripped of foliage. Power lines broke and lashed through the air, blasting anything they touched. They resembled enormous deadly vipers spitting sparks and flame.

Some residents, like Peter Coombe, ventured out, joining a group of partygoers in a convoy of cars to 'have a look at the cyclone from Fannie Bay'. A tree fell on the convoy. Coombe went home, but realised he would have to help a neighbour with a severely gashed arm and an hysterical woman who was also bleeding. He put them into his Peugeot sedan and headed off down the Stuart Highway towards Darwin Hospital. It was raining so heavily that he had to drive at a crawl. 'The rain was horizontal and it was pitch black,' he said. At Goyder Road, about two kilometres from his home, he ran into an unexpected traffic hazard. 'All of a sudden I hit a house!' he said later. 'It was right in the middle of the road. I knew that because I was following the white line. It was a complete house still with its roof on and fairly intact. It still had its banks of louvres in place. I wasn't going too fast so it wasn't much of an impact. I backed up and carefully drove around this house and continued on into the hospital.' When he returned, the house was gone.

Others sheltering in their houses were forced to move from their first position as windows and louvres were shattered and debris was blown in. Some people found that once corrugated iron rooves peeled off, the rain then poured through plaster ceilings and then the ceilings would collapse under the weight of water. Many saw timber from roofing struts and walls pierce their refuge and threaten to impale them. They moved from one side of their house to the other when the wind changed direction. In screaming winds over 150 kmh, rainwater squirted through closed louvres—many bending beyond belief without breaking—and drenching everything. It became freezingly cold. Low air pressure, high wind and torrential rain were turning Darwin into a very large air conditioner. Few people had been 'dressed for the storm', the hot sultry nights had been inducing most people to sleep in the nude or with very little on, and that was hardly helping, now that warmth was a priority.

Forestry officer Laurie Gwynne and his wife Shirley were in their home of the past six years, a high-set three bedroom house in the northern suburb of Wagaman, with their daughter Tahnee, two, and son Damian, one. By midnight it was obvious the storm was very very serious. The house was moving on its piers and starting to break up. At about 1 am Laurie said, 'It's going to go.' Laurie was wearing swimming togs and a T-shirt and Shirley a short dress and underwear. Tahnee wore summer pyjamas and Damian wore a baby suit. Nobody had shoes on. In one huge gust the lounge furniture was sucked through the partition of the louvred wall and thrown over the small front balcony. The rest of the house began to break up. It was time to move downstairs. Laurie moved to open the front door and as he did so it was sucked off the hinges. He took the children downstairs, braving the gale. Shirley had trouble getting her feet to move. She saw their black and white cat sucked off the balcony landing. Then she herself was blown off, landing in the front yard. Laurie said, 'I was beyond worry now we were fighting for our lives.' He crawled into the yard and found his wife, now injured by the fall and by the impact of airborne concrete blocks. Her feet had deep penetration wounds from nails. 'The noise was deafening, terrifying,' Shirley said later. 'The rain was so heavy I was almost drowning. I couldn't breathe for the water in my face.' The family crawled painstakingly towards their downstairs laundry and storeroom. After a few terrifying moments they eventually got onto the down-wind side of the buildings. They could not get inside—they would have to have gone directly into the wind, which would have invited sure death, so they huddled with their children on the outside.

The First Wind, as it became known, blew for about three hours, peaking between 1 am and 2 am. On *Assail*, Lieutenant Chris Cleveland and crew, who had been placed on standby for search and rescue work, spent two hours desperately trying to stay on the storm mooring. By 1 am the boat was starting to drag its heavy hawser lines and the 7.5 tonne concrete mooring buoy. The pressure was so great that at 2 am the steel cable broke and Cleveland realised his best chance was to make for the open sea, trying to ensure that there was no collision with any other vessel in the anchorage area. 'We crash-started the engines when the cable broke and tried to leave; however, the initial wind direction laid the ship on her beam-ends twice and I feared further attempts would capsize her,' Cleveland said later. The Assail was rolling at least 80 degrees and the navigation sidelights went underwater several times. Visibility was a little over a metre. The propellers were as much out of the water as they were in and the echo sounder seemed to be pinging on the wavetops. The combined force of the wind and rain stripped the foremast of its top coat of paint. There was solid water halfway up the superstructure. One wave lifted the stern out of the water and another smashed the propeller. Cleveland decided on a 'racetrack pattern' between Mica Beach and Doctor's Gully, directly into and then away from the howling winds.

On *Advance*, Lieutenant Peter Breeze had been tracking the tropical cyclone on his ship's radar all afternoon and thought Tracy looked 'like a bad one'. He had decided to anchor in the harbour rather than attaching to his mooring buoy because he feared that conditions became bad enough, 'we might not be able to get ourselves away from the buoy.' By about 1 am *Advance* was starting to drag anchor so he fired up his engines and decided like *Assail* that his best course was to steam out to sea, into the gale. The *Attack*, commanded by Lieutenant Paul de Graaf, started dragging about the harbour, still secured to its mooring buoy. It almost came into contact with one of the wharves, and the crew, desperately manoeuvring managed to avoid colliding with a prawn trawler.

The *Arrow*, commanded by Lieutenant Bob Dagworthy, was riding out the storm in the harbour. One of the ship's company had counted about 17 prawn boats, two ferries and a schooner anchored behind them in Darwin's inner harbour before the cyclone struck, and soon after the fiercest winds struck—at about 2 pm—he turned and saw no craft at all. The *Arrow's* troubles began when its mooring line and 160-metre anchor chain partly snapped. While it was still half-attached, Dagworthy started the engines. The *Arrow* was rolling violently. The chain snapped and the windlass was torn from the vessel before it disintegrated. Unable to gain headway, Dagworthy decided to run the boat up onto the wharf so the 19 crew could jump off. The *Arrow* was driven into the outer corner of Stokes Hill Wharf, rolling heavily in crashing waves. Dagworthy took to a lifeboat and was at the mercy of the lashing winds for the next 13 hours. Crew members jumped for the wharf, clinging for their lives in absolute darkness to whatever they could, which was probably the oysters and coral encrusting the wharf. Their clothes were ripped off by the wind and rain. Petty Officer Les Catton was struck by flying cargo, knocked unconscious and blown back into the water, where he drowned. Another sailor, John Rennie, also drowned. As the boat sank, four sailors who were swept into the water against the wharf pylons and struts were severely lacerated. Those on the wharf decking faced danger from steel cargo containers, some 'the size of a room', being 'tossed along like children's toy blocks'. Once off the wharf, the sailors made their way to a deserted car park. Some vehicles, such as that of the assistant harbour master, Colin Woods, had been blown onto their sides. The men took refuge where they could to avoid flying objects.

Between 2.30 and 3 am, depending on where people lived, those who wished to marvel at Nature's phenomena might have had a chance to observe the surreal atmosphere at the eye of a cyclone, but not all would have had the chance. In some areas, like the Central Business District, the eye did not pass directly overhead but off to a flank. As it did so, the wind changed direction. The eye of a tropical cyclone is like a huge chimney. Inside that hollow column there is very little wind, no rain and very little cloud. Consequently there is also very little noise. It is an area of extremely low pressure. In Tracy's case this has to be estimated, since the Bureau of Meteorology's barograph stopped recording at about 947 millibars, which was when the barometer dropped below the bottom of the paper and the instrument was damaged. Some brave souls ventured out into the street looking in awe at the devastation. Many thought that the eye was 'totally still' and 'dead calm'. In fact the wind was still moving at about eight kmh, but in the circumstances it seemed windless.

At Ludmilla, Alan Grove's three young children had slept through the First Wind. Alan peered out to see what he could in the lightning flashes, but his view was blocked by a small rise in the ground. He ventured outside. 'It was eerie,' he said later. 'It felt deathly still. I met my neighbours and we chatted. The house across road was badly damaged, but the owners were away. It was strange and unsettling because we all knew it was coming back.' Graham Clark was sheltering with his family in Wagaman. He could not believe what he saw in the illumination of the lightning. 'There were definitely several black tornadoes inside the cyclone,' he said. He knew tornadoes did not exist in the Southern Hemisphere. In fact it was a phenomenon associated with severe tropical cyclones, but only rarely reported. Dianne Ferguson was in a married quarter on the RAAF base. 'It was completely still,' she said later. 'I could hear voices, I heard someone yelling for help and a woman screaming.' Her husband Bob looked outside with a torch, then came back and said nothing except that there was glass 'all down the hallway'. Just up the road, Josephine Foreman heard neighbours screaming. 'There was a strange light and the lightning in the background reminded me of St Elmo's Fire,' Foreman said. The eye, which had now shrunk from 13 kilometres in diameter to eight or nine kilometres, began to move in a trochoidal fashion north of the airport and head through the northern suburbs.

The Second Wind came suddenly from the opposite direction, picking up all the debris from the First Wind and turning them into deadly missiles. Many houses that had survived the First Wind, though in a weakened state, had little chance of surviving the second. Alan Grove was wondering where to go. 'Within and under a minute it hit and it was a sound much deeper than the First Wind, like a heavy roar,' he said. 'Instantaneously we knew something catastrophic was coming. We put the kids in the lounge room between some mattresses, but that very quickly got too wet and so we moved to the bathroom and then moved again when a tree came through the side of the house.' The Second Wind reached an estimated speed of just over 300 kmh. The instruments failed when the gauge reached 295 kmh. The rain gauges also failed. Some people were picked up and hurled through the air at lethal speeds. A woman became airborne in her bathtub and was deposited two doors from her home. She lost nearly all her fingers, which had been hanging onto the edge of the tub. Structures already weakened by the first onslaught were now subjected to continuous strikes by lumber, metal and furniture. Huge objects—domestic refrigerators, baths and cars—became airborne. In the suburb of Larrakeyah, Julie and Heikki Tam found the entire upper structure of their home blown away, leaving only the hardwood floorboards. They hung grimly onto a toilet pedestal and downpipe, which was all that was left standing.

In Lee Point Road in neighbouring Wagaman, Tricia and Graham Clark had decided to retire for the evening and 'sleep through the storm', Graham having to get up for an early start next day. They had two children, 19-month-old Sharon and 3-month-old Barry. During the First Wind the Clarks had been chased from room to room and finally into the hallway as their rented home disintegrated. They had just made the decision to stay where they were when the Second Wind descended with a roar, ripping the remains of their home apart. Every wall and stick of furniture was now gone. In Tracy parlance, all they had left was a 'dance floor'. They crawled across the dance floor to the bath, the only other thing remaining. Tricia had filled the tub with water, but it was now empty. The couple talked to each other about dying. Not long after another huge gust slammed into them and they were blown off the floor, along with all the floorboards. With their babies in their arms, they were hurled through black, wet, whirling space. Graham landed in a neighbour's backyard with Sharon still in his arms. Tricia landed somewhere else, on her back, gashing her shoulder to the bone, but still clinging to Barry.

Graham crawled, carrying Sharon koala-like under his body. He found the family car under the remains of their house and put Sharon in the front seat. As the car interior light came on he could see that young Sharon had blood matted over her entire body. 'I had to clear her eyes so she could see,' Graham said later. 'She was totally naked. Her nappy had been sucked off her'. He turned the car headlights on, then started crawling on the ground again, looking for his wife and son. The wind whipped the muddy ground into fine dirty spray, making breathing difficult. Crawling over broken glass, smashed timber and jagged iron, he found Tricia, still protecting Barry with her body. He carried Barry and led Tricia back to the car. In the dim light inside the vehicle, they realised all their clothes had been ripped off and they were covered in blood and mud. Graham grabbed a shirt from the back seat. Intended as a Christmas present , it was quickly ripped into strips to bandage Tricia's shoulder. Then the car became their refuge.

At Rapid Creek Chris Kingston-Lee, his wife Roslyn and their family had got through the First Wind and Chris had collapsed exhausted into bed. Then the Second Wind hit. The roof started peeling off, taking most of the ceiling with it. Roslyn got under the bathroom sink. Chris covered her and their son, TJ, with blankets. The dog huddled behind Roslyn, under the sink with a look on its face that, according to Chris, conveyed the message: 'You can bite your arse! I am not moving!' Chris sat in his bathtub. 'Fibro sheeting fell through the open ceiling and into the bath and so I covered myself with that,' he said. 'The noise was just incredible, it was whistling and screaming. The rain was hitting us like we had the shower full on in the room.'

In her low-set concrete house at Jingili, Karen Jurek heard the roar of the Second Wind. 'I thought that this was it—we would die,' she said later. 'Sheets of iron were now tearing off their roof. In fact the entire roof was lifting off the pre-cast concrete walls including some of the trusses.' In nearby Nakara, John Woodcock and his family and parents abandoned their house. Their cars were in the open and had lost all their windows. They decided not to get into the wind but to use a concrete block wall to protect them from the rain and mud. John saw refrigerator doors flying past. All the trees were flattened. Nothing over two metres was left standing in his backyard. His neighbour's Land Rover was over upside down under his house.

In the suburb of Alawa, John and Sue Ryan and their three-month-old son Daniel were in their high-set three bedroom government house, but felt the house rock and shake on its pylons and believed it was about to totally disintegrate. The couple crawled out onto the landing, struggling with all their might against the gale-force wind. They went down the concrete stairs, using the wall of the house to provide some protection as they headed for their concrete block storeroom. John was on all fours, clinging to Daniel, who he had hidden under his body. Once in the storeroom the Ryans thought they were safe. But less than 30 minutes later, an incredibly strong wind gust blew in the storeroom wall. The Ryans had placed Daniel in a pram. Concrete blocks weighing some 300 kilograms fell onto the pram, but a solid piece of timber panelling used for a tool rack spread the force of the falling bricks. It saved Daniel's life. They retreated to their Volkswagen sedan and crouched inside as it rocked violently and took direct hits from debris. John did not think much of the accommodation, but he had little choice. His other car, a utility, had had its roof caved in by a falling floor. Sue, who had cut her feet on smashed louvres, tried to breast-feed Daniel but found that she had dried up.

Laurie and Shirley Gwynne, sheltering outside the laundry and storeroom of their home in Wagaman with their two children, felt the Second Wind come and tried moving to the opposite side of the buildings. A neighbour's above-ground pool, containing about 40 000 litres of water, collapsed and the ensuing deluge swept baby Damian from Shirley's arm. Shirley crawled despairingly in the darkness after him. She tried screaming to Laurie for help, but the words themselves were ripped from her mouth. 'I panicked and I can remember screaming in absolute terror,' she said. 'He weighed about 15 kilograms and was the biggest, fattest baby and that was probably why I lost hold of him.' She got to the other side of the storeroom where her brand-new Mazda, a Christmas present, was standing. As she put her feet under the front of her car she felt Damian. She frantically clutched the boy to her chest, not knowing whether he was alive or dead. Getting into the car was simply not an option because they were unable to make the two metres into the wind and the sedan was locked. Their open Mini Moke offered no protection and so Laurie screamed at Shirley to climb into the trailer whose sides offered some minimal cover. Above their heads on a rack was a four-metre dinghy. It had almost broken loose from its cradle and was endangering the family. Laurie kicked it completely off the cradle. 'The wind caught the dinghy and it went up into the air like a sheet of paper and was never seen again,' he said.

Then they heard a faint cry. It was a neighbour who had just moved into the street. She pleaded for help. A wall had collapsed on her husband, trapping him from the waist down. He was holding their baby. It was impossible to contact the rescue service. Laurie, who had found a pair of trousers and some boots, realised he would have to assist by himself. 'I went with this woman and was obviously loathe to leave my own family but you just can't leave people,' he said. 'It took ages to get out of the trailer and crawl back to her house using the gutter for protection.' Laurie searched in the dark and found a piece of timber to lever up the wall and get the man and baby out. It took all of his strength to just get into the house, but he rescued them both, then led the family downstairs and put them on the down-wind side of their storeroom before making his way back to his home. 'The wind had dropped from 250 kmh to 249 kmh,' he said. He tried running across to his family's trailer but only made it 15 metres when a piece of corrugated iron hit him, luckily upright when it did so, and carried him across the street into a front yard, breaking all his toes. He crawled slowly back across the street and with all his strength climbed back into the trailer where he, Shirley and children spent the rest of the night—almost three hours.

At about 4 am Chris Cleveland and his crew on *Assail*, riding out the storm in the open ocean, their progress hampered by a 20 centimetre hurricane hawser wrapped around the port screw, felt the wind veer rapidly to the north-west. Cleveland decided to steam towards Bathurst Island but to reverse direction and return to Darwin when the wind eased. The return to Darwin Harbour at 6 am, presented a dreadful scene. Where there had been some 50 sea craft there were now only five, two patrol boats, two trawlers and one tug. The rest were sunk, missing or run aground. Cleveland saw that his arm was covered in huge bruises from where they had been wrapped around the binnacle as he tried to stay upright in the wheelhouse. By now the cyclone was some distance away. By 5.30 am, it was heading south of town towards Humpty Doo, completing a rampage that had lasted up to six hours.

As more light seeped through the misty, drizzly rain early on Christmas Day it revealed damage on a scale that had never been experienced in Australia's short recorded history. People began emerging from their wrecked houses, from under rubble and out of cars, and walked dazed through block after block of what had once been Darwin suburbia. Laurie and Shirley Gwynne found nothing left of their house save for the stairs and the balcony railing. The damage in the northern suburbs had been acute, but almost 90 percent of the city had been destroyed. More than fifty people had lost their lives on land, mostly as a result of having been crushed, haemorrhaging from cuts caused by flying iron or glass, or being impaled, often by timber from roof struts. Others had been killed by trauma after being blown into the air and against an object. Sixteen had been lost at sea.

There were degrees of survival. Nick Paspaley found his pearling boat relatively undamaged, but it had broken its anchor lines and was pushed high up into the mangroves in Sadgrove's Creek. *Clipper Bird* had been driven ashore at Doctor's Gully. HMAS *Attack* had lost its struggle and had been driven ashore, ending high and dry at Doctor's Gully, some four or five kilometres from where it had tried to stay at its mooring buoy. It was holed at three places in the hull, having in all probability encountered *Clipper Bird* or the unmanned *Jenny Wright*, which had sunk about 60 metres away.

For almost everyone who survived Tracy, there was at some stage during the storm a moment when they thought that they, their families or their neighbours were in deadly peril. Many people had thought there was a good chance that they would not survive until dawn. It was 'the longest night of my life,' said Diane Kerntke. Greta Quong said later, 'I thought I was going to die. The noise was so loud we couldn't talk.' The storm had been capricious. Karen Jurek's husband, Kevin, saw that other houses of similar construction to his own at Jingili had 'basically survived the storm'. Some people had survived through determination, courage and willpower. Others had been lucky. In most cases it was a combination of personal application and luck.

It was a time for soul-searching. Shirley Gwynne said of husband Laurie, 'He was in total control.' Laurie said that was not so. 'I caved in and Shirley bounced back,' he said. 'After dawn I sat on a heap of rubble and cried . . . I went grey in one year.' Other married couples had held hands and told each other of their love. Others just looked into each other's eyes because it was impossible to talk. Countless couples said they had prayed for the first time since they were children kneeling by their beds. Moving to seek shelter during the storm had been extremely difficult in darkness so profound it was, as one Darwinian described it, 'as black as the inside of a dog's guts'. No one had been able to stand upright. The gales had made movement above a crawl on all fours extremely hazardous, and moving away from cover ran the risk of being killed.

Although other cyclones in Australia have caused greater loss of life, mainly at sea among the pearling and fishing fleets of earlier years, none has caused damage of the magnitude suffered by Darwin. About 20 000 people were rendered homeless. The damage bill was estimated at $500–600 million in contemporary values. Not one house had been left undamaged. Most had been wrecked. Every backyard was littered with debris. In many cases almost every window or louvre pane in the premises had been broken. The airport had been knocked out of commission, its radar hanging crazily upside down and off its mount. All the 50-odd light aircraft at the airport had been destroyed and piled in a couple of tangled heaps at the end of the runways. The roads were virtually impassable unless one had a front end loader to scrape away the piles of debris. If there was a clear road there was a good chance one could not get very far because of sharp nails and shards of glass. It was eerily hushed. After the roar of the Second Wind it was now deathly silent—not a cry of a bird or whirr of a cicada could be heard.

Darwin Hospital had to cope with hundreds of casualties. Its casualty reception floor was full of water and stained red with blood. Temporary morgues were set up in suburban police stations. Everyone was in shock. It was too much for many people to comprehend, to assimilate and come to grips with easily. All reference points were gone. People got lost trying to find their own street. Most of the telegraph poles in Lee Point Road were bent at right angles about 500 millimetres off the ground. Most people compared it with Hiroshima. There was now an enormous health risk and medical services had all but been reduced to nil. Darwin needed to be evacuated. The Federal Government quickly declared a national disaster. The head of National Disasters Organisation, Major General Alan Stretton, flew in on Boxing Day to oversee the re-establishment of essential services and local government in what was a massive national effort. Records were set on aircraft flying people out of Darwin. A Boeing 747 claimed a record 674 souls on board on Sunday 29 December. By New Year's Eve only about 9000 people remained in Darwin. For many hundreds of people it was such an ordeal that they packed up and left Darwin, never to return. The search for bodies continued for months after the cyclone. Some 18 months later harbour master Carl Allridge reported the discovery of 'one-and-a-half bodies'. The whole body was identified as that of a Japanese fisherman. The prawn trawler *Booya* was never found.

Many found it difficult to believe the low casualty count, given the enormous amount of destruction. One theory that does appeal is that if the cyclone had not hit in the early morning hours when it did, more people might have lost their lives trying to do things they did not do that night because they could not see. Several people were killed and many more injured when they moved outside of their shelter during the storm. Houses had come apart with disarming ease—the style of residential house typical in Darwin had a lot to do with that. Cyclone bolts would not have mattered, since many a house was left with a dance floor and dozens of bent bolts pointing skywards. What was needed was some greater protection for the occupants. The Darwin Reconstruction Commission adopted a 'bunker' approach for a short time, but concluded that reduction of window sizes and other requirements was going too far, that it was not so much the lack of building strength but the intensity of the wind borne by a very deep pressure system that had done the damage. Harbour Master Allridge was convinced that a lock was needed to protect smaller craft. His suggestions were taken on board.

Today in Darwin millions of dollars worth of pleasure craft and commercial vessels can take refuge at Cullen Bay behind a storm-surge-proof lock. When Tracy hit there was no tidal surge that normally accompanies a cyclone experienced in Darwin, since the tides were out—this prevented a lot of coastal damage. Darwin is now more prepared than ever for cyclones. Houses all contain a storm shelter made of concrete that is near the bathroom/toilet area. The houses are made stronger, and the mets have even greater ability to predict cyclones with more advanced technological aids like geostationary satellites.

There were several factors that contributed to the devastation that Tracy caused: the apathy created by Cyclone Selma, the time of day Tracy hit, and the circumstances of Christmas Eve. Had they been different, the result would have been different, but not necessarily any better. What could have been present, though, was a serious appreciation by administrators and people in general that in this region of climatic extremes, a direct hit by a cyclone was always on the cards.

13

The Brisbane Floods, 1974

Centenary bridge between Kenmore and Jindalee untrafficable because of being struck by a barge.

Brisbane Police log, 10.30 am, 27 January 1974

Floods are nothing new to Brisbane. Since the earliest days of white settlement in the 19th century, they had visited the city regularly, wreaking havoc and destruction on its homes, citizens and infrastructure. Creekside flooding had been a problem since the first free settlers began arriving in what had until then been a convict village. The combined catchments of the Bremer and Brisbane Rivers in prehistoric times had deposited truly massive quantities of water into the Brisbane River. Evidence enough for this can be found in the geological record of the Brisbane suburb of Indooroopilly. Four floods in the European history of Brisbane had indicated the potential dangers: a flood in 1867 that swept away the original Victoria Bridge, and three successive floods in 1893 that stranded a ship in Brisbane's Botanical Gardens, washed away the Indooroopilly railway bridge, washed away the northern end of Victoria bridge and carried the stranded ship back into the Brisbane River. People still came to live along those waterways that drained the steep hills around Brisbane. Why did they do this?

The answer lies mainly in the economy of the day, which was largely based on the pastoral industry that was burgeoning in the settlement's hinterland. There was also a need for a ready water supply. Pastoralists did not raise cattle primarily for food in those early years of the 19th century; the demand in the days of horse transport, horse-power and lighting by candle was for harness leather and tallow, and these were the staple products of the Brisbane settlement as it tanned the hides of cattle and rendered fat from the carcasses. To serve the processing end of the pastoral industry, tanneries and rendering works mushroomed along Brisbane's creek flats to take advantage of a ready supply of the enormous amounts of water these processes demanded.

With no public transport, the workers for these labour-intensive works built their homes within walking distance of the flood plains of the creeks. Extended families continued to make their homes there, and organised housing subdivisions and commercial developments followed the natural progression of roads, utilities and other infrastructure into already settled areas.

The continuing problems this caused for the next 130 years were highlighted by an engineering study of flooding in Brisbane creeks in 1973. In March 1973 the engineers, Cameron, McNamara and Partners, reported to the co-ordinator general that as well as the direct and indirect losses caused by creeks flooding, there were important sociological consequences that could not be evaluated in monetary terms. 'Repeated flooding has left some families living in poor conditions,' the report said. 'These families lack capital to fully restore flood damage, to lift their houses, or to sell their houses at a price adequate to purchase alternative accommodation.' They said families already near the poverty line became trapped in a situation of periodic flood damage and their standard of living continued to deteriorate as the quality of their housing was continually degraded. Severe emotional distress was often the result.

The Cameron McNamara report noted that within 50 years of the establishment of Brisbane, the flooding problem triggered by lack of planned development and restriction of natural waterways had been largely alleviated. 'But the historic flooding problem . . . is now in various stages of repetition on a larger scale . . . for many of Brisbane's larger creeks,' it warned. The engineers noted that a major flood had occurred in the Enoggera-Breakfast Creek system in 1931, but another flood in 1967 had resulted in much higher damage because of more intensive development and the existence of more expensive machinery within the zones of inundation. The June 1967 flood had caused $1 760 000 worth of damage; another in February 1972 had cost $1 450 000. More government and city council control over land usage in the creek catchments was needed, the engineers observed.

Flood mitigation schemes for the Brisbane Valley went back almost as far as the beginning of white settlement. Typical examples included those of an engineer named George Phillips who in 1901 advocated upstream dams, the straightening and deepening of the Brisbane River in its lower reaches, and the cutting of canals to enable floodwaters to by-pass the city. 'We should endeavour to regulate and improve the estuary, certainly as far as Victoria bridge, and ultimately all the way to Ipswich by widening and deepening the navigable channel and cutting off the principal bends and points to shorten the distance the water has to run and also to reduce the resistance offered to the passage of water in flood time,' he wrote. 'The entire removal of Kangaroo Point is pre-eminently desirable, not only as the chief obstacle to the free passage of floodwater but also with a view to improving the Port of Brisbane in the very heart of the city.'

One of the problems associated with any rare disastrous event has always been the difficulty in persuading potential victims of the danger. By 1966 a very efficient flood warning system had been developed, but problems with the dissemination and interpretation of warnings, coupled with some reluctance by the community to accept reality, meant that the full gravity of the situation might not necessarily be conveyed.

By January 1974 factors seen in retrospect to have contributed to the disaster had long been at work. The weather systems were both complex and persistent as well as being unusual. The wet season in northern Australia is not normally established until early in January, and the associated monsoonal airflow is usually confined to the northern part of the continent, but by mid-December 1973 the monsoonal trough was already well established over far northern Australia. It continued a steady southward progression during January 1974. Near-record rains had fallen over a large part of Australia. Cyclone Una had moved south over the sea parallel with the Queensland coast in December, dumping huge amounts of rain that had left the coastal mainland sodden. An Australian Weather Bureau analysis showed that this combined with remarkably strong and persistent monsoonal flow to cause heavy rains over a large area of Queensland, the Northern Territory, and northern parts of Western Australia. Nearly every Queensland river had been in flood except the Dumaresque, on the south-east border.

Incredibly enough, the storm that was to trigger so much human suffering and loss began as a puff of cloud no larger than a golf ball over the Coral Sea, thousands of kilometres from Brisbane. Weather bureau observers on Willis Island, 2000 kilometres north-east of Brisbane, detected the embryo storm as their barometers began to fall on 21 January. It was a weak low in the monsoonal trough near Willis Island. During the day the low intensified further. By late 23 January, the low, now code-named Cyclone Wanda, had re-curved to a south-west track and was moving towards the Queensland coast. By the next day it was off Mackay and gaining strength, and mainland observers were tracking it on their instruments as atmospheric pressures dropped along the Queensland coast. Later that day the disturbance was producing 100km/hr winds. Weather bureau chief Arch Shields was to say that Wanda never developed an 'eye', and therefore was never really a cyclone at all, but the distinction became a very academic one.

Flooding began with heavy rain over the Stanley River catchment on 24 January, in association with the decaying Wanda. That night the weather bureau announced that Wanda had moved inland near Gympie and heavy rain was falling on the Stanley and Brisbane River watersheds. At 11.20 pm that night Raymond Roy Davidson, 29, from the Brisbane suburb of Wacol, and Hazel Dulcie Afflick, 40, were killed in a head-on collision while driving in blinding rain and gale-force winds in Wacol. These were regarded as the first flood deaths. By daybreak on Friday Brisbane's notorious creek floodplains were awash and cars were stalling in floor-deep water. Police were called to their first emergency when rising winds tore the roof from a house in Nundah, an inner northern suburb. The weather bureau warned of expected serious flooding in Kedron Brook and Enoggera Creek, the main river tributaries on Brisbane's north side, on the high tide at 2 pm. The warning was spot on. At 1.59 pm the first evacuations from the low-lying suburban areas of Windsor began. Forty minutes later rescuers were calling for a boat to evacuate a woman and her children. Calls began to come in for sandbags to build flood levees. Cribb Island, on the northern Bayside, reported water undermining houses. People were starting to move to emergency shelter in church halls and public buildings.

Flooding was occurring in the upper Stanley River, and by 3 pm on Friday rain had saturated all the Bremer catchment. By 9 pm significant run-off was occurring in the Bremer and Upper Brisbane Rivers and Lockyer Creek. Record rains in the Ipswich area caused unprecedented flooding and the Bremer began to rise at an exceptional rate in Ipswich. As dawn broke on Australia Day, floods were rising in the suburbs of Oxley, Corinda and Woodridge. Ipswich came into the picture as the Bremer rose towards record height. Families were being rescued in the racecourse area. Caravans had been washed from a van park into a swift-flowing creek at Goodna. Four people had been rescued from trees and another was missing.

After crossing the coast, Wanda continued on its southwest track towards Dalby, but continued weakening at a rapid rate and disappeared as a feature of the weather chart. It provided the initial rains that saturated the Brisbane River catchment and forced the monsoon trough south to Brisbane itself, where it persisted for several days. The other important weather system was a large anticyclone in the Tasman Sea. This remained almost stationary during the period of the floods and stopped the normal eastward movement of weather systems, thus preventing any dry air mass from moving in over Queensland and clearing the weather. The high also steered Wanda onto the Queensland coast and influenced the movement of the monsoonal trough.

As the high tide ebbed the creek flooding receded, but heavy rain was now cascading from the mountain ranges that hedge the 13 600 square kilometre Brisbane Valley, and the die for Brisbane's worst ordeal was cast. Just before midnight on Friday radio stations began broadcasting warnings for people living in low-lying parts of the Gold Creek and Moggill Creek catchments to move to higher ground; heavy rain at Enoggera and Mount Nebo was pouring floodwaters into the creeks.

Calls to police flood headquarters began to escalate in the early hours of 26 January. An elderly woman had been washed away at Ashgrove. Help was needed with evacuations at Indooroopilly and Herston. At Herston a man had tried to rape a woman. A car had been swept away at Arana Hills. At 1.20 am a caller advised that a car had been washed into a creek from a bridge at Inala. A man and woman had escaped, but on a causeway over Oxley Creek, Inala, two-year-old Shane David Patterson, from Yeronga, was torn from his father's grasp and drowned. Water was 2.5 metres deep in a house at Newmarket, and other houses were being evacuated at Tennyson, Windsor, Kedron and Wilston. Telephone poles were being washed away at Inala. A pregnant woman needed help at Kenmore. Boats were being torn from their moorings and whirled down the Brisbane River.

Hazel Tew, of Margate, saw horizontal rain as she drove through it to get to her work in the city telephone exchange, where 100 operators manned boards around the clock during the emergency. 'It was a madhouse trying to get calls through,' she wrote later. Amateur radio operators had worked around the clock to provide emergency communications when telephone systems became inadequate, and established a 50-operator network that covered the Brisbane Valley from Mt Crosby to Pinkenba.

Richard Webber, who had been controller of civil defence in the Northern Territory, was asked to set up a flood command centre at police headquarters. He arrived there and asked a superintendent what he was to do, but the police officer said he had no idea. 'He said, "You are the expert, here is our operations room and it is entirely at your disposal," gave me his telephone extension number and left. We set up and ran that operations room 24 hours a day until the end of the flood; it was run like a war room—telephones ringing with information and details of emergencies, people logging each piece of information to plot the rise of the floodwaters on a map of Brisbane, people co-ordinating with the civil defence headquarters in Fortitude Valley, the police, ambulance, the armed services, volunteer groups, newspapers, radio and television.'

According to the weather bureau, the imminence of a flood higher than 1893 was not apparent in the city reaches of the Brisbane River during the daylight hours of 26 January. A minor flood height of 3.5 metres occurred at the port office gauge on the high tide at about midday, caused mainly by runoff from local creeks and a persistent storm surge caused by high winds in Moreton Bay. With the enormous contribution from the Bremer and continuing high rainfalls in Brisbane, the river continued to rise. 'It was the heavy rain that fell over most of the Brisbane Valley, principally during the period between 3 pm Saturday and 3 pm Sunday, that was responsible for converting a minor level flood in Brisbane into one of major proportions,' the bureau said.

The Bremer River rose more than 10.5 metres during Saturday. Because of water backing it up in the Brisbane River, the Bremer River height remained above 19.2 metres for 39 hours. Carmel Benham, of West End, saw the flood through the eyes of a frightened child. 'I was eight when the flood came,' she said a long time later. 'It rained for a long time; we just sat on the veranda of our Ashgrove home watching the creek rise higher and higher until it broke its banks. The creek looked like a river; during the night of January 25 my grandfather heard something outside the window and got up to open the door. The water flooded in; he woke up Dad, then they woke the rest of the family. The only way out was by the kitchen window, and Grandfather and Dad helped the older ones out; I was so scared I didn't want to get out.'

There were added complications. Though the main flooding was in the Brisbane Valley, there were three periods of intense rain in the Brisbane metropolitan area that caused severe local flooding in three separate waterways—Moggill Creek, Enoggera Creeks and Kedron Brook. During the evacuation of a caravan park in the suburb of Newmarket, Robert Adams, 56, suffered a fatal heart attack. As the day progressed police lost count of the number of rescues they were called on to carry out. There were many instances of heroism. When an amphibious army vehicle struck a power line at Jindalee, Queensland Government cabinet minister Bill Lickiss, who was aboard, dived into the water to rescue one of two soldiers who had been thrown from the boat by the electric shock. Although he risked his own life to save them, both men perished.

During the crisis, Brisbane's two daily newspapers attempted to keep abreast of the situation but there were some deficiencies in their coverage, largely because of disrupted communications and general confusion. There was a rush of interstate media to Brisbane causing a mass of information to be released in one form or another. It was no time for a reporter to stand idle. This writer at the time was news editor of Brisbane's *Sunday Sun*. My own house was flooded, but I did not miss a day's work.

The flash floods began to wane after midday, and many people thought—wrongly—that the worst was over. The real ordeal was just beginning.

The enormous amount of water that had cascaded into the Brisbane Valley from surrounding mountains was swelling the Brisbane River and rolling towards its confluence with the Bremer, which was approaching previously unknown heights, flooding Ipswich before contributing its waters to the Brisbane flood. As the two floods met, the greater volume in the Brisbane backed up the Bremer like a weir. By 9 pm Saturday water was back in the houses it had left during the afternoon, and the City Council warned that higher levels were on the way in Brisbane. At 10.30 pm the Brisbane River broke its banks at Indooroopilly. Fifty minutes later it was spilling floodwaters into Yeronga. At midnight water was entering houses at Kenmore. At Ipswich, the Bremer was rising by 30 centimetres an hour.

The rumours about Somerset Dam began at 1 am Sunday. Bogus police were reported to be telling Ipswich people via loud hailer that Somerset Dam had broken. Had the rumour been true, flooding would have risen to a height impossible to cope with. The dam stood on the Stanley River spanning a gorge six kilometres above its confluence with the Brisbane. It had been commissioned as a water supply impoundment in 1943 for part flood mitigation in 1950, and for full flood mitigation in 1956. Rain in the Stanley River catchment was a major contributor to most Brisbane River floods, but up to 25 percent of the total floodwaters passed through Somerset Dam and could be controlled. Under favourable circumstances the dam could be shut down and the entire flow of the Stanley River could be stored while the peak of the Brisbane River flood passed the city. Water was then emptied slowly from the dam over a period of about two days in readiness for the next flood.

As 27 January dawned, the Brisbane River continued to rise, reaching 4.5 metres above its normal level by 9 am. Flooding had begun in the new showcase western suburb of Jindalee. Coronation Drive, the riverbank road that led to the leafy south-western suburbs, was disappearing under water. Most people believed that the Somerset Dam would save the city from a major submersion, but another drama was developing.

At 5.17 am an anonymous caller telephoned police headquarters to report that the newly-built 60 000 tonne tanker *Robert M. Miller* had broken loose from its fitting-out wharf at Kangaroo Point and was floating down the river crosswise. Simultaneously the tug *Neptune* was reported to have also broken her moorings and was sweeping down the New Farm reach. Eleven minutes later a police car radioed that the tanker appeared to have been anchored in midstream in the New Farm reach and was stationary. As the huge ship—the *Robert M. Miller* was the biggest vessel ever built in Brisbane—swept down the river dragging two anchors, she posed an enormous threat to high-rise apartment buildings towering only metres from the water's edge on the New Farm side.

Bill Dransfield, a marine engineer who managed the Evans Deakin shipyard where the *Robert M. Miller* had been moored at the fitting out wharf, recalled the drama 27 years later. 'We had been at the shipyard all of Saturday and left about 5 pm when it seemed the worst danger had passed,' he said. 'I was in bed at my Mount Gravatt home about 5 am when the shipyard watchman phoned to say the *Robert M. Miller* had broken her moorings. I asked him how he knew that. He told me, "I just saw her disappearing down the river near New Farm." The situation was pretty serious, but I had to laugh at the way he said it.' Dransfield alerted other shipyard workers by telephone and drove the 20-minute trip to meet them at Kangaroo Point. 'We could see the ship near the East Brisbane side of the river, and one anchor appeared to be holding,' he said. 'We had arranged the anchors so that if the ship got loose one would break and the other would cause her to slew towards the side of the river where the current was slower, and that's exactly what happened.'

At that time a man came down the river in a five-metre launch. Dransfield hailed him and commandeered the vessel to chase the tanker. 'There were four or five of us, a senior engineer named Bill Pennell, Bob Norris, who was a rigger and materials handler, another rigger named Fred Cotton, and one or two others including the launch owner. Fred climbed a rope that was hanging over the side of the *Robert M. Miller* and let the gangway down. When we got aboard we found that one anchor had gone and the other was hanging on a broken clenchpin. I got our scaffolding bars and jammed them in the anchor chain and we wired the capstan up so that it couldn't move. Bill Pennell went below to get the engines ready, and we got them started about lunchtime. We kept the ship facing upstream with the engines going dead slow. The river current was enough to give us steerage, but every time we saw a significant piece of debris coming we gave the engines a ten-second burst that enabled us to swing away from it. We were dodging houses, trees, horses, barges, pianos, cattle—you name it. One big barge hit the hull and punched a hole in it.'

There was no food aboard the ship, and no one could sleep. Tugs that had to fight their way upstream against the flood did not arrive to give their assistance until next morning. 'I was an engineer, but I was on the wheel, and by then everyone was calling me captain,' Dransfield recalled. 'We were on the ship for four days before we could leave.' The emergency crew in fact steamed the equivalent of a voyage to New Zealand without actually moving a metre—in a ship that was still unfinished and which had had no sea trials. It had been purely fortuitous that the ship was being readied for engine trials when the flood came—and her fuel tanks had just been filled for that purpose. Dransfield disclosed that if he had not been able to control the tanker, his plan was to strand it on a sandy beach under the southern end of the Storey Bridge. At the end of the day there was no recognition for the *Robert M. Miller* heroes. Dransfield said, 'We didn't care; we were just relieved that everything turned out okay.'

While the *Robert M. Miller* drama was unfolding, the flood was raging on along the entire length of the river's city reaches. A whole street was going underwater at Chelmer. Floodwaters were threatening a road tanker full of nitric acid at Rocklea. More than 40 people were huddled on an island near the Regatta Hotel at Toowong. Water was rising rapidly at Jindalee, and a major evacuation was under way at Woodridge, where police were spread so thinly that the police station phone was being manned by a civilian volunteer. The police log continues: 8.19 am: Four adults, four children, including two babies, require help to leave houses at Archerfield; 9.09 am: Caller advises that woman in Turley St,

Fairfield, who lives alone and won't leave her animals, may lose her life if not evacuated soon; Centenary bridge between Kenmore and Jindalee untrafficable because of being struck by a barge.

Centenary Bridge was Brisbane's newest cross-river link. The barge that had cannoned into it after being swept downstream from its moorings was wedged firmly under the edge of the carriageway, and was threatening to wreck the whole structure. At 8.55 that night an attempt to sink the barge— a former minesweeper with a double hull—with explosives failed. Firemen then pumped water into the explosives-laden vessel until it sank and swept upside-down under the bridge before exploding downstream.

By midnight on December 27, after more than three days of drama, rescue workers were showing signs of exhaustion, and now the flood was threatening the city itself. The Queensland Institute of Technology was slowly filling with water at Gardens Point and water was knee-deep in the city watch-house. Water was a metre deep in Albert and Mary Streets and was rising in Charlotte, Albert, Elizabeth and Creek Streets. Evacuation calls were coming thick and fast from St Lucia, Yeronga, Moorooka, Jindalee, Indooroopilly, Kenmore and New Farm. At the tide peak the flood level at the port office was 6.34 metres—two metres above the level generally considered the starting point of a serious flood.

The weather bureau later reported, 'In the five days from January 24 to January 29 total rainfalls in the Brisbane Metropolitan Area ranged from 500 millimetres (19 inches) to 900 millimetres (34.6 inches). Among five-day totals were 1318 millimetres (50.6 inches) at Mount Glorious in the catchment of the middle reaches of the Brisbane River, and 819 millimetres (31.5 inches) at Newby, near the headwaters of Oxley Creek. Near continuous rain with some heavy falls continued over the Brisbane Valley during Saturday, January 26, and Sunday, January 27. Although rainfalls in 1893 were less than in 1974, the flood peak in 1893 was higher because of the absence of Somerset Dam. In the 24 hours to 9 am on January 27, 1974, a total 341 millimetres (13 inches) fell at Ipswich—the highest ever recorded there.'

People were at last beginning to accept the warnings that had been given, and most evacuations from further threatened areas were complete. The dangers remained, however, sometimes unrecognised until it was too late. Citizens Military Forces Corporal Neville Barry Hourigan, of Sunnybank, and Captain Ian Kerr, of Aldersley, were on an army amphibious LARC vehicle, carrying out evacuation work at Bellbowrie. The vehicle hit high-tension wires. Both men were thrown from the vehicle and both died. Other tragedies were revealed only when the waters receded. The body of a man whose name was never published was found at Milton.

With rescues put to one side, the logistical problems of supplying the evacuees with shelter, food, clothing and cooking facilities began. As the floodwaters receded, people began to move tonnes of wrecked furniture and other household items from their homes. Trucks were needed to cart it away to dumps, disinfectant was needed to cleanse the stench from thousands of sodden homes. The rotting carcasses of drowned animals had to be disposed of, and volunteers were needed to hose, scrub and shovel the muck away. They in turn had to be protected with anti-tetanus injections, given in thousands by roving bands of medical workers.

Brisbane's Lord Mayor, Clem Jones, had been in Adelaide at a local government conference when the floods had come. Unable to fly directly back to his home city, he had arranged a flight to Maroochydore, from where he had travelled by truck through flooded roads, reaching Brisbane on the Sunday morning. He was observed to have cried quietly when he saw what had happened to his beloved city, but the Lord Mayor, always a man of action, went personally to check levels of the Brisbane River at Tennyson. Then he came to the moment of crucial decision: whether or not he was going to close the floodgates at Somerset Dam so as to stop any water from the Stanley River reaching Brisbane.

More than a quarter of a century later, controversy still surrounds the question of whether or not those gates should have been left open. Engineers argued then, and argue still, that the closure was a useless gesture that posed an enormous risk of another storm following the first and catching Somerset Dam full of water and therefore unable to impede the Stanley's contribution to a second flood. They calculated that the Stanley River water would have taken at least a day and a half to reach Brisbane, and by that time the flood peak would have passed through the city. Such a repetition of storms had caused three ensuing floods within a month, which had inundated Brisbane in 1893. If this recurred, and the Somerset Dam was full, it would potentially be catastrophic. As it turned out, the engineers were almost to be proved right. Jones ordered the gates closed. He told a later media conference that he had made the decision to allow floodwaters to fall more rapidly in Brisbane. 'I have no regrets about the decision, and there were no recriminations against those who opposed it,' he said. 'The floodwaters were just sitting in Brisbane, and I realised something had to be done to get them down as quickly as possible.'

The flood peaked at 6.6 metres on the Port Office gauge on the high tide at 2.15 am on 29 January. Ironically, it showed that the flood warning system developed from 1966 had well and truly worked—it was the level predicted 21 hours earlier. The trouble was that dissemination problems and complacency had robbed the warning of its full value. By the time the storm dissipated, 8500 homes from Brisbane to its sister city Ipswich were flooded. An inland sea stretched 200 kilometres west from of the coast. Aiden Sutton, 50, who had left his civilian job at Queensland Police Headquarters to go to his home at St Lucia to collect his spectacles, was found there dead.

If people could be confident the water would not rise any further, the receding waters signalled a new set of problems. The great cleanup was already on in earnest in upstream suburbs that had dried out earlier and in Ipswich. The cleaning up had not been without complications. In some creekside suburbs, residents had been driven from their homes by creek floodwaters early in the deluge and had returned to them next day to begin the cleanup, only to find themselves driven out again by backup floodwaters from the Brisbane River. Additionally, there was always an opportunity for a little mischief. Ian McAlpine, of Albany Creek, recalled the kids he and his mates caught stealing from flooded homes. They were swimming from house to house picking up articles left on the tops of wardrobes and cupboards by those who had fled, and pushing the collection around in a floating wooden box.

On 30 January the bodies of three men whose names were never reported were found as floodwaters receded from South Brisbane. When the waters finally receded, the toll was enormous. More than 6000 homes were either wrecked, missing, or full of slimy, stinking silt and debris that would take months of hard toil and heartbreak to clean up. In Ipswich, a community of 67500 people, 39 homes had been destroyed completely. Damage in Brisbane and Ipswich totalled about

$200 million. Twelve people had drowned and several elderly people had suffered heart attacks while being evacuated from homes. Scores of families had been torn apart. Stress victims were queued up at psychiatrists' doors, and some older house-holders had suffered financial loss beyond redemption within their lifetime. Carmel Benham said, 'We had to wait in the backyard for help; we lost everything, and stayed with our babysitter for two weeks while my parents fixed up our house. People helped my parents to get the mud out and get things together, and we went back to the house when it was clean again. I was so scared I didn't want to get out of the car and kept saying, "No, there is water in there." I am still afraid of living near a creek when there is a lot of rain.'

Whether it was a fully-fledged cyclone or not, Wanda brought a monstrous deluge, the like of which Brisbane residents had not seen for 81 years. Nature appeared to be taunting the saturated folk of southern Queensland, in partic-ular Clem Jones. Only a week after the Australia Day floods, Cyclone Pam cartwheeled down the Queensland coast while Somerset Dam was still holding Stanley River floodwaters. Pam had a cloud mass that covered more than two million square kilometres. Fortunately, it veered off into the Tasman Sea before it could dump its billions of tonnes of water into the Brisbane Valley. Had it dumped that water into the valley with the Somerset Dam gates closed, Clem Jones would not have been in a comfortable position.

There was point pondering on what might have been. Jones quickly began organising relief and formed an appeal com-mittee, headed by Lady Mayoress Sylvia Jones, that raised nearly $5 million. It was this appeal that showed the gen-erosity of those not affected by the flood. Brisbane's weekly *Sunday Sun* newspaper ran an appeal the weekend after the floods began with a front page banner headline, 'For God's sake give!' Half the paper's 400 000 readers responded to the suggestion that they place a one dollar note in an envelope and send it in. The *Sun* had to put on special staff to open the mail and fill scores of cardboard cartons with currency to be handed on to the Lord Mayor's fund.

There was also some sardonic humour, including the laughter directed at a much-vaunted long-range weather fore-caster. He had been featured in the weeks leading up to the flood in a television advertising campaign selling a garden watering system—he was predicting one of the driest sum-mers in Brisbane's meteorological history. Daryl Wyatt, at the time a deli owner in the suburb of Kenmore, decided to sell his precious stock of fresh milk only to mothers with babies in arms. 'Some of my regular customers became mothers overnight, and one matron demanded milk because she could not drink her tea without it,' he said later. Pearl Arnold, Red Cross disaster co-ordinator, remembered someone phoning in to donate a set of false teeth. 'Strangely, she said, only an hour before we had had an inquiry from a man who had lost his false teeth while being evacuated and hoped the Red Cross might have a spare set.'

There was no lack of people willing to assist. A multitude of volunteers came in off the street to offer assistance. Noel Wanmer, of Kangaroo Point, writing of his experiences to a Brisbane newspaper many years later, recalled a beautiful teenage girl who arrived at his home while he and some help-ers were shovelling silt from it. 'She was wearing a beautiful white dress. The skirt was pulled up and draped over one arm, and she was carrying her shoes; her legs and much of the dress were plastered with the muck through which she had been plodding from a railway station a couple of kilometres away' he recalled. 'She explained that she was on her way to a birthday party, but would not have been able to enjoy herself without having done something to help.'

What about setting up in life again? Was there any money to fund it? What about insurance? There were going to be problems. Before 1974 most urban Queensland householders had insurance policies that said they were covered against loss and or damage by 'storm and tempest.' Most of them believed that this term included flood. How wrong they were. The waters had not cleared from their flooded homes before they learned that insurance companies meant water that had not touched the ground when they talked of 'storm and tempest'; once rain had reached the ground, they said, it became 'flood'—and very few people were insured against that. Of the 39 homes lost in Ipswich, virtually none except a few financed by the War Service Homes Commission, which insisted on flood insurance, had been adequately insured.

In 1974 a report by Anne L. Quinnell, the then executive officer of the Queensland Disaster Welfare Committee, said, 'The financial position of many of these people is hopeless in the extreme and has caused consequent problems within the families.' Of the flood victims in general, 'increased financial commitment because of the inadequacy of compensation in meeting loss has caused frustration, anxiety and depression, as has delay in repairs to houses. As expected, those with greatest financial loss and least financial resources are experiencing most difficulty . . .'

A Snowy Mountains Engineering Corporation investigation of the floods said, 'It is known from flood damage surveys that very few residential homes were insured against flood. A study at Jindalee found that only 25 out of 280 (flooded) homes surveyed had flood cover. Most of these were Defence Service homes.' Respondents to a survey of the flood at Indooroopilly used words such as 'shock', 'confusion', 'bewilderment', 'depression', 'disbelief', 'panic', 'fear' and 'anxiety'. The corporation report noted, 'As not many of the thousands of residents affected believed that they could be inundated, the reaction to the sudden devastation was not surprising.' Besides the immediate emotional problems caused by the flood devastation, physical injuries were inflicted on people during evacuations and 12 people lost their lives in the Brisbane area. In the weeks and months following the floods, studies showed many cases of shock and mental illness attributable to the flood.

'Other intangible damage may become apparent in the coming years. Typically, in flood-affected areas land values become depressed unless flood mitigation works are carried out. The expectation of further flooding causes a feeling of insecurity among the residents and discourages property improvement. The long-term effects may be to produce areas with lower material living standards and a depressed social atmosphere. Although direct and indirect damage in 1974 was put at $178 million, actual damage in Brisbane and Ipswich would have been much higher because of severe flooding of major tributaries in both cities.'

A Jindalee flood survey reported that more than 800 of the suburb's 1100 to 1200 homes had not been affected. 'With few exceptions, those residents who were affected were sustained by the majority who were not,' the report said. 'The speed and efficiency with which local business and community activity is recovering offers an example of the resilience of all affected people in the face of one of the major national disasters of the modern era.' The survey said the average cost to Jindalee flood victims ranged from $7600 for fully-submerged houses to $1100 for those who experienced relatively minor flooding.

What were the chances of this disaster recurring? The weather bureau said that, statistically, the 314 millimetres (12 inches) that fell in Brisbane city on 26 January was a 'once in 100 years' event, but explained, 'This does not mean that Brisbane will not experience such rain again until 2074. Indeed, there is about a ten percent chance of recurrence before 2024.' The Wivenhoe Dam, designed purely for flood mitigation, has been built downstream from Somerset Dam since 1974 and has added vastly to the system's capacity to hold and release floodwaters without causing undue increases in the level of the Brisbane River. Meteorological studies have suggested that the investment is timely. The studies suggest that rainfalls in excess of those of 1974 are possible, and that without the Wivenhoe dam built since 1974 even greater floods could be experienced in the city.

The weather bureau reported in late 1974, 'Meteorological studies suggest that rainfalls well in excess of those of 1974 are possible. Therefore it seems certain that unless major flood mitigation schemes such as the Wivenhoe Dam are carried out, floods even greater than those of 1974 will again be experienced in Brisbane.' The Wivenhoe project is now a reality; the huge dam stands on the Brisbane River near Fernvale, well below the Somerset impoundment, but it is many river kilometres above the Brisbane's confluence with the Bremer and therefore unable to control floodwaters contributed by that stream and its major tributary, Lockyer Creek. So how safe are Brisbane and Ipswich?

The Snowy Mountains Engineering Corporation says that construction of Somerset Dam has already had a significant effect on floods in the Brisbane Valley. Although the dam has a catchment of only 13 600 square kilometres, it believes flood-producing rainfalls are frequently highest over this part of the Brisbane catchment. Without Somerset Dam, it says, floods as high as 1974 would have been experienced in 1955. The 1974 flood would have been nearly one metre higher without Somerset.

The weather bureau suggests that in situations where the major floodwater contribution occurs below Somerset and Wivenhoe Dams, there would be considerable problems in deciding when to empty floodwaters caught in those storages. If floodwaters were retained in the dams for too long, not only would there be major and prolonged flooding upstream from the storage, but the dams would be useless for flood mitigation downstream in the event of a repeat of excessive rainfall. It seems that while the flood mitigation system now in place gives a reasonable degree of protection from heavy rains above them, its effectiveness against heavy and prolonged falls on the lower Brisbane, Bremer and Lockyer catchments would be negligible for Brisbane. However, it might afford some relief to Ipswich by reducing the 'back-up' effect of the Brisbane at its confluence with the Bremer, thereby allowing the Bremer's waters easier escape.'

How prepared are relief services to cope with another disaster, should it occur? Perhaps Anne Quinnell of the Queensland Disaster Welfare Committee should have the last word:

'The benefits of combining resources through the Queensland Disaster Welfare Committee have been obvious, and in the early period (of the Brisbane flood ordeal) provided quite essential order to a chaotic situation. Such a chaotic situation may in fact occur again . . . in the urban area if the next disaster does not occur for another eighty years.

Inherent in the task of pre-planning now facing the Queensland Disaster Welfare Committee is the difficulty of planning for an uncertain event. However, the difficulties involved in organising a recovery service from the ground up during the impact phase of a disaster may spur welfare personnel in Queensland to continue to plan, even for an uncertain event. Unfortunately, it is likely that disaster will strike again. Hopefully, the welfare sector will never again be as unprepared as it was in January, 1974.'

14

The Sydney–Hobart
Yacht Race, 1998

This is not what racing is supposed to be. Difficult, yes.
Dangerous, no. Life-threatening, definitely not.

Larry Ellison, owner of Sayonara, *winner of the 1998 Sydney–*
Hobart race

They crossed the 225 kilometres of water separating Tasmania
from mainland Australia in numerous ways, by sailing ship
and steamer, by longboat and kayak, and many, many times
by yacht. The trip across Bass Strait was always hazardous,
the strait representing the convergence of currents down the
east coast and often fierce southerlies and breakers building up for hundreds of kilometres hitting relatively shallow
water. It was the scene of some horrific shipping catastrophes
in 1835 and 1895, in which a total of 631 people died. If size
and motor power of modern ships averted such catastrophes,
the allure of adventure brought more victims, as in the case
of Tony Dicker, 39, who set out in 1986 to row solo across
Bass Strait. Getting into difficulties, he radioed for help and a
would-be rescuer drowned trying in vain to save him.

In sailing terms, in the era of round-the-world races, the
Sydney–Hobart jaunt is relatively short, but it is a challenge,
a test for yachts and yachtsmen, making it a prime candidate
as a premier blue water yacht race. Yacht races were being

conducted across Bass Strait at least as early as 1907. In 1945, as a form of escapism from the grind of World War II, the first official Sydney–Hobart race was conducted, taking yachts 1166 kilometres down the coast of the mainland, across the strait, along the east coast of Tasmania to Tasman Island, across Storm Bay and up the Derwent River. The event was organised by the Cruising Yacht Club of Australia (CYC), but there were problems from the start. The fleet was hit by two fierce gales and rather devastated. *Winston Churchill*, then only three years old, took shelter and the skipper had to put his arm in a sling. Over the years skills and standards improved. What initially took a week eventually took less than two and a half days for *Morning Glory*, setting a record in 1996.

Conditions often did blow up, and the boats often took refuge, sheltering at Eden on the far south coast of New South Wales or at Gabo Island, sometimes retiring from the race. Through more than half a century of annual races there were few fatalities. In fact, until 1998 there had only been two, both related to injuries or misadventure: one yachtsman had been lost overboard, another had sustained head injuries from collapse of rigging. In 1979, however, a yacht, *Charleston*, sailing across Bass Strait in heavy conditions to compete in that year's Sydney–Hobart, disappeared with five on board. There were years when the majority of starters dropped out. In 1993, when the fleet was hit by ferocious winds and seas, causing large-scale retirements, helmsman John Quinn, thrown overboard with his lanyard broken and sustained only by a life vest, trod water for five hours before a rather miraculous rescue.

The Sydney–Hobart is classified by the International Sailing Federation as a Category One race, where competitors were required to race 'long distances well off-shore where boats must be self-sufficient for extended periods of time, capable of weathering storms and dealing with emergencies without the expectation of outside assistance'. The only other Category One race in Australia was from Sydney to Lord Howe Island. There is little doubt that such events can turn nasty. The 1979 Fastnet race in Britain, from Cowes to the south-eastern tip of Ireland and back, was busted up on the south-west tip of England by a huge storm, which rolled 80 boats and killed 15 sailors.

Fastnet taught some valuable lessons to the international sailing community. Boats being entered into such an event had to have professional surveys of their stability and capability to withstand tough conditions. There was a code of requirements, known as the International Measuring Standard (IMS). One of the critical requirements was that there had to be a 'limit of positive stability', meaning the maximum angle a boat could tip from upright and still be able to right itself immediately. The greater the angle the more stable the boat, and the quicker it would normally take to become upright if it became inverted. Even with such rules and regulations, there is still need for astuteness and commonsense.

For the Sydney–Hobart of 1998, the limit of positive stability was 115 degrees, but if a boat had raced in the event before and had a limit less than that but more than 110 degrees, it was allowed in. This was the so-called 'grandfather' clause. Bruce Guy, owner of *Business Post Naiad*, had some difficulty with requirements. His initial IMS certificate, which had a limit of positive stability of 112.9 degrees, making the boat eligible under the grandfather clause, was outdated. Guy had added and subtracted from the boat, including removing some lead ballast, reducing the net weight by 300 kilograms.

He had a new measurement done, and the limit of positive stability was only 109.5 degrees. Yet another measurement was done, and this showed the limit of positive stability to be only 104.7 degrees. The Cruising Yacht Club accepted the final IMS certificate. In the coroner's inquest that followed the race, the acceptance of *Business Post Naiad* was described by the CYC as an 'administrative oversight', but, coroner John Abernethy said, that was not good enough, even though he heard evidence that the final measurement was probably not correct and the limit of positive stability was more likely to have been 109.5 degrees.

In 1998 there were 115 starters crewed by a total of 1135 sailors, representing millions of dollars in investment and great eminence for the winners. The Bureau of Meteorology had been studying weather patterns with the aid of several computer models. One model was the American MRF system. Another was based in continental Europe, another in Britain, and a further one was an Australian LAPS regional model. The models took in thousands of pieces of information, collated them and presented forecasts, but because the databases' analyses varied, there were sometimes significant variations in what they could forecast. In 1998 the MRF system predicted that a severe low would form in Bass Strait at the time of the race. The European and Australian models produced 'softer' scenarios, the Australian model putting the low pressure system east of Tasmania. Because the US model was regarded as rather 'bullish', predicting serious scenarios that did not come into being, the other models were preferred. It was most unusual for a storm of that ferocity to form in Bass Strait in mid-summer.

On Christmas Eve, a Thursday, there was normal excitement, banter and good cheer. Forecaster Ken Batt gave the Christmas Eve weather briefing wearing a Santa Claus hat. He said to the 250 assembled skippers and navigators that all the computers were saying 'different things', which brought laughter. He said, 'I think I am actually pleased I am working over this Christmas [instead of sailing in the race]. A low might be on the cards and I draw your attention to this area [a low pressure marked on the map].' He said there were likely to be thunderstorms and a southerly change which could 'kick up a fairly nasty sea fairly rapidly' and it could 'kick up a seven or eight or nine-metre sea, which is not chickenfeed.' He said the forecast would be 'fine-tuned' and otherwise to have a 'merry Christmas' and an 'outstanding and safe race'.

The vagueness of the forecast did not satisfy all of the people assembled, but they were ready for heavy conditions. The Sydney–Hobart never had never been a race for wimps. Everyone had Christmas Day off, and it was hoped that the situation would clarify itself by Boxing Day. On Boxing Day morning the computer models all agreed that a low was forming, but they disagreed on where and when. The European and British models were not predicting a low as severe as the US model was. Forecaster Brett Gage put together weather 'packages' to be distributed to the departing crews. The forecast then was for a 'strong wind warning' with winds from 25 to 33 knots (a knot being one nautical mile, or 1.85 kilometres, an hour), but at about 10 am Batt told him the forecast had been changed to a 'gale warning', which was for winds from 34 to 47 knots, so the weather information was amended. Batt told those who asked that there was a front building 'down south' and that it 'could turn nasty'. Roger Badham, a weather forecaster providing a service for private clients in the race on this occasion told his clients there would be a southerly change. He said later that he was relying on the model that put the low pressure system east of Tasmania.

However much attention was paid to the models, they remained simply forecasts. Accurate prediction of weather had certainly been helped by the invention of the computer, but no forecast could be perfect. Badham, who had been providing his service for the race for 12 to 15 years and was highly regarded, said later that one would never know the exact scenario until it actually happened.

The fleet set off at 1 pm, with plenty of fanfare and a race-start collision between the maxi, *Nokia*, and *Sword of Orion*. The collision damaged some of *Sword of Orion's* deck stanchions but not badly enough to put the boat out of the race. *Sayonara*, the 1995 winner, led the fleet out of the heads and immediately caught a good north-wester blowing so well that it burst *Sayonara's* spinnaker. With its spinnaker replaced, *Sayonara* reached its highest speed ever, 26 knots, and *Brindabella*, an aspiring winner with more sail area, reached 31 knots, which helped in its duel with *Sayonara*.

Back on shore the Bureau of Meteorology finally realised that things were serious, and that the fleet was heading for a huge storm. Batt, who had sailed in the 1993 race, felt physically ill. He told the coroner's inquest, 'I felt tears welling up and went down there to my office and sat there. I felt quite emotional about it.' He said to others, 'There's going to be a shit-fight in Bass Strait.' At about 2 pm Brett Gage said, 'I would be surprised if the race went through without at least one person dying as a result of this event.'

Formally speaking, action was taken. Peter Dunda, a supervisor in the bureau's Sydney office, sent out a faxed warning to the Australian Maritime Safety Association, the CYC, the

Eden Coastal Patrol, commercial radio stations and fishing fleets. The official storm warning went out at 2.50 pm. It went to the *Young Endeavour*, a Royal Australian Navy square rigger that was acting as the Telstra Control relay vessel. It said, 'Storm warning is current south from Merimbula. Gale warning is current from Broken Bay.' A storm warning was the highest level of alert. A storm was defined as having winds in excess of 48 knots. The scale was open-ended. The winds could be as high as 90 knots, which is more than 160 kmh.

There are no 'cyclones' in the southern climes. Cyclones are weather phenomena associated with the tropics. The word 'hurricane' is used in other parts of the world for tropical cyclones. To the layman the word 'storm' is ambiguous. It could denote just thunder and a sprinkle of rain. As it later transpired, yachtsmen in the race did not have much better knowledge. Some thought 'storm' a lower order of seriousness than 'gale'. Most did not realise that the predicted wind speeds were an average only over a ten-minute period and that there could be gusts which were 40 percent higher. Most did not realise that predicted wave heights were also an average of the highest one-third of waves over a ten-minute period and that waves could be encountered that were 80 percent higher. This was an ignorance that was shared, sadly, by some in the race administration.

Whether the bureau men could have done more to spread the message has been debated since, but the consideration for safety ran head-on into the ferocity of the competitive spirit. The rules were strict, especially about unauthorised communications. There were to be scheduled weather forecasts and scheduled radio communications, known as 'skeds', when boats contacted Telstra Control and reported their positions. The first sked would be at 8.05 pm on Saturday night, seven hours after the start of the race, and after that at three pre-scribed times a day, 3.05 am, 2.05 pm and 11.05 pm. There was provision for a three-minute 'listening watch' every half-hour on high frequency (HF) and very high frequency (VHF) radios. This was for yachts in distress. At 5.45 am on Sunday, when the yacht *Magleri Wines* asked Telstra Control for a weather update, a member of the Race Management Team supervising the race, Mark Robinson, said the boat would have to wait for a regular bulletin.

The yachts had life rafts. They had radios and Global Positioning System (GPS) beacons and Emergency Position Indicating Radio Beacons (EPIRBs) that could guide rescuers to them. From there, judgements about whether to continue, pull out or take shelter were left to the skipper of each boat; but that system, of course, was vulnerable to human failings. Patrick Sullivan, director of the Bureau of Meteorology's New South Wales operations, believed a storm warning would cause many competitors to drop out. It turned out to be a false assumption.

Batt, Gage and Dunda realised that people had to be warned. Gage rang the CYC personally. But there was nobody there apart from a woman who identified herself as 'Lorraine', and she did not appear to take in 'the gravity of the situation'. He asked for Phil Thompson's mobile number, but Lorraine said she did not have it. He rang the Sydney–Hobart Media Centre and spoke to another woman who also did not appear to understand what was being conveyed. That afternoon Badham discovered the storm warning on the Internet and realised how serious things were. He realised that there would be 'particularly nasty conditions', in which yachts could be broken up. There would be a lot of damage, and there would be withdrawals. He tried ringing two of his clients by mobile phone, though this was against race rules, but could not get through. He had done this, he said later, because he knew the crews were inexperienced and he wanted them to know what they were in for.

There was also the comfort, regardless of the initial communication difficulties, Gage said later, that there was '22 hours lead-time' before the boats hit the rough weather and surely, in all that time, with an official storm warning being broadcast, it would become general knowledge. Formally the weathermen had done their duties. Coroner Abernethy was to find, though, that there could have been more urgency and determination in their efforts to get the message through, but ultimately, the question has to be asked, 'What more do you have to do?' The fact was that the warning had gone out. Batt said in evidence that he had 'preached to yachtsmen' the need to 'interrogate every single piece of weather information you can get.' It was not the weather bureau's fault that there was too little interrogation and too much gung-ho on the part of the competitors.

After the start of the race, the Race Committee of the CYC was replaced by the Race Management Team. This had eight members, including Phillip Thompson, the CYC's sailing manager and effectively the hands-on controller of the race; Mark Robinson, the CYC's sailing administrator; Bruce Rowley, the CYC's general manager; Matthew Elliott from the CYC; and representatives of the Racing Yacht Club of Tasmania. The race committee attended the start of the race, then made arrangements to travel separately to Hobart the next day, to make preparations for the end of the race, but on the Boxing Day afternoon and the following day when race committee members were in transit, a dangerous vacuum was developing in control of the race.

Storms, in the minds of seamen who understood them, were things to be avoided. Captain Crispin George, RAN, was to say later that no ship, no matter how big, came out of a storm unscathed. Yachts in severe storms were small, vulnerable and fragile, but Phil Thompson, though he was appraised of the storm warning, was not disturbed. He said later that he had read nothing in the forecasts on the day of the race that was alarming to him. He said after the race when asked to give his account. 'At the time of preparing this state-ment, I read the 14:50 forecasts and I am still of the view it contains nothing of particular concern.' Matthew Elliott, of the race management team, had later to admit that not even he knew at the time that a storm warning was the highest category. He thought there were two other categories: severe storm and hurricane. He had certainly heard the forecast that night, but had been focussing on other things, in particular the positions of the boats at that stage in the race.

The storm warning was read out over the radio by Telstra Control during the 8.05 pm sked on the Saturday night. It said, 'Warning, repeat, warning. There is a storm warning current south from Merimbula and there are gale warnings, repeat, gale warnings, current south of Broken Bay.' It went on to say that in the waters south of Merimbula, winds of 30 to 40 knots were expected later that night, changing west-north-west to between 40 and 55 knots later on Sunday. Extreme conditions were expected to last until Monday night—two days away. What was not passed on, said Alun Hill, counsel assisting the 2000 coroner's inquest into the race, was the fears the weather bureau had expressed. Why was it not done?

On *Sword of Orion*, Robert Kothe interpreted the warning to mean that there would be winds of 40 to 50 knots, and he thought he could handle that. He said later that he expected some gusts might have gone up to 65 knots, but he could have lived with that, too. He believed that he could get more precise weather information and make a more informed decision later.

The yachts made good progress down the south coast, but already there were indications of trouble ahead. On Saturday night Mark Rudiger, crewman on *Sayonara*, saw the barometric pressure drop from 1008 millibars to 930 millibars in less than four hours. The low settled between midnight and 3 am Sunday and started spiralling. In the early hours winds had become so fierce that most yachts had dropped their spinnakers. The freakish nature of the weather was being experienced elsewhere, such as high winds inland and mid-summer snowfalls in Victoria and New South Wales, all associated with the low pressure system. In the fleet, winds shifted from north-west to west.

Back on shore, at 2.45 am Phil Thompson read the weather bureau forecast that had been released half an hour earlier. The forecast repeated the storm warning and said that seas in the south would be producing waves of four to five metres, but even Thompson did not know that 40 percent had to be added to the upper speed to allow for gusts and that 80 percent had to be added to the wave heights, which were also just an average over a set period. He calculated the fleet was some 480 metres north of the low and that it was moving east-north-east so the fleet would miss it; 40- to 50-knot winds, though unpleasant, were not unusual for the race. He believed the winds would not last long and would then moderate. He expected some retirements as the fleet made its way down the New South Wales coast, but he also expected that, the winds being as they were, there might be a new race record.

At 6 am wind speeds at Wilson's Promontory, the extreme southern tip of mainland Australia were being measured at 79 knots, with gusts up to 94 knots, and even though an allowance had to be made for the exposed position of the wind gauge there, it indicated that conditions were becoming serious. The race crews needed no convincing. Waves were nine metres high—as high as houses. *Sayonara*, entering Bass Strait at dawn, experienced a lull in conditions and for a while thought it had passed the southerly front, but then the winds increased again and the crew realised it was no front. They had gone through the eye of what would have been a cyclone in the tropics. This far south it was a storm, but a cyclonic one. At 7 am Hugo van Kretschmar, commodore of the CYC, hearing the forecast, decided his boat should retire. At 8 am, *Sword of Orion's* crew saw a thick back cloud stretching like a sausage from one end of the horizon to the other.

Back on shore there was no knowledge of this by people who should have been acutely aware. Matthew Elliott caught a flight from Sydney to Hobart. He was followed at 8.30 am by Phil Thompson and Mark Robertson. They planned to meet at the Royal Hobart Yacht Club and listen to the 2.05 pm sked. Elliott, arriving at the Royal Hobart Yacht Club at 11 am, set up computers and went off for an hour's briefing.

At sea, on the *Sword of Orion*, crewman Steve Kulmar felt the conditions build up from 10 am onwards. The wind gauge at one point measured 82 knots. Kulmar urged Kothe to turn back, but Kothe was reluctant and wanted to get better weather information. They waited for a weather forecast at noon, but when it came it was in their opinion disappointingly vague, failing to indicate precisely where the low was centred. By 11 am, winds were hitting 65 knots and occasionally gusting to 80 knots. *Team Jaguar Infinity III* abandoned the race and motored back towards Eden, but a rope washed into the sea by a wave became entangled round the propeller, stopping the boat. *Miintinta*, which had done a round trip to America and two Sydney–Hobarts, motored back towards Eden but its motor died when it was in sight of land and the crew were left to bail manually.

The sea had become a cauldron, with shrieking winds and waves coming at all angles, threatening boats whether they chose to keep going or tried to turn back. The waves increased in height, some towering over boats like multi-storey buildings, and breaking at the top. *Doctel Rager* decided it was time at least to give a hint that things were not well and radio to Lew Carter at Telstra Control that they were being buffeted by 50- to 60-knot winds, with gusts up to 70 knots. It was an unusual thing to do. The competitive streak was so fierce that normally information about strong winds made other boats head for the area where they were being experienced. And after *Doctel Rager's* 12.38 pm broadcast, another yacht radioed asking whether the report was authentic.

Within an hour, *Secret Men's Business, Wild Thing, She's Apples II* and *Terra Firma* all confirmed that conditions were serious, *Terra Firma* saying it was experiencing winds of 60 knots. At 1.32 pm *Wild Thing* said it was abandoning the race and at 1.39 *Secret Men's Business* followed suit. At 1 pm, Glyn Charles, a former British Olympic representative in yachting, now part of the *Sword of Orion* crew, told Kulmar he thought the boat should retire. Kothe resisted. At the 2.05 pm sked, *Sword of Orion* broadcast to the rest of the fleet the conditions they were experiencing. The message was, 'I just want to tell you a bit about the weather we are experiencing down here . . . It's a little bit more difficult to forecast . . . we are experiencing 50- to 65-knot westerlies with gusts of 78 knots. Over.' *Yendys*, about three kilometres astern of *Sword of Orion*, confirmed the information.

At Hobart, the race management team, having heard the 2.05 pm sked, realised at last that the race needed closer attention. They radioed Lew Carter, asking him to broadcast to the fleet that it was the responsibility of each skipper to make a judgement as to whether the boat should remain in the race, but by then the opportunity the race management team had to play any meaningful role to avert the disaster had passed. It was now time for damage control, even if the formalities of competitive racing were still being observed. Carter told the fleet, 'Attention is drawn to Rule 4.7. A boat is solely responsible for deciding whether to start or continue racing . . . The CYC is not responsible for any damage or injury either ashore or at sea. I ask all skippers, before proceeding into Bass Strait or wherever you're proceeding, to give it your utmost consideration as to what you're doing. And talk about it with your crew.'

About 20 yachts abandoned the race as a result of the broadcast, but getting back was no piece of cake, at least for some. If they sailed north, the breakers were coming from behind, which was even more dangerous. *Team Jaguar Infinity III* rolled and lost its mast. *VC Offshore* rolled and issued a mayday. At 2.15 pm Standaside, hit by a wave that might have been 30 metres high, rolled and crew member Mike Marshman found himself underwater, trapped in the rigging. He remembered the warning not to get out of his harness and managed to wriggle free. Seven other crew, attached by their lanyards, scrambled back onto the boat. One other, John Culley, did not have his harness or a lifejacket but was fortuitously swept back towards the boat by a wave and scrambled aboard. The crew radioed they were in trouble and another competitor, Siena, with its motor working, diverted to give help. Its skipper, Ian Moray, said later that he had registered winds of 80 knots. The white foam was blowing so fiercely that the crew could not look at it without wearing goggles. Almost everyone was suffering injury. On *Siena*, crew member Timothy Evans was thrown heavily and broke two ribs. *Siena* reached *Standaside*, which was sinking, and stood by while a helicopter took the crew off.

At about 4 pm, *Solo Globe Challenger* met a wave it could not handle. Tony Mowbray, its owner, said in *Fatal Storm*, Bob Mundle's book on the race, 'I opened my eyes and I looked up and I could see the water curling over us. We were literally in the tube of a wave. It was just a phenomenal, unbelievable situation. We could see it was breaking over us . . .'*Solo Globe Challenger* was knocked over and just missed capsizing, but the crew were injured. *Midnight Special* was heading back to Eden.

On *Kingurra*, which had competed in 14 Sydney–Hobarts, American John Campbell was washed overboard and knocked unconscious. As the crew dragged his limp form back on board, he slid from his lifejacket. Plunging back into the water, he came to, but saw the boat pulling away. Throwing a lifebuoy was impossible because it was in the face of 70-knot winds. He was struggling in the sea when a winch operator, Barry Barclay, on a police rescue helicopter, called to the scene, miraculously saw him. One of the helicopter crew, David Key, was winched down and struggled to get to Campbell and put a harness around him. The rescue was successful, despite a temporarily jamming winch and fuel supplies that only had a matter of minutes to run by the time the helicopter got to Mallacoota.

At 4.40 pm, *Sword of Orion* turned back to Eden. Kothe had said he would retire if the winds reached 60 knots and now they were experiencing close to 70 knots. The boom was secured apparently firmly to a stanchion on the starboard side. Because the boom extended a metre beyond the point where the helmsman was standing, Glyn Charles, who was then at the helm, had to step back to allow it to pass. The motor was engaged, but now, they were heading north and the waves were breaking dangerously behind them.

At about 5 pm *Winston Churchill*, owned by Richard Winning, encountered a wave that Winning said was 'a great deal higher than the top of the mast so, it would have to be 60 feet and I saw, you know, it was not so much the size of the wave that concerned me as its steepness'. The yacht started to climb the wave. Winning hoped it would get to the top, but the grand old stager did not have the speed, and the wave seized it half-way up and hurled it onto its side, smashing it and breaking over it, throwing Winning and crew member John Dean overboard, secured only by their lanyards. John Stanley, another crew member, said it was 'like hitting a brick wall'. The main batteries were partly submerged, unable to give enough power to start the motor. Winning, his GPS no longer operable, broadcast a mayday using the one working bit of equipment, the VHF radio, and estimated his position. His call was picked up at 5.21 pm by Gary Ticehurst, manning the ABC's helicopter, who was then hovering over Standaside. Winning had to give an estimate of his position: 'Twenty miles southeast of Twofold Bay.'

With the deck of *Winston Churchill* now partly submerged, the crew took to two lifeboats, a four-manner and a six-manner, and got into them. They tied them together and activated their one EPIRB, but the seas quickly separated the rafts and some 20 to 30 minutes later, *Winston Churchill* went below the waves.

At about the same time *Sword of Orion*, fleeing north, was caught by a wave at least 12 metres high, which came from the rear left, picking up the boat, smashing it into the water and turning it over, in the process ripping the boom from where it had been lashed. The boom swung viciously towards the port side, catching the wheel and shearing the top off it. In all probability it hit Charles, most likely inflicting mortal injuries and ripping him out of his safety harness.

When the boat came upright it had lost its mast. Darren Senogles, who had been on deck, looked around immediately for Charles and saw to his horror that he was in the water 15 to 30 metres behind the boat, with no lifejacket. He screamed to him to swim, but Charles appeared to have been seriously injured. He threw six strokes weakly, trying to get back to the boat, and then he stopped. Senogles tried tying ropes together to reach him, but more waves came and then Charles was 100 metres away and reaching him was impossible. Charles remained in view for five or six minutes. He was last sighted at 5.10 pm. Steve Kulmar activated the man overboard button and the EPIRB. Robert Kothe wanted to broadcast a mayday. The VHF aerial had been attached to the mast and Senogles had to put up another one. It was 20 minutes after the capsize that Kothe was able to get away the call for help and to say there was a man overboard. The boat was badly damaged, the motor having come off its mounting blocks and its fuel line cut by falling stairs. The crew cut away fallen rigging.

By that time the Australian Maritime Safety Authority issued a general mayday for Bass Strait. Soon afterwards *Winston Churchill* had reported that the boat was sinking. There were then 16 EPIRB distress signals being emitted and 13 boats were listed as being in trouble. At 5.48 pm, *Young Endeavour* turned towards the point Winning had indicated in his broadcast. There was some confusion over the position. At 5.57 pm a civilian search pilot, Neil Boag, said he had seen a yacht much further to the south which he thought was *Winston Churchill*, but it turned out to be another yacht. *Winston Churchill* was no more, and the only thing to look for was two tiny rubber rafts bobbing about in fading light in that massive sea.

At about that time *Business Post Naiad* was hit by a huge wave and overturned, revolving 360 degrees and emerging badly damaged, with its mast smashed. Four crew members on deck were washed to sea, but the lanyards connecting them and their harnesses to the boat held firm. The boat sent out a mayday that was relayed to Telstra Control. The crew activated their EPIRB and put the motor on, trying to get to shelter at Gabo Island.

At about 6.30 pm the crew of the stranded *Sword of Orion* saw Richard Purcell's *Margaret Rintoul II* in the distance and launched flares to attract its attention. *Margaret Rintoul II*, its motor not working, was having its own battle. Every wave it encountered was a challenge. The task was to survive that one, and the next, and the next. To turn around, using only sail power, and to try to get close to another boat in those conditions, was hazardous in the extreme. Purcell's main concern, according to his later account, was the safety of his boat and crew. He told crew member Colin Betts to radio Telstra Control that that a flare had been sighted. Then he elected to sail on—a decision that was later to plunge him into bitter controversy. Colin Betts did put his call through to Telstra Control at 7.05 pm. Seeing *Sword of Orion* was mastless, he assumed it did not have a VHF aerial and therefore did not switch his VHF radio on. In fact, *Sword of Orion* with its makeshift aerial was on the VHF, on its emergency channel.

As was pointed out by Abernethy, *Margaret Rintoul II* could have fired an answering flare to reassure *Sword of Orion's* crew that they had been seen. *Sword of Orion's* mayday call was picked up by pilot Neil Boag, who took down the position given by Kothe and went to the area to make a desperate but fruitless search for Charles.

At 2.30 am, Garry Schipper, a Victorian police officer on *Challenge Again*, was caught as he unclipped his lanyard to move to another position on the boat. He was thrown off but grabbed a torch and was able to signal his position, an action that helped the crew to save him. Just before dusk *Kingurra* was rolled 360 degrees. John Campbell, 32, from Seattle, found himself overboard without a lifeline and had to swim back to the boat. Peter Jourbert, the 74-year-old engineer who had designed the boat, ruptured his spleen, broke half a dozen ribs and punctured his lung.

Darkness descended and the storm continued to rage. The yacht B52 was turned upside-down and crew members Mark Vickers and Russell Kingston found themselves trapped underneath. A wave lifted the boat and Vickers, having unclipped himself and wearing no life vest, was swept 40 metres. He swam back. The boat was turned upright but its mast was broken and both its motor and radio would not work. A Navy Sea King helicopter came but decided it was too difficult to take the crew off the deck. They would have to get into the water to be rescued. Rescues were perilous for everyone concerned. The pilots had to watch the waves to ensure they themselves were not hit. The rescuers winched down found themselves underwater, being tossed about by waves. When the surviving crew from *Sword of Orion* were taken off they had to get into the water, and Robert Kothe almost had his head split open by the hull of the abandoned yacht being washed towards him. At one point he actually put out his hand to fend it off.

At about 11 pm another monster wave hit *Business Post Naiad*, which overturned again, this time remaining upside-down for five or six minutes. Robert Matthews, who had been on deck, struggled to release his harness from its tether but the pressure from the boat being propelled upside-down through the water made it difficult. A shaft of air came in. He took a gulp of breath, then made his way to the surface, clinging to the yacht for dear life. When the boat came upright it soon became clear that Phillip Skeggs, who had also been on deck, had not made it. Whether he had not been able to undo his harness or whether he had been entangled in ropes was not clear, but he had drowned.

Business Post Naiad's crew put out the two life rafts in anticipation of having to abandon ship. In the course of preparing the rafts Tony Guy suffered a massive heart attack and died. Putting the life rafts into the water was not the best course of action. The life rafts carried water to give them stability and that weight resisted being dragged by the yacht. *Business Post Naiad* put out a mayday call and a Navy Sea King with lights and the ability to operate at night, went out in search of it. The waves were still nine metres high. At 3 am *Business Post Naiad* was hit by another huge wave and the crew saw to their horror that the life rafts had gone. The pressure had been too much for the rope and its connections.

The lifeboats containing the crew of *Winston Churchill* were left to the mercy of the elements. In the six-manner were John Stanley, John Gibson, John Dean, Michael Bannister and James Lawler. In the four-manner were Richard Winning, Bruce Gould, Michael Rynan and Paul Lumtin. The rafts, supplied by RFD Australia Pty Ltd, skipped over the waves like a beach ball, hardly comfortable for anyone inside. At about 12.30 am Monday, the six-manner was tipped upside-down and the occupants, standing on the canopy with its inflated tubing, found that the raft was more stable in an inverted position, but there was no air, and it was felt it was too dangerous for anyone to take his life vest off and climb outside to right the raft. A collective decision was made to cut a small hole in the top so that they could breathe. Ten minutes later the raft was righted, but the hole in the bottom was a problem.

Twice more the liferaft was rolled, the second time at about 2 am when the entire canopy was sheared away and the breathing hole had become a slit extending from wall to wall. What the men had not realised when they made the cut was that they were destroying the integrity of the floor, which maintained the shape of the raft. Five men were effectively hanging onto a ring of rubber. Gibson clipped his safety harness to the tube, an action that almost certainly saved his life. When a huge wave hit it and swept it 300 metres, three of them, Dean, Bannister and Lawler, were washed away, leaving only Stanley and Gibson clinging to the remains of the raft.

The four-manner was also turned upside-down, but Richard Winning decided to take the risk and twice went outside without lifejacket to right it. The raft had other troubles, including a tube that deflated and a missing part to the pump. A slit developed, caused by some equipment, but the four remained with the raft and worked hard with a makeshift pump connection to keep it seaworthy. They drifted all night and into Monday.

Helicopters rescued *Business Post Naiad's* surviving crew at 8 am Monday. *Naiad* was abandoned with the bodies of

Guy and Skeggs still on board. *Sword of Orion's* surviving crew were taken off by two helicopters and the yacht itself abandoned, never to be recovered. The crew of *Midnight Special* were rescued by a Victoria Police helicopter and the yacht was so badly damaged it was written off. The crew of *Miintinta* were taken off by a trawler, *Josephine Jean*, after which the yacht drifted away and sank. *Solo Globe Challenger* had three crewmen lifted off by helicopter, including Tony Purkiss, who had a broken leg and jumped into the sea with lifejacket to be winched up. Two other crewmen were taken on board the frigate, HMAS *Newcastle*, and a skeleton crew continued to motor *Solo Globe Challenger* to harbour before being met by a trawler that had been sent by an insurance company to bring the boat in. *Team Jaguar Infinity III* was also towed by trawler to Eden.

At sea, Richard Winning's crew, drifting all day Monday, saw an aircraft in the late afternoon and fired flares, but the black colour of the raft made it difficult to pick out from the air. Alun Hill said in the coroner's inquest that it would have cost the life raft manufacturers nothing to have made the raft in a different colour. He and his colleagues were rescued by helicopter at some time after 5 pm. The remains of the six-manner, with Stanley and Gibson clinging to it, was seen by air after darkness descended, when one of the survivors shone his strobe light upwards, and the two were rescued at about 8 pm. *Naiad* was recovered by the navy with the bodies of Guy and Skeggs still on board. Though equipped with life vests, none of the three washed from the *Winston Churchill's* six-manner survived. The body of Michael Bannister was recovered by the navy early on the Tuesday morning, and that of James Lawler less than an hour later. The body of John Dean was never found. Naiad was broken up and its remains deposited on a rubbish tip. Of the 115 starters, 43 made it to Hobart. In the disaster operation, a total of 55 sailors had been rescued and 20 boats towed to shore. Five boats, *Winston Churchill, Sword of Orion, Standaside, Midnight Special* and *Miintinta*, had sunk. The rescue effort had involved about 1000 personnel, 25 aircraft and six vessels.

Sayonara won line honours, completing their crossing in two days, 19 hours and three minutes, but there was hardly much to celebrate. In his book, *The Proving Ground*, Bruce Knecht quotes billionaire Larry Ellison, owner of *Sayonara*, saying, 'This is not what racing is supposed to be. Difficult, yes. Dangerous, no. Life-threatening, definitely not . . . No race I've ever done has been anything like this. It was like sailing through the eye of a hurricane. The seas were enormous, and the wind made noises we'd never heard before.'

In the coroner's inquest, John Abernethy found that *Margaret Rintoul II* would not have been able to find Glyn Charles 90 minutes after he went overboard even if it had diverted, but he found *Margaret Rintoul's* response deficient in other ways. *Margaret Rintoul II* could have made radio contact. It could have sent an answering flare. Abernethy found that the members of *Winston Churchill's* six-man raft were justified in the circumstances in making the incision that destroyed the raft. He made a series of recommendations, in particular recommending the improvement of the quality of the life rafts. He said that the Mae West personal floatation device was unsuitable and that the harnesses and lanyards had been unsatisfactory. His major criticisms were reserved, as they should have been, for the management of the race, where attention, continuous hands-on monitoring, communications and coordination had been grossly deficient.

15

The Sea King Disaster, 2005

Sea King helicopters were tough, reliable machines that had proved themselves many times. Introduced into service in the Royal Australian Navy in 1974 as a replacement for the Westland Wessex to provide anti-submarine capability, they were to prove themselves worldwide. In Britain's campaign in 1982 to retake the Falklands, they were, along with the magnificent Sea Harriers, the aircraft of the moment. The second-in-line to the British throne, Prince Andrew, flew from HMS *Invincible* as a Sea King co-pilot. In the Balkans wars, HMS *Ark Royal* carried 17 of them, and they excelled themselves providing logistical support, casualty evacuation and performing other tasks. Sea Kings were used in the 2003 invasion of Iraq, among other tasks, flying from HMS *Ocean* to the Al Faw peninsula. (This writer, as a war correspondent, was winched off an Australian warship in the Arabian Gulf and flown to Abu Dhabi in a Sea King.)

By December 2004, when the Australian warship HMAS *Kanimbla* sailed to assist in tsunami relief operations at

Aceh in Indonesia, ship borne helicopters had long been an indispensable part of naval operations. They had been used in military operations such as East Timor and the Solomon Islands, in civil emergencies such as bushfires and rescues during the Sydney–Hobart race disaster. Maintained by units such as at 817 Squadron RAAF, at HMAS *Albatross*, Nowra, they had since 1999 been deployed at an increasing rate.

Helicopters could do things never before seen in history. They could come from nowhere, allow things to be done quickly, and disappear. Author Michael Caulfield says in his book, *The Vietnam Years*: 'It was rapid medical evacuation of a kind never seen before on a battlefield and it worked. Most casualties made it to hospital within 30 minutes and the blood loss and shock that had killed so many in past wars was kept a little more at bay.' But they were no cinch to handle, no more than horses in the field of conflict. The helicopter never really 'wanted' to fly, unlike fixed-wing aircraft whose aerodynamic shape had already been conceived in nature. Mechanically, going almost against the order of nature, helicopters were always going to be an engineering challenge. Above all, their designers and maintainers had to factor in the immense mechanical stresses inherent in the acceleration, deceleration, lifting, descending, turning, hovering and endlessly vibrating.

There was an inevitable attrition rate, in overseas service and in Australia. A number of Sea Kings were lost in the Falklands, one ditching while performing a risky transfer of supplies to a ship at night, another due to a systems malfunction, another because of an altimeter malfunction. In 1987, one crashed while trying to land on the USS *La Salle*. In 1990, a Sea King ditched while making a routine training flight from the USS *John F. Kennedy*. Some of Australia's original 13 Sea Kings suffered mishaps at the outset of their service, mainly due to a chronic problem of loss of gearbox oil. In 1989, one ditched into the sea during exercises off Darwin. In 1995, another crashed into a tree at Bamaga Sea on Cape York, remaining suspended in the branches while rescuers had to extract the seven on board, all of whom had been injured, three seriously. The shock of the impact in that particular incident had not been absorbed by the tubular aluminium and stretched canvas seats. By 2004, only seven of the original 13 RAN Sea Kings were still in service.

Orders for new fleets of modern military aircraft ran into billions of dollars, so the existing fleets had to be kept going as long as possible. Questions were being raised after 30 years as to whether the Sea Kings were simply too old. The head of the Australian Defence Association, Neil James, said the Government should have spent money earlier to replace them. But the Sea Kings had a longer designated life than that; they were designed to last more than 30 years. Aldo Borgu, a military analyst with the Australian Strategic Policy Institute, was to say that while the Sea King was based on an 'old platform', that did not mean it was a flight hazard.

From the outset, Australia's Sea Kings did not incorporate the most up-to-date technology. They were not equipped with frangible couplings, devices developed during the Vietnam War to prevent helicopter engines continuing to pump fuel after a crash. (Such couplings were adopted in Sea Kings by the Canadian Navy.) The Australian Sea King went through a technical review in 1994–95, when changes were made to its main frame, but no consideration appears to have been given to frangible couplings. The passenger seating, shown up for its flimsiness in the Bamaga crash, should have been given very serious attention. Tests in the United States showed they were prone to collapse in low-speed crashes. An inquiry into the Bamaga crash concluded that passengers would not have been as seriously injured had there been 'crashworthy' seating and proper body harnesses instead of simple lap-belts that would have reduced injuries to the thorax and torso and the limbs which would otherwise flailed about.

Installation of crashworthy seating in Sea Kings raised questions of cost and weight, and convenience. Every kilogram of weight meant more fuel and less manoeuvrability of the aircraft. A less efficient aircraft meant, in military logic, transfer of risk to personnel somewhere 'further along the line'. In May 1998, the Defence Science and Technology Organisation said crashworthy seating 'might benefit' Sea King passengers. In October 1999, the then Chief of the Air Force, Air Marshal Errol McCormack, said 'most defence aircraft cannot and do not conform to civilian aviation standards'. As a compromise, a decision was made that year that, till further notice, Sea Kings would not fly passengers. But there were pressures to have the Sea Kings resume that role. That was what they were meant to do.

In 2003, a memo was signed in the name of the then Director-General of Technical Airworthiness, Air Commodore Noel Schmidt, took up the question of crashworthy seating. New seats would be 'difficult and expensive to install [causing a] possible reduction in capability/accept risk', it said. Schmidt was later to say that he had not seen the final document, signed in his name by a subordinate. He did say that he had been satisfied that the risk assessment had been properly carried out. The then Maritime Commander, Rear Admiral Raydon Gates, was later to say that he had a huge volume of work and had to rely at times on the advice of subordinates. In accordance with this, he persuaded the then head of the Defence Force Airworthiness Authority, Air Marshal Angus Houston, to have the ban on Sea Kings passengers lifted. Commander Carl Capper, manager of Naval Aviation System Program Office (NASPO), said later that nothing was done to improve the safety of the Sea King passenger seating because there had been no direction to do so. Lieutenant Matthew Vesper, counsel assisting in the later inquiry, said the 'Bamaga recommendations' on seating had been tossed around 'from agency to agency' and 'effectively abandoned'.

If the flimsy seating was retained, it was necessary to make doubly sure the aircraft would not crash. But in March 2003, a Transport General Technical Air Services audit of the maintenance standards within the squadron was damning. It said the maintenance regime 'compromises the integrity of technical airworthiness'. That went to Commodore Geoff Ledger, then head of the Australian Navy Aviation Group. (Incidentally, unrelated to that report, one Sea King was found in November 2003 to be in need of extensive maintenance. This was Sea King N16-100, maintained by 817 Squadron. It was found to have had extensive cracking in the area where the gear box and the blades were attached, and accordingly was taken out of service. A major part of the frame was replaced.)

All Sea Kings faced heavy demands. The years 2002 and 2003 were particularly busy, straining maintenance resources. Commodore Ledger had problems in maintaining qualified staff and standards at all levels. On the shop floor, an attitude developed that whatever else was done or not done, aircraft had to be available on demand and this was done in what was later described as a 'high workload, low supervision environment'. The Sea King was scheduled to be replaced under a 10-year Defence Capability Plan, but that was not till 2013.

Concern continued to be expressed. In February 2004, Lieutenant Commander Bradley Hock, Acting Fleet Aviation Engineering Officer at 817 Squadron, said in an internal report that 817 Squadron 'isn't manned and has insufficient assets to operate four concurrent bases'. There was, in his view, a 'can do' attitude irrespective of management issues. To say this squadron is ready to meet the challenges in 2005 is incorrect, unless command was depending on new personnel brought on board to address the many problems and turn them round before an accident', he said. Hock said there had been recommendations for change of practices but there was 'no physical proof' that anything had been done. Other squadrons had similar problems, in particular 816 Squadron. Hock recommended that in the second week of March, there be a 'health check' on important areas of 817 Squadron.

Hock's report was apparently never seen by the commanding officer of 817 Squadron, Commander James Tobin, and no follow-up check was ever carried out. But Tobin was concerned anyway. On 13 August that year, he sent an email to a senior officer at maritime headquarters, Commodore Nigel Perry, telling him that 'a small but significant number of errors' were creeping into the maintenance program. Perry concluded that there was indeed 'a systemic problem' affecting the maintenance regime in the squadron, and he informed Commodore Ledger. He did not brief the Maritime Commander Australia, Rear Admiral Rowan Moffitt. Moffitt was to confirm later that no warnings were passed on to him. He said had he done so, that 'would have caused me to ask probably a lot more probing questions, particularly at the time as we embarked upon an operation which was going to entail, in all likelihood, high operational tempo, from two Sea Kings, in that squadron.'

In September 2004, Tobin sent another email to Perry saying there had been 'three to four years of continuous operations' endured by the squadron, resulting in 'a slight tendency to cut corners to ensure a high rate of availability'. This was leading to 'a number of silly mistakes' as well as 'a number of issues being missed'. Perry contacted Ledger. On 12 November, Tobin wrote a minute saying there were problems with 'squadron management', that the squadron was inadequately manned and resourced and said that 'no-one in command has the balls to say enough is enough'. For this reason there was 'an embedded culture of shortcuts and workarounds', and unless things improved, there would be 'an accident'. The minute went to both Perry and Ledger. Perry was later to say that he did not see the minute at that time. 'Because of the turnover of staff . . . correspondence such as this can go unattended for a number of weeks,' he said. The minute was supposedly also passed onto Rear Admiral Moffitt. It was received by someone on 21 November and endorsed: 'No further action'.

After the Boxing Day tsunami in Asia in 2004, HMAS *Kanimbla* was ordered to prepare for a relief operation. It was to take two Sea Kings, an Army Landing Craft detachment and a joint service medical team. The deployment was to be called Operation Sumatra Assist. Shortage of time meant that a routine pre-embarkation inspection of the Sea Kings was waived, including an inspection of Sea King N16-100, which had clocked up 7200 hours flying time. Waiving such an inspection was a 'highly irregular' procedure, a later witness, Naval engineer Brad Willis, was to say. The 'pack up kit' for on-board maintenance of the helicopters was packed hastily, and it did not include some items. *Kanimbla* left Sydney on New Years Eve, 2004, farewelled by revellers on the banks of

Sydney Harbour. On board as part of the Sea King detachment were Sea King pilot Lieutenant Paul Kimlin, 29, who had flown missions during the Iraq War, and Lieutenant Jonathan Curlewis, 23, who had done his rotary wing training in 2003 and was embarking on his first mission. One of the Sea King tactical coordinators was Matthew Goodall, 24, a survivor of the 1998 Sydney-Hobart yacht race. Loadmasters included Leading Seaman Scott Bennett, 36, married with two sons and looking forward to promotion as a petty officer, and Leading Seaman Shane Warburton, a 30-year-old communications operator, in the Navy for 13 years, who had volunteered for the mission.

Squadron Leader Paul McCarthy, aged 30, had joined the mission to lend his considerable expertise as a doctor. He had joined the RAAF in 2001 and had served in Kyrgyzstan, East Timor and Iraq, and had assisted in the aftermath of the Bali bombings of 2002. He had once rowed with another doctor in a race across the Atlantic, finishing second in a time of 45 days. For Sumatra Assist, he was appointed to the Aeromedical Evacuation Coordinator. Also on board to handle the multitude of sick and injured people was Lieutenant Matthew Davey, 31, a medical graduate who had joined the Australian Army Reserve in 2000 and had served in East Timor. Other medical personal included a RAAF nursing sister, Flight Lieutenant Lynne Rowbottom, 43, an East Timor veteran, Petty Officer Stephen Slattery, 39, married with two children and two grandchildren, medical assistant RAAF Sergeant Wendy Jones, 40, veteran of East Timor and the Middle East and another medical assistant, Leading Seaman Scott Nichols, 32.

Commander George McGuire took command of the *Kanimbla* on January 30, 2005. He had to be appraised of many things. But he was not made aware of the continuing maintenance problems with the Sea Kings. N16-100, code-named Shark 02 for the operation, was due for a service on board ship but was put on restricted usage so it could transport the then Prime Minister, John Howard, during an official visit. That done, it could be serviced.

On 4 February, Leading Seaman Daniel Viero took out the vital control mechanism, the rear-aft bellcrank in the mixer unit. The mechanism was in an awkward position, difficult to get access to. Getting it out, he noticed there was too much lateral movement by the five-centimetre bolt within the mechanism. The bolt was worn. He brought that to the attention of a superior. It was discussed, but paperwork was not done and proper procedures not followed. There was no spare bolt available. A decision was made to reinstall the fore-aft bellcrank as it was. Doing such maintenance on a ship, in operational conditions, was challenging to personnel, but that was nevertheless what they were trained for. They should also have been properly prepared. But the tool that should have been used to apply to correct torque during reinstallation of the fore-aft bellcrank had not been put into the pack-up kit. Leading Seaman Ian Fairweather, doing the reinstallation, had to rely on his memory to select the correct torque. It was later found that he did not apply the correct torque to any of the fore-aft bellcrank connecting bolts. For a reason never explained, Fairweather apparently did not insert a split pin. The recommended split pin was 3/32 of an inch in diameter. A fully functional, correctly torqued bolt and nut would have been safe enough without a pin. The pin, a simple piece of equipment that might have cost 50 cents in a hardware store, was there as a failsafe device. It was very important that the fore-aft bellcrank not fail.

Shark 02 went back into service, presumably with a castel-
lated nut in place, but no split pin to ensure the nut stayed in
place. Commander McGuire was unaware of the reinstallation of the worn bolt. There was no paperwork in which any
concerns were recorded. Dr Ray Southin, a consultant metal-
lurgist, was to say that the nut, unrestrained by a split pin,
must have come off at some point, probably shaken by the
aircraft vibrations, and worked itself loose. When that was
was 'anybody's guess'. It could have come off in the first couple of hours of flying after the service. For the next 38 hours,
the bolt rode in its socket, moving backwards and forwards,
the movement facilitated by the worn threads, moving slowly
upwards, to the point where it would separate.

After service in Aceh, HMAS *Kanimbla* made its way
home, stopping at Singapore on 24 March for rest and rec-
reation. Shark 02 sat in its hangar, its work apparently done.
Had there been no further call for it, it would have undergone a post-operation maintenance when it got back to base,
and at that point the state of the bolt and nut in the fore-aft
bellcrank would almost certainly have been discovered. But
events were to intervene, the clock was ticking, and the top
brass were unaware of what was looming. They could hardly
be said to have been complacent. On 28 March, Ledger wrote
to Rear Admiral Moffitt, saying there were serious problems
with maintenance, and he was not being told 'till the very last
moment' about serious incidents. If there was a disaster, he
said, he was the one who was going to have to answer for it,
adding: 'I am happy to raise a couple of . . . issues, in particular that I believe unacceptable.'

That very day, a second earthquake struck, hitting Indonesia with the island of Nias near its epicentre. The *Kanimbla*
was diverted to assist in a second humanitarian operation,

Sumatra Assist 11. Paul McCarthy, who had completed his mission and returned to Australia by air, was immediately deployed back to the ship to assist. Matthew Davey had also returned home. When he heard about the earthquake, he volunteered to go back. Back at naval headquarters, Rear Admiral Moffitt, having considered the concerns raised by Commodore Ledger about aviation safety, was in a more relaxed mood. In his reply to Ledger, dated 31 March, he said: 'Geoff, I suggest that you sit on the idea until the last few months of your tenure, there is little receptiveness or capacity in taking on such work examining the organisation that is at the moment with the focus firmly on sea change, but in the new year, with a new regime settling in, the timing might be better.'

Oh, time! If only there was enough of it! Napoleon once said: 'You can ask me for anything you like, except time.' In Commodore Ledger's case, the time available to contemplate Admiral Moffitt's note of reassuring words was four days before events took over.

Kanimbla arrived off Nias in the early hours of 2 April and immediately began operations. Shark 02 did three initial missions, including one where it picked up an Australian aid worker, Frank Tyler, from the Nias village of Gunung Sitoli. Working with a non-government organisation, the International Medical Corps, Tyler was concerned about the village of Teluk Dalam, where more than 100 casualties had been reported. He had with him 12 boxes containing butane gas cylinders, each of 250 grams, which he wanted to get to Teluk Dalam. He put them onto the helicopter. Such inflammable substances should not have been put on the helicopter. Petty Officer Jeff Webber, one of the crew who picked up Tyler, said later that Tyler had told him that the boxes contained 'medical supplies'. When asked whether they contained anything inflammable, Tyler had said: 'No'. Tyler himself, according to later evidence, said he had not known it was butane, that he had thought it was camping supplies or medical equipment. Shark 02 had to go back to the ship. There, the boxes containing the butane were placed in the hangar.

The next mission was to be an aero-medical evacuation. Shark 02 was loaded with medical equipment, including a stretcher. The butane cylinders were loaded. It was required that there should be a safety briefing for passengers. How extensive that was is a moot point. The overriding assumption is that nothing is going to happen. (This writer, taken as a journalist on a jet trainer from Williamtown in New South Wales years before, had a safety briefing, in which the flying officer quickly pointed out things that could go wrong. 'And if everything fails,' he said, 'it's not your day!' Then there was a laugh and we took off.)

On the occasion of the mission from *Kanimbla*, Shark 02 was to deliver a medical team to the village of Tuindrao, deliver medical supplies to the International Medical Corps at Teluk Dalam, together with the butane, and transport casualties and medical attendants to *Kanimbla*. It departed with 11 people on board, including Kimlim as pilot, Curlewis co-pilot, and Goodall, Bennett and Warburton as crew. The six passengers were McCarthy, Davey, Rowbottom, Slattery, Jones and Nichols. Helmets were in short supply and two of the passengers, including Shane Warburton, were not issued with them.

Just after 4pm local time, the helicopter approached the football field at Tuindrao. Shark 02 flared in the normal way, pushing its nose up to slow the forward motion. As it hovered at 15 metres, everything appeared normal. It was being watched by crew of the second Sea King, Shark 21, still airborne. A local, Waris Waruwa, saw the aircraft as low as seven metres above the ground and saw a child running towards it, anticipating that in a very short time, it would have been on the ground. Then the bolt in the fore-aft bellcrank, which had been rattling round loose for however long, finally came out of its casing. Its departure destroyed the link with the controls. The pilots could no longer do anything. Warburton said later: 'The movement started to change and we went into a nose-dive. It felt the tail had kicked up. I was looking forward through the cockpit.' Nichols braced himself for the crash, grabbing the seat below him with his left hand and reaching out with his right. The helicopter hit the ground at a speed of 50 kmh. It took just three-and-a-half seconds to crash after it began to malfunction. Warburton said: 'On impact the cockpit caved in towards us. I vividly remember the sound of the cockpit. It sounded like glasses breaking, metal twisting and was extremely loud.'

The Sea King cartwheeled on its propellers before hitting the ground again, snapping off the tail motor. Those on board, with no more restraints than the flimsy seats with their lap belts, had no way of stopping the shock throwing their bodies and limbs being thrashed about. The belts would have caused abdominal and or spinal injuries. Some of the passengers might have 'porpoised' over the lap-belts, others 'submarined' under them. Some were probably knocked unconscious by the shock. Those who were not, or came to, were stunned or injured by the initial impact, or perhaps hurt by sharp objects thrown about. Everything loose would have become a projectile, including the stretcher on the floor. Those on board capable of thinking might have thought of getting out. But they could not move, or could only move with agonising slowness, restrained by their injuries, perhaps blocked by dislodged equipment.

Denah Giawa, a 20-year-old primary school teacher, started running away. Then he looked back, saw smoke coming from the wreckage, and an arm. 'I started running towards the aircraft and others started running as well,' he said later. 'As I was pulling the first person away, I saw he was holding on to his friend's head.' The first person pulled away was Shane Warburton, the only person on board who was physically able to get himself out. He had been calling for help and trying to pull Nichols free. The locals dragged Nichols out. There was no time to rescue anyone else. Leaking fuel or engine oil coming into contact with hot metal sparked a small fire.

An aviation medical specialist, Major Jack Randell, said in later evidence that those on board had about three minutes to get clear before the helicopter exploded. When the explosion occurred, the entire aircraft went up. Eight of the 12 butane bottles exploded, as did oxygen cylinders. Even the high-pressure carbon dioxide in the life vests exploded, going off, it was said, 'like a .410 shotgun going off beside you'. The heat was so intense that it broke the victims' bones.

Nichols came to lying on the grass. His right leg, doubled back behind his body, had been almost torn off. Taken to a nearby building, he saw a local boy look at the leg and start dry-retching. Other locals were praying beside him. 'That made me realise I was severely injured,' Nichols said. The crew of Shark 21 radioed *Kanimbla* and rendered whatever other assistance they could. A Singaporean Chinook arrived. Nichols and Warburton were evacuated onto the *Kanimbla*. Warburton regained consciousness in the ship's intensive care unit. 'The medic was upset and I started to realise something terrible had happened,' Warburton said. 'I asked the medic what had happened and he told me I had been on a helo the day before with a medical team and it had crashed. I asked how everyone was. The medic told me that nine others had died. I was devastated and quickly realised that what I thought I had just dreamed was reality'. Commander McGuire went on the agonising task of retrieving the bodies. 'I was commanding officer and that was where I felt I should be,' he said later.

The bodies were salvaged and returned to Australia. An investigation got underway, led by Wing Commander Pierre Blais, who with his team found the fore-aft bellcrank bolt separated from the casing. There was no sign of a split pin. Wing Commander Chris Crowley, Commanding Officer of the RAAF School of Technical Training, said later: 'It appears there was a fastening device not fitted'. The split pin had been a widely used, very simple and very successful design. It was 'extremely unlikely, if not impossible', for it to have failed. The separation of the bolt, unrestrained by a nut and split pin, was prima facie the cause of the crash. It was quickly confirmed that the victims would have had little chance of surviving. The seats had collapsed in the crash and the victims had sustained 'flailing injuries'. They had not rendered incapable of the exertion required to get out of the wreckage quickly. It was later contended that had they had crashworthy seating, seven of those on board would have survived. A forensic pathologist, Dr Paul Botterill, found that some of the victims had breathed in soot, indicating that they were alive after the crash. As it was, Botterill had difficulty determining the cause of death because he could not determine which bone fractures had been caused by the accident and which had been caused by the heat of the fire.

The Australian services responded with due care and compassion for the families of the victims. A board of inquiry was established. And naturally enough, flaws in maintenance became the topic of the day. When people looked, they found plenty to talk about. In November 2005, a commander doing a final inspection of an 817 Squadron Sea King helicopter prior to its departure found that a split pin that should have been in the tarpaulin hinge in the tail section was missing. He checked the maintenance paperwork. The paperwork said a split pin had been inserted. It turned out that the chief petty officer had said the split pin was not necessary because the part had only recently been serviced. That was passed on to the leading seaman who in turn had passed it on to the able seaman. The leading seaman had asked another leading seaman to do the paperwork to say there had been an inspection and everything was in order.

When all this came out, the then squadron executive officer, Paul Moggah, said he was 'knocked for six' and at a loss to explain how it could have happened. Commander Tobin said that when he heard about it, he had 'felt like smacking my head against a wall'. 'I just cannot believe that people are still around who think this is acceptable,' he said. Warrant Officer Mario Cinello said that he felt like giving up, because all the education processes had been put into place, but were not working. 'I clearly don't know what to do,' he said. When on 8 December 2005, a routine inspection of Sea Kings disclosed another maintenance problem, the helicopters were grounded till further notice. A defence spokesman said: 'As a result of a series of subsequent technical investigations, which concluded in December 2005, the root cause of unserviceability was determined to be an incident of inappropriate maintenance in 817 Squadron. As a precautionary manner, the Maritime

Commander has suspended Sea Kings till the matter has been fully investigated.'

But there was still pressure to keep them going. The then Minister for Defence, Brendan Nelson, arrived at the naval base HMAS *Albatross* on a Sea King and announced that the program for replacing the Sea Kings had been accelerated, from 2013 to 2010.

The Board of Inquiry began at Sydney's Randwick barracks in September 2005. It had appropriate legal representation for all parties, with the former NSW Opposition leader, Peter Collins, a Naval Reserve officer, liaising with family members. The inquiry, under Commodore Les Pataky, took 111 days, heard from more than 160 witnesses and produced 10,000 pages of transcript evidence. It was obvious that some individuals would be singled out for blame. Some senior officers argued that in the modern world, the complexity of operations was so vast that the doctrine of executive responsibility for officers was not really applicable. There were similar representations for maintenance staff on the *Kanimbla*. Lt-Commander Caroline Needham, a counsel representing Leading Seaman Viero, said it would be counterproductive to blame individuals for organisational deficiencies. There were, she said, 'poor design, gaps in supervision, undetected manufacturing deficiencies and the maintenance failures, unworkable procedures, shortfalls in training and less than adequate tools and equipment', that had been present in 817 Squadron for years.

On 21 June 2007, releasing the inquiry report, a grim-faced Chief of the Defence Force, Air Chief Marshall Angus Houston, flanked by the Chief of Navy, Vice-Admiral Russ Shalders, and the Commander of the Australian Fleet, Rear Admiral David Thomas, faced a media conference. The

Board found, predictably, that there had been lamentable maintenance failures, not just in the last maintenance of Shark 02, but across the board. There had been 'a complex interaction of individual and systemic failings', across the entire defence force and parts of the Australian Defence Organisation, and senior commanders and managers 'did not fully understand their responsibilities for airworthiness'. The 'misunderstanding and ignorance of individual responsibilities was seen to significantly influence the performance of relevant personnel at all levels in the Defence Organisation'. The Navy's lofty stated commitments to safety were not matched by action. Personnel did not understand the safety rationale behind many airworthiness rules. There were 'competency issues with technical tradesmen, aircrew and managers at all levels'. The board found that on the day the doomed Sea King was last serviced, on board the HMAS *Kanimbla* two months before the accident, there had been a 'series of errors, oversights, inadequate supervision, repeated non-compliance with maintenance regulations, and poor communications'. Shalders told the media conference: 'The navy accepts full responsibility for this terrible accident'.

There were hostile media questions on the subject of whether Houston and those beside him should resign. No, Houston was not doing that. But he was personally committing himself to implementing the report's 256 recommendations on how the system should be improved.

Many individuals had been exposed to criticism, though not all. Rear-Admiral Moffitt, it was decided, had not been made aware of the problems and had not had a chance to heed any 'alarm bells'. Of the 10 personnel singled out for adverse mention, the senior commanders did not state publicly what would happen to them, but for those named, including senior officers Ledger and Tobin, and maintenance staff like Viero and Fairweather, there was plenty to occupy their minds in the months ahead. Aid volunteer Tyler was referred to the Australian Federal Police.

It was clear enough from the evidence that none of the officers adversely mentioned were unmindful of their responsibilities. But as had always been in the military, there was a huge gap between raising concerns and having something done. Recommendations going up the chain had run the gauntlet of rank, prioritisation, personal views, shortage of resources and bureaucratic fog. Inevitably, once something had 'happened' that fog became a menacing cloud. Those in its shadow would have to do the best they could. Nine people who went on that last flight of Shark 02, assuming as they did that everyone else had done their job, had no chance to do anything.

Conclusion

'If you had your time over again, is there anything you would do differently?' It's a safe bet that if that question were put to anybody, anywhere, the answer would be in the affirmative. Things have happened that most of us profoundly and bitterly regret. Some of us are fated to live through the utter horror, the mind-numbing shock, when time seems to stand still. A father looking for his three-year-old son found him at the bottom of the family swimming pool. A female police officer in southern New South Wales pointed her pistol at her colleague's head in jest and heard it discharge. A group of young people, spending the entire night partying in Coonamble in north-western New South Wales, decided to travel back to Dubbo the next day with one of them, who had also been partying, driving. The car crashed and all were killed—probably because the driver went to sleep. In the aftermath, questions can always be asked. Why did the family have to have a swimming pool, knowing there was an infant in the home? Why did the policewoman have to regard the pistol as a plaything? Why didn't the group of young people assign one of them as the driver and tell her to go off and have a good sleep instead of partying? It is always so simple in retrospect. In the privacy of one's own mind, the thoughts come over and over again: 'If only I had done this . . . If only that other person had done the other thing . . . It was such an easy thing to have avoided.' But alas, the moving hand writes on. The dead are buried, the newly-crippled learn to adapt to life, and individuals found guilty of negligence or reckless-ness are usually called to account.

There is always, in the aftermath of these calamitous events, an appreciation of the factors that led up to the event. So often the person whose actions might have avoided the tragedy was under pressure from costs, time, personalities, politics or inadequacies of equipment. At other times, there was always an acceptance of the danger and an assumption that safety mechanisms would prevail. For years in Epping, in Sydney's north-west, a horse-float was parked outside a home in Car-lingford Road. It was parked there legally, and the assumption was that all the time, day and night, drivers would see it. One night a driver did not. A group of detectives, returning from a late-night call-out, hit it with fatal results. In other cases there is acknowledgment of the dangers, but the person or people involved gamble that they can compensate for it by extra attention and application, and their gamble fails. On 13 May 1999 a long-distance truck driver, Michael Gordon McKenzie, pushing himself beyond his limits, keeping himself awake by what was described as a cocktail of stimulants, set out for a journey out of Sydney in a prime mover loaded with steel. He had already undertaken huge journeys and had had very little sleep, but felt he had to keep going because of the huge finan-cial pressures on him and his family. A few kilometres west of

Parramatta, on the Great Western Highway, he did not realise there were red lights ahead of him, at which six other vehicles were waiting. He crashed into two of the vehicles at a speed of 70 kmh, killing two people. Convicted of driving in a manner dangerous to the public, causing death, he was sentenced to two-and-a-half years' imprisonment. The judge expressed sympathy, but could not excuse him.

When such acts, omissions, gambles or whatever failings may arise are translated into situations where scores or hundreds of lives are at risk, the factors are the same. We have focused on disasters relating to Australians. The world has numerous other examples to put forward. If only the pilot and co-pilot of Air Florida's Flight Palm 90 had decided on 13 January 1982 that the ice and snow conditions were too severe for them to take off, given their own lack of experience in operating aircraft in such conditions, the catastrophe that followed might have been avoided. Instead the plane stalled shortly after takeoff and crashed into the ice-covered Potomac River, killing 78, leaving only five survivors. If only the pilot of the KLM jumbo sitting at one end of a cloud-covered runway at Teneriffe in the Canary Islands on 28 March 1977 had not succumbed to impatience and tried to take off without getting clearance. He hit a Pan Am jumbo on the runway in front of him and in the resulting conflagration, 583 people died. There is little that could be learned from these overseas disasters that could not be learned from our own.

In the aftermath of disaster there is one thing we can always be sure of. There is plenty of time and plenty of expertise available for us to learn from the event. Often it is found that these dreadful mistakes are really just the outcome of systematic failures over a long time, and that there could have been such a disaster many times, except that in the past the time and placement did not come together in a critical way. The way the system works, the person who makes the mistake is usually the one who has to bear all the blame. So often, that person is a victim too. A most important safety mechanism is the vigilance of those in regulatory positions who see, perhaps, that there has been a near-miss and embark upon a study to find out why that situation developed in the first place. An even more important safety mechanism is the intelligence of those in regulatory authorities who can embark upon such studies even before the near-miss, but such wise forethought and perception is often lacking.

There have nevertheless been improvements over the years. At the forefront of that have been the trade unions. In recent years, with the impetus of workers' compensation legislation which imposes a financial penalty on employers who neglect safety, there is greater awareness of public liability, so much so that public officials decline to hold events that years ago they might have organised without the slightest concern. Activities with a degree of danger associated with them simply don't happen any more. I remember as a boy going to the local show where other boys participated in a sideshow event featuring two donkeys. They were invited to try to vault onto the donkeys from behind without being kicked. The animals could certainly kick. One was unmountable, the other was possible to mount if you were quick enough. Both kept their hind legs in the direction of the boys. These days, with full appreciation of liability, such things don't happen. We now see instances of public carnivals and other events cancelled by considerations of the cost of public liability. The cavalier attitudes of the laissez-faire economic system, where both management and workers accepted risks to health and safety as a consequence of earning a living are long gone.

There is ample evidence that people are more aware of safety than they used to be. Company safety officers now put up statistics telling workers how many accidents there have been per man-hour worked. Trade unions preach safety endlessly to their members. This writer did an interview with Bob Groves, a retired miner-turned-cartoonist living in Broken Hill, who has dedicated much of his life to passing on the message, in cartoon form, that workers in the very dangerous industry he worked in must at all times be safety-conscious. The National Safety Council has adopted a 'systems approach' to such questions. The various State Emergency Services, the NSW Rural Fire Service and its interstate counterparts, and other emergency organisations have been given more and better equipment. Public education has improved. Water safety is taught at schools. The states have set up traffic accident research agencies and road safety authorities to study every accident where the vehicle has been so badly damaged it has had to be towed away. Cars have been made more crash-resistant. Road safety campaigns are endless. State authorities have long accepted that roads whose dimensions were set in the horse and buggy days were never adequate for the demands of fast, heavy motorised transport, and painstakingly, at the cost of millions of dollars, highways have been widened and divided.

Inevitably, new situations will develop. Crowds at rock concerts such as Sydney's Big Day Out on Australia Day 2001 can become too big and pressures too intense and ultimately, someone will be crushed to death, like Jessica Michalik. Crowds at football matches have been seen overseas to go so badly out of control that people are crushed to death. More and more, as the demands of modern life intensify, people are going to have to put their faith in safety mechanisms. Very

Fast Trains have demonstrated the potential for catastrophic malfunction, as has been seen in the 160 kmh derailment at Potters Bar, north of London, on 10 May 2002, when seven people died. Air traffic can only ever grow and become more intense and planes will become bigger. It has already been seen how high-rise buildings can become death traps. Life has to go on and the world must continue to develop. There are more people, there is more movement, the world becomes increasingly complex. There is always going to be an element of risk with everything. The only word of caution, which might come from the lips of thousands of victims, is that we must always think ahead.

The Authors

Malcolm Brown is a staff reporter on the *Sydney Morning Herald*. He was born in Dubbo, NSW, in 1947. Following university studies, where he gained a Bachelor of Arts degree from Sydney University, he began his journalistic career with the *Daily Liberal*, Dubbo, in 1969 and, following National Service, started on the *Herald* in 1972. In his career, he has worked as a general and crime reporter and has served as correspondent in Newcastle, NSW, Brisbane and London. He has had other overseas assignments in New Zealand, Fiji, Germany and the Arabian Gulf. He is co-author of four previous books, *Justice and Nightmares*, the bestseller, *Australian Crime: Chilling Tales of Our Time*; *Rorting, The Great Australian Crime* and *Bombs, Guns and Knives: Violent Crime in Australia*. Malcolm is married with three children. He edited this book and contributed the chapters on Mt Kembla, Canberra Hospital, HMAS Voyager, Black Hawks, Granville, Thredbo, Maccabiah, Sydney–Hobart and the Sea King crash.

Ken Blanch was born in Sydney in 1927 and grew up in the Blue Mountains and at Grafton. He entered journalism with the Grafton *Daily Examiner* in 1944 and worked on the *Cumberland Argus* at Parramatta and the Sydney *Daily Telegraph* before moving to Brisbane in 1949 to join the afternoon daily, *The Telegraph*. After 16 years he entered the Australian Regular Army with the rank of captain and did a tour of duty as public relations officer to the First and Sixth Battalions, The Royal Australian Regiment, (1RAR and 6RAR) in Vietnam in 1966. Blanch then joined the *Sunday Sun* in Brisbane and reported on crime and politics before becoming in turn chief of staff, news editor, computer systems manager and acting editor. He then moved to *The Courier-Mail*, where his duties included leader and feature writing and reporting assignments such as the Chamberlain case, the 1987 Fijian coup and the crime crisis in Papua New Guinea in the mid-1980s. Awards include the Australian Journalists' Association gold honour badge, Most Significant Contribution to Queensland Journalism, and the Order of Australia Medal (OAM) for services to journalism. He retired from newspaper writing at the age of 70. He contributed the chapter on the Brisbane floods.

Stephen Downes, journalist and author, has worked on Fleet Street and in Paris for the French news agency Agence France-Presse. He covered the 1973 Middle-East War and interviewed Bjorn Borg when he was a promising junior. He later held many positions at the *Age*, including education editor and leader writer. Since 1977 he has specialised in restaurant reviewing and food writing. His work has appeared in many of Australia's major daily newspapers and magazines, including the *Australian Financial Review* and the *Sunday Age*. He writes weekly columns on food and restaurants for the Melbourne *Herald Sun* and the *Weekend Australian*. A freelance journalist since 1986, he has also presented regular television and radio segments. A pioneer in business-etiquette training, he coaches executives and MBA students in the deft skills required to gain quick rapport of the right kind with clients and colleagues. He has written several books, a major history of the development of Australian restaurants and cooking entitled *Advanced Australian Fare*. He contributed the chapter about the Ash Wednesday bushfires.

Bill Hitchings has been a newspaper journalist for more than 40 years, during which time he has covered several major international and national stories. Having started his working life as a fireman on the railway, he began his newspaper career in the Welsh valleys, moved to daily journalism and then to London and Fleet Street before emigrating to Melbourne, where he worked for The Herald and Weekly Times for more than 30 years. In that time, he was involved in several noted stories—including the Chamberlain case, the Springbok tour of New Zealand, the Ethiopian famine, a host of inquiries and royal commissions and the West Gate Bridge collapse. It was said by editors of Bill Hitchings that when a big inquiry came up, just assign him to it and don't worry about another thing, because he would always come up with the goods. Hitchings has written five books, including a biography titled *Eric and Martha: A life of deadlines*. He contributed the chapter on the West Gate Bridge collapse.

Bernard Lagan was born in Palmerston North, New Zealand, in 1953. He was educated by the Sisters of Mercy and by the Christian and Marist Brothers. He started his journalistic career as a copyboy on the *Dominion* newspaper in

Wellington, NZ, in 1964 and stayed with the paper for 13 years. He was named New Zealand Journalist of the Year in 1982 for a portfolio of work that included a series of articles for New Zealand's DC-10 crash. In 1987 he took up a position with the *Sydney Morning Herald*. With the *Herald*, Lagan worked in the State and Federal bureaus as a political reporter. He travelled widely for the *Herald* and covered such traumatic events as the Hoddle and Queen Street massacres in Melbourne and the Snowtown murder case in Adelaide. He also covered the 2000 coup by George Speight in Fiji. Lagan served as chief-of-staff on the *Herald* and left in 2001 to take up life as a freelance journalist. He has had articles published in the *Bulletin*. Lagan is married with one child. He contributed the chapter on the Mt Erebus disaster.

Ken Longworth has been a journalist with *The Newcastle Herald* for most of the period since 1966. As a specialist writer on transport and industry, he won five Prodi Awards for best feature writing in northern NSW between 1974 and 1989. One of the Prodis was for a series probing into the reasons for the shipwreck near Newcastle in 1974 of the 70 000-tonne Norwegian bulk carrier *Sygna*, the largest ship to be wrecked on the Australian coast. In 1989 he was named Northern NSW Journalist of the Year. Since July, 1989 he has been the *Newcastle Herald's* chief leader writer. He has also worn the hat of the *Herald's* theatre critic since 1976 and is the chairman of the City of Newcastle Drama Awards (CONDA) Committee. The Convocation of the University of Newcastle presented him with the 1995 Newton-John Award, an honour given to a graduate of the university for his or her contribution to the community. He contributed the chapter on the Newcastle earthquake.

Gary McKay was born in 1947 in Perth WA and moved to NSW in 1957, where he completed High School in 1964. He worked for the AMP Society as an insurance clerk and trainee computer programmer and was called up for National Service in 1968, serving as a platoon commander in Vietnam, where he was awarded the Military Cross. He signed on after his National Service and saw service in Malaysia and in Darwin during the clean-up after Cyclone Tracy. He began writing in 1983 while still a soldier and has produced a series of books, some dealing with the Vietnam War. Following his retirement from the military in 1995 he has devoted himself full-time to writing. One of his most recent books is *Tracy*, a historical account of Cyclone Tracy. He is married with two children. He provided material which has been adapted for the chapter on Cyclone Tracy.

Acknowledgements

We are indebted to the assistance of the following people for gathering the information and for checking and proofing the copy: Grace Brown, university student; Bernard Collaery, solicitor, Australian Capital Territory; James Dalton, engineer; Colin Elterman, industrialist; the Rt Rev. Dr Tom Frame, Anglican Bishop of the Australian Defence Force; Jeremy Gormly, barrister; Richard Hogan, Australian Defence Force Media Liaison; Alan Kennedy, journalist; Dr Stuart Piggin, Master of Robert Menzies College, Macquarie University; Vicki Sanderson, historian; Mark Slater, secretary of the Granville Train Disaster Memorial; Mt Kembla Public School; Clive Woosnam, schoolmaster; the NSW Railway Historical Society; the library staff of the Melbourne *Age*, *Newcastle Herald, Sydney Morning Herald,* the Melbourne *Herald-Sun* and the Victorian Parliamentary Library.